Mr. Banff

The Story of Norman Luxton

Susan Warrender

Front Cover: Norman Luxton (c1902)
Eleanor Luxton Historical Foundation, Banff, Alberta
Back Cover: Banff Avenue (c1908)
Glenbow Museum, Glenbow Archives, NA-5329-9
Cover Design: Alice Lee/Oakville, Ontario
Editor: Deanna Pratt/ Calgary

Printed and bound in Canada by Blitzprint

First printing June 2003

Includes index.

ISBN 0-9733238-0-9

Published by
Alistair Bear Enterprises
P.O. Box 56002
Airways RPO
Calgary, Alberta, T2E 8K5
1-403-256-8000/ email: mrbanff@telus.net

www.mrbanff.com

Mr. Banff

The Story of Norman Luxton

Susan Warrender

To my friend

Rob P.

The greatest guy in the world

(He made me say that)

Acknowledgements

I wish to thank all those who encouraged and assisted me in the research and financial assistance required to complete this book. To Guy Mathias (past archivist of the Maritime Museum of B.C.), the amazing staff and archivists at the Whyte Museum in Banff (special thanks to Lena, Don and Elizabeth), and all the staff in the archives and library of the Glenbow Museum and the Castell Library in Calgary. To my researchers David Parker (Victoria), Bonnie Bridge (Winnipeg), Ellen Opie (Tracy, California), MaryLynn Pulschar (Minneapolis), and Steve Douglas of the Maple Leaf Legacy Project. Special thanks to Bill and Judi Ormond of Victoria, Susan Freeborn (Luxton) of Calgary, Elsie Harris of Banff, Simon Begent of England, David Bentley of England. For Ruth Manning and Jamie Stephenson who took many trips to Banff and Victoria with me to do research, and all my friends and family who had to listen to me talk incessantly about Norman for several years including Joe Kinshella, Leszek Wrobel, Bill Dennison, Douglas Manning, Kathy Beever, and Neil Warrender. Most of all I must thank Norman Luxton for keeping every letter, scrap of paper, receipt, and diary for over 60 years. Norman this book is for you, I hope you like it.

If you are ever in Banff and want a home away from home I would be happy to recommend the Blue Mountain Lodge, managed by Greg Sproule. There was always a lovely room and a warm greeting waiting for me when I arrived for yet another week of research.

Permission for photographs contained in this book were generously provided by the Eleanor Luxton Foundation, the Glenbow Museum of Calgary, the Provincial Archives of Manitoba, and the Maritime Museum of B.C.

Table of Contents

Introduction

It all started with the merman, half man half fish, and he sat in a case in the back of the shop. It was in Banff, Alberta on a weekend in the mountains when I first wandered into the little souvenir shop. Inside the "Indian Trading Post" was all manner of souvenirs pertaining to Banff and the local Indians. The shop was very old and high on the walls were various stuffed heads of animals native to the park. As I wandered through the shop I found, tucked away in the back, a large, glass display case. Inside the case was some sort of skeletal remains of something that was meant to be a sort of mermaid but obviously male. The sign on the case said the history of the creature was unknown. Curiosity got the better of me and I inquired further at the cash desk. It was there they told me that the shop had originally been owned by a Norman Luxton but they knew little else. Rumour had it that Norman (who was the taxidermist responsible for all the mounted heads I'd seen earlier) had got drunk one evening and along with his brother made the creature out of spare animal parts. The helpful cashier suggested that perhaps the museum next door could tell me more, it was after all the Luxton Museum.

So armed with my new information I toured the museum and although it was interesting, it was all about the history and culture of the local aboriginals and nothing at all about a merman. There was a small write up on Mr. Norman Luxton and the article mentioned that Norman had circumnavigated the globe in a canoe in 1901. Circumnavigated the globe in a canoe? Now that was an interesting story and far surpassed the Indian display or the merman. If this man from the town of Banff had really circumnavigated the globe why had I not heard of him? Why, in fact, was he not the most famous man in Banff, if not Alberta? I was now determined to find out more about this fellow so I went home and typed in the word "*Tilikum*" on the Internet and I found that the canoe still existed in Victoria, B.C. in the Maritime Museum there. Supposedly there was a book all about the voyage in their gift shop. A quick phone call later and I had secured my own copy of "*The Venturesome Voyages of Captain Voss.*" The book was written by Captain John. C. Voss who had sailed with Norman Luxton on that fateful journey.

From the moment I finished that marvelous book I never looked back. I have spent several hundred hours, since that first day, doing research on the boat, Norman Luxton and Captain Voss but it is Norman that this book is about. I have not attempted to recreate the *Tilikum's* voyage as it is best to read the two books already printed on this subject. The first is the Voss account as mentioned above. It was reprinted in 2001 as "*40,000 Miles in a Canoe*" by McGraw Hill. The second book was from Norman's diary and published in 1971 by Norman's daughter Eleanor. It was republished in 2002 under the title, "*Tilikum - Luxton's Pacific Crossing*" by Key Porter Books. These two books cover Norman's life over a period of seven months (while on his voyage), the book you now hold covers the other 85 years of his life. Norman was an amazing man with an even more amazing life and so it is with great pride that I bring his story to you.

ONE

Mutiny

Crouched inside the tiny 5-by 8-foot cabin of the old Indian dugout canoe he quietly ate his pork and bread and sipped slowly on the steaming coffee. When he was done he washed up the dishes and then reached over and opened the small locker. Nestled among the medicines, camera, dishes, and ammunition lay the 22 long-target Stevens pistol. He placed the ammunition in a small sack and took the pistol in his hand. Methodically he loaded the pistol and then quietly stepped out the cabin hatch.

At the helm was Captain John "Jack" Voss, a 42-year-old Danish sea captain, reputedly the best small craft sailor in the world. There was no disputing that fact but the young man could take no more. Approaching the captain from behind, he held the pistol against the back of Voss's head.

"Beat it below otherwise I will shoot you dead and I won't report you missing either, but as a damned pirate that I had to kill to save my own life. Go and go fast!"

Without a word Voss left the helm and quickly climbed through the small opening into the cabin. The hatch was kicked shut behind him. Voss was ordered to throw out the padlock, to which he complied, and with that the cabin hatch was closed and bolted shut.

It was 3:00 pm on September 29, 1901 and the tiny craft was bound for Samoa. The 24-year-old handsome young adventurer, Norman Luxton, and the seasoned old Captain Voss had been at sea since leaving Vancouver Island on May 21, 1901 in their attempt to circumnavigate the globe. Equally headstrong and opinionated, there were often violent outbursts; the clashing personalities had increasingly become a problem between them. Voss had earlier threatened to kill Norman and it was a threat the young man took seriously. With Voss now secured in the cabin the tiller was tied so the boat could steer itself while Norman caught a few hours of much- needed sleep. When he awoke he unlocked the cabin hatch and accepted the cooked meal that Voss had prepared. Later that evening Norman spotted land. It was too late to attempt to reach the shore so the anchor was dropped, the lantern hung on the mast, and Voss was again locked inside the cabin.

Still concerned for his safety, Norman prepared a document that said if he, Norman Luxton, were to disappear on the remaining journey to England that Captain Voss should be held for murder unless he could prove himself innocent. The following morning Norman made Voss sign the document and upon landing in Apia, Samoa the document was left in the safekeeping of an English chemist named Mr. Swan.

The journey continued, and by October 16 the canoe was bound for Suva, the capital of Fiji. Voss was sound asleep and Norman was at the helm at 2:30 am, on that fateful morning. Suddenly in the darkness, there was the terrifying sound of breakers, certain death to a sailor. The waves smashed against the small coral reef. Without further warning a wave lifted up the small canoe and ran it aground, leaving it at rest in the middle of the reef. The impact threw Norman off the boat, landing him in a lagoon full of sharks. Fully awake, the young man began treading water, salt water stinging his eyes and filling his mouth. Thinking he might find a shallow spot in the centre of the lagoon, away from the jagged coral, he began to swim. Finding no shallow spot in which to rest, Norman decided to stay near the edge of the reef and hoped to somehow hang on. As each wave crashed over the reef, Norman was thrown back into the centre of the lagoon and repeatedly he would again try to swim back to the edge. Coral tore the skin from his shins, arms, and elbows and each excruciating pain told him he had lost another toenail. Exhausted from swimming, Norman clung on desperately to whatever bits of coral he could, praying that morning would come and Voss would find him.

Voss had awakened when the canoe hit the reef and immediately called out for Norman but there was no answer. It was too dark to search and with no response from his repeated calls, Jack decided to wait until morning. As the sun came up Voss began searching and some time passed before he found the body. Norman lay face down in a sandy spot, a puddle of seawater having formed where it had run out of the lungs and innards. There was no point in getting upset; Norman could be buried later, for now there was a badly damaged boat to contend with. Voss returned to the vessel and began patching her up as best he could. While doing an inspection on the extent of the damage, Voss heard a noise behind him. Slowly he turned and saw the most horrific sight. Voss took in the gruesome picture though he couldn't really believe what he was seeing. In front of him stood what was left of Norman. The entire front of his body was raw, he was devoid of any finger or toenails and his knees were scraped down to the bone. He resembled a raw slab of meat one might see hanging in a butcher shop. Jack quickly left his work and attended to Norman, covering the young man with Vaseline and sweet oil bandages. Norman was deeply in shock and unable to register pain. Too exhausted to move, he laid inside the cabin while Voss fixed up the boat. By the third day coral poisoning set in and Norman's body began to swell. The canoe was almost in as bad a shape as Norman but Voss worked hard to fix her up. While in search of coconuts to eat, Voss found an enormous pile of human bones stacked high under a banana tree. Reaching into the pile he grabbed a skull to take back and show Norman. There was no telling how old the bones were but Voss didn't want to wait around to find out. It was time to leave and soon Voss and Norman set sail on the tiny *Tilikum*.

Voss was happy that Norman was alive as he prided himself on the fact that in all his years at sea he had never lost a sailor. He nursed Norman by applying salve and bandages and then quickly set their course for Suva Harbor. Once landed, Norman checked into the nearest hotel and immediately sent for medical assistance. The doctor arrived and quickly assessed Norman's injuries. Norman was advised that to continue the journey would mean certain death and that it might be best to take a steamer to Australia, giving the time needed for the wounds to heal. Although hesitant to give up his quest to sail around the world, Norman knew the doctor was right. It was up to him to find himself a replacement. That evening Norman entered the bar of the hotel and overheard a young man saying, "I would not be afraid to sail her anywhere!" The voice belonged to a clean-cut, fine-looking young lad who was boasting to Voss of his ability to sail a small craft. Jack Voss agreed to take the young chap in Norman's place if Norman paid the sailor's wages. The agreement was made and 24 year-old Louis Begent of Tasmania signed on as the *Tilikum's* newest skipper.

Norman left on a steamer for Sydney, just 1700 miles away, now confined to his cabin while he recuperated. He looked forward to his arrival in Sydney where there would likely be letters from home. He hoped his parents, William and Sarah, and his many siblings were all well. As he lay in his bunk, he thought back to his childhood, remembering warm summer days fishing and canoeing the rivers near his childhood home of Winnipeg.

TWO

The Early Years

In the distance you could hear the painful shriek of the Red River Carts, a sound unmistakable even from miles away. Hundreds of settlers piled their belongings in the rough wooden carts, mounted on a wooden axle connecting two enormous wooden wheels. Without benefit of oil, the wooden axle and wheels ground against each other, causing the horrific squeal as the carts rolled along, each cart having its own distinct howl. The new settlers were coming to Fort Garry, a small dusty town with a telegraph line and a stagecoach that ran three times a week.

It was 1871 and one of those carts belonged to a young man by the name of William F. Luxton and his wife Sarah Jane. They had left their home and livelihood in Seaforth, Ontario and were making their way west. The little family included two young sons, William F. Jr. (born 1867) and Henry (born 1870).

William was born in Devonshire, England on December 12, 1844 and immigrated to Canada at the age of 11. The family settled in the beautiful and charming town of St. Thomas in Elgin County. At the time the small town was home to just 1,000 people. William attended the common and grammar schools and in a few short years was a teacher himself. William proved to be an excellent teacher and enjoyed his work but his true passion was writing and soon he set his sights on journalism. At the age of 22, William started a small paper called the *Strathroy Age* with a partner, the Hon. G.W. Ross (who later became premier of Ontario). It soon became apparent that the news business was in his blood and in no time William was hooked. He wasn't satisfied with one little paper and soon expanded by purchasing the *Seaforth Expositor* and founding the *Daily Home Guard/Journal*. Busy though William was, he also had time for romance and in April 1866 he married Sarah Jane Edwards of Lob, Ontario. Sarah had been born on December 12, 1846 in Brampton, Devon in England. The new couple settled in the little town of Seaforth in 1869 and William was the town's first librarian. Seaforth library contained not only books but also games and billiard tables. Life was good for the young couple and they were happy in the new town. Perhaps the little family would have led a quiet life but fate, as it often does, had other plans. One day a letter arrived that would change their lives. The *Toronto Globe* was offering William a position as journalist. His job would be to cover the story of the "New West," as yet an unknown land. They wondered if William would be willing to relocate and be their new correspondent. Sarah and William discussed the offer and agreed that it was too good an opportunity to pass up. Belongings were gathered and packed tightly into their cart and soon the Luxtons were on their way to Winnipeg, Manitoba or Fort Garry as it was more commonly known.

The Luxtons had only just arrived in the little prairie town when William was taken ill. He began to run a high fever and suffered stomach pains, headache, and loss of appetite. At first it only seemed like a simple dose of the flu but as it got worse Sarah decided to summon the local doctor. A diagnosis of typhoid fever shocked the family and William was immediately taken to a little private hospital on Albert Street. To the relief of his family, he recovered in just a few short weeks but William was certain that the illness was a bad omen. He thought that perhaps they had made a bad decision in coming out west and should immediately return home to Ontario. As they began to pack their things, fate again stepped in by way of the Winnipeg school district.

There was no school in town and no taxes to pay for one but that wasn't going to stand in the way of three local school trustees. Archibald Wright, Stewart Molvey, and W.G. Fonseca approached William and asked if he would consider staying on as a teacher. It meant a modest teaching salary but along with the money from the *Toronto Globe* it was just too good an opportunity to turn down. The trustees had managed to scrape together $600 and got busy building Winnipeg's first school on Argyle Street. On October 30, 1871, the little one room school house opened its doors. Inside there were freshly painted desks set in neat little rows, each proudly displaying a brand new inkwell. Thirty students attended that first day with William as teacher, standing behind his new lectern. William was a kind-hearted man with a good sense of humor and usually he arrived at school wearing an old farmer's suit. He was in no way pretentious and soon gained the respect of his students. He believed that learning could be fun and his classes were interesting although discipline was enforced.

That same year William had met John A. Kenny, a retired farmer, and convinced him to go into partnership. John had a spare $4,000 in his pocket from the recent sale of his farm, and he agreed to use the money to start up a local newspaper. They called it the *Manitoba Free Press*. The school season ended on December 22, 1871, and William decided to resign from his teaching post and devote his time and energy to establishing the newspaper. Suddenly life was looking good and Sarah gave birth to her third son, Harry A. Luxton.

William prided himself in being an honest man and upright citizen. His primary goal in writing and publishing a newspaper was that it would be honest and no politician or businessman could pay to sway his opinion. William and John had found a decrepit old shack at 555 Main Street and set up shop. It wasn't a bad shack if you didn't mind that the foot deep Red River mud oozed in the door and seeped into the furniture. There was also the threat the one wall would cave in at any moment. A typewriter was neither affordable or a necessity so the men wrote all the copy by hand. What money they did have was put towards a new printing press, the first power-operated press northwest of St. Paul, Minnesota. It was an exciting day for William and John when the new press arrived by paddle-wheel steamer. Before the first issue went to press there were already 200 subscribers signed up, anxiously awaiting the first copy.

November 9, 1872, saw the first issue of the *Manitoba Free Press* roll off the press. The headlines included the re-election of General Ulysses S. Grant and the latest rage in military equipment, a very impressive 31-inch blade sword for the U.S. Army. The news from Toronto was that street signs were being erected bearing the name of each street. The little eight-page, once weekly journal, was a success and renamed the *Winnipeg Free Press*. William served as editor and went on to use the paper to promote education and to provide general interest stories on the state of the city and of the country.

Shortly after publishing began, a young woman named E. Cora Hind applied for a job. William was shocked and could not imagine himself having a woman as a coworker so he turned down her application. Cora later became president of the Winnipeg Grain Exchange and would receive an honorary doctor of law degree.

By 1873 the little paper had a circulation of over 1000. Advertising rates were set at $200 a year for a daily ad and 12¢ for a single ad. Along with topical news stories, there appeared illustrations and several witty puns showing off William's very silly sense of humor.

You really couldn't help but get a chuckle from some of the zany puns that William slipped into the little paper.

"The beaver on the new police badges looks more like a gopher than a beaver. But then, the police Gopher people."

"Charlie Alloway is with us again. He has been Alloway to Montreal."

"Thirty American whisky traders were arrested by Inspector Macleod and his Mounted Police in the Rocky Mountains. They were fined $200 and their liquor spilled on the plain. If the buffalo visit that quarter we will likely have plenty of "corned beef."

"Being Monday, the butcher downtown got on a clean apron and thought he was dressed to kill."

More often than not, the top news story involved the latest misadventure of the stagecoach. When it wasn't stuck in the mud or falling off the pontoon into the river, it was getting lost or falling through the ice. The arrival of spring brought the steamboats, bringing passengers from Minnesota. It was always an exciting day when the first steamboat of the season arrived.

Winnipeg now boasted door-to-door water service, the running water supplied via a 40-foot hose running from the river. The town had grown substantially in a short time and William believed that the time had come to incorporate Winnipeg. Incorporation was essential for the town's prosperity and would give the community the power to deal with sanitary and fire matters. Drains and sidewalks could also be built. A committee was established, with William as secretary, and together they drafted an act of incorporation, which would go before legislature in March of 1873. The problem was that if the town were incorporated the provincial legislature's income would decrease substantially. Dr. Bird, speaker for the legislature, did his best to stop the incorporation. When introduced, most of the act was struck. A second committee was appointed to go to back to the legislature, with the amended act, to express the anger of the citizens. The matter was reconsidered and the original bill was restored. Again, Dr. Bird ruled the amendment out of order but minutes later the good doctor was suddenly called out of the meeting on the pretext that one of his patients was dying. The doctor was then taken just a short distance away where he was tarred and feathered. The hot tar caused critical injuries to Bird but he survived initially. The burns were severe and Bird's health continued to deteriorate. He repeatedly sought medical help over the next few years but died of his injuries in 1876.

After the attack on Bird, the protesters took to the streets and soon the cabinet minister advised the committee to prepare a new bill which he would carefully consider. The new bill was passed and Winnipeg was incorporated on November 8, 1873. That same year William and Sarah celebrated the birth of child number four, a little girl they named Nellie.

William was well known for his teaching, editorials, and political activism so the next logical step was to run for politics. On the ballot for mayor in 1874 were two well-known names, William F. Luxton and Francis Evans Cornish, former mayor of London, Ontario. Corruption was rampant and friends of the candidates were happy to cast multiple votes. William begged his friends to mark only one ballot but supporters of Mr. Cornish were not quite so ethical and were more than happy to vote repeatedly to ensure their candidate got his majority.

Election Day dawned clear and frosty with all business suspended except for the hotels and saloons which did a roaring business. With only 382 names on the voter's list it soon became apparent that Cornish's supporters were up to mischief. There were 562 votes and only 382 voters. Cornish came in with 383 and Luxton trailed behind with 179 votes. Luxton immediately called for a recount and Cornish was found with 172 repeat voters although Luxton did have 5 repeat voters of his own. Once the legal votes were tallied, Cornish won by a narrow margin of 34 votes.

Remembering his bout with typhoid fever, William was soon involved in the founding of the Winnipeg General Hospital. The little hospital that William had recovered in had long since shut down and now patients were put up in boarding houses and hotels. William used the newspaper to crusade for a new hospital, suggesting that perhaps the Manitoba government should foot the bill. The government refused and so the now-desperate citizens decided to raise the money themselves. Mr. Fonseca, who had started the first school, came to the rescue. He offered his hall free of charge. Soon a grand concert was held, followed by a bazaar and numerous church collections. The fundraising which began in 1873 lasted two years by which time the citizens had raised over $1,700 and the government at last agreed to add another $500 to the pot. The Winnipeg General Hospital opened on October 2, 1875, but the fundraising was far from over; the building was there but supplies were needed. Donations were solicited for everything from cordwood, food, ice, and milk, to old bed linens. December saw the addition of an ice house, morgue, and coal house.

Winnipeg grew rapidly and William's newspaper was now coming out daily. New shops of every variety had sprung up as did a jail, a courthouse, and the new hospital. It was an exciting time because everyone knew the railway was coming.

On November 2, 1876, William and Sarah Luxton celebrated the birth of their fourth son. They named him Norman Kenny Luxton, "Kenny" in honour of John A. Kenny, partner in the *Winnipeg Free Press*. The new baby was a fine-looking little chap and before his first birthday, a public holiday was declared on October 9, 1877, to announce the arrival of the railway. The town was booming and hotels were jammed, many bars and gambling joints made fortunes overnight. William's paper struggled to keep up and began running a morning edition. The success of the paper meant a move to a new, more spacious office and so the operation moved into a two-storey building on McDermot Street. The street would later become known as Newspaper Row.

With five children at home, the Luxtons were a busy family, but in the summer Sarah took the children out to her mother's farm. Sarah's mother, Sarah Jane Edwards, lived near London, Ontario, with her son Jerry. Sara Jane was a formidable woman and was well known for her gardening talents. The children adored Grandma who was as intelligent as she was amusing and they loved their summer visits to the farm.

Little Norman especially loved his summers with Grandma. When the Luxton children entered the kitchen each morning, the table would be covered in roses and peonies from the garden. Grandma would arrange the flowers in pitchers and fill them up with water right up to the blossoms and buds. She said it was so the flowers could be come "fully charged" with water. After a few minutes she would pour off most of the water and add a spoonful of sugar. The pitchers were then taken out to the ice cold stream that ran through the old milk house. Later in the day Grandma would use the flowers to make bouquets and wrap them in damp cloths. These bouquets were then distributed to invalids and new mothers in the area. There were never enough flowerpots for all the bouquets so Grandma would use metal cans that she would coat with beeswax, followed by a thin layer of birchbark which she glued into place with clear shellac.

Norman and his brothers and sister loved to feed earthworms and berries to any little birds they found. Grandma told them that if a baby bird was found alone that they should wait for half an hour to see if the mother would return. If the mother did not return they could then feed the birds and take them inside for the night. Always the next morning they had to take the baby bird back to where they found it in case its' mother was looking for it.

Although Sara loved birds, she hated slugs with a passion. The children would often watch her putting stale beer in saucers around the garden. The morning usually found the saucers full of dead slugs. Uncle Jerry always told the children that he never quite knew if the slugs drowned or died of acute alcoholism. In either case it was a waste of a good beverage, as far as he was concerned. The only alcohol ever allowed in the house was for the slugs and Sara always bought her beer one pint at a time.

Uncle Jerry was a great storyteller and the children gathered around to listen to his tales of horror. A favourite story of the Luxton children was the gruesome story of a Dutch sailor who lived in the mid 1800's. One morning the young sailor was very hungry and came across a garden where he found what he thought were onions. He soon got busy digging up the "onions" and ate them for his breakfast. Unfortunately the "onions" were in fact seven prize tulip bulbs taken from a tulip dealer's garden and were worth over $3,500. The hungry sailor was hanged.

As much as Norman loved Uncle Jerry's tales of horror he preferred stories and legends of the Indians. His first real friend in Winnipeg was a native Indian and he was in awe of their ancient ways and culture. Norman's idol was Louis Riel and Norman fancied himself to be a lot like his hero. He wanted to also be a friend and advocate of the aboriginal peoples.

While on the farm the children often managed to contract poison ivy. Grandma would send Jerry off to any swampy place he could find in search of snapweed. He would return with handfuls of the weed and Sara would vigorously rub it on the children's skin. The old Indian remedy worked like a charm.

Norman loved to fish and hunt, and worked hard to perfect his skills as a marksman. Often Norman would play hooky from school and head up to the mouth of Devil's Creek near Lake Winnipeg, where he would hunt with his buddy, Ashley Hines. Before long, Norman was an excellent shot and began entering competitions. After winning many local competitions he decided to try his luck at the most famous competition of the day—the Championship of Western Canada. The finest shots entered this contest and came from as far away as Minnesota and the Dakotas. To Norman's thrill and amazement, he won.

Canoeing in those early days gave one a sense of independence and Norman loved his canoe. Often on a school day Norman could often be found paddling about on the many lakes and rivers around Winnipeg. Sometimes he went alone but often he was with his best friend George Grieves, a day of fishing was always better than a day in school. George was a naturalist and taught Norman a love for nature and the art of taxidermy. Boring though school was, there was one teacher who Norman adored. Her name was Agnes Laut and she taught Norman the importance of reading and writing. She introduced him to the works of Rudyard Kipling, and the wonderful stories of adventure captured Norman's imagination. Perhaps someday he would have his own exciting adventures to write about.

The Luxton family had continued to grow, and in 1878 Norman had a new baby brother named Louis. He was followed in 1880 by Olive "Ollie" and George in 1881.

In 1884 Norman's family built a luxurious home at Armstrong's Point on Assiniboine Avenue. It was a very lovely area with grand homes and the Luxton house had a huge veranda that wound its way around the entire house. It was certainly big enough to house the now-large family of six boys and two girls. The staff included a nurse, horseman, cook, and groom. The home was located at 40 Westgate and later would serve as the French Consulate. Assiniboine Avenue was just west of downtown in an exclusive area of privilege and wealth. The house had everything one could want, including a conservatory that served as the summer kitchen. Sarah and William had one room each and there was a nursery for the little ones. The older children each had their own rooms and Norman was eager to decorate his. On the walls were pictures from the "*Boys Own*" paper and on the sloping walls were painted scenes from Burlesque shows. The back stairs always served to trip up little George who had a habit of falling down them. Fireplaces could be found upstairs and down and there was a separate room for the maid.

The family was at last complete in 1886 when the final son was born on February 2. His name was Harold Malloch Luxton but he went by the name of Malloch. Norman loved his younger siblings and often played "bear" in the upstairs linen closet with George, Ollie, and little Malloch.

In 1891, at the age of 15, Norman's father gave him the job of sweeping the floors at the newspaper office. Norman was also taught how to set type on the old printing press. The newspaper office had expanded and was now housed in rather grand quarters at 300 Carlton Street. It was a good job, but for a young man full of adventure it was just too confining. At the age of 16, Norman said goodbye to his family and headed off to Rat Portage, Ontario.

The Rat Portage First Nation had signed the Northwest Angle Treaty of 1873 and by 1875 had selected their reserve lands. The reserve they chose was on the north shore of Lake of the Woods, near the fur trade post of Rat Portage. For a time this small community staged a border dispute with both Manitoba and Ontario, both of which laid claim to the town. For this reason both provinces had jails in the town and all mining and timber titles were held by both provinces. Rat Portage would later change its name to Kenora in 1905. The name change was due to the Maple Leaf Flour Company who refused to build in the town as they didn't want the word "rat" on their bags of flour. Actually the "rat" was for muskrat as the area was well known for its muskrat trading. But Rat Portage it still was when Norman arrived. Soon after his arrival, Norman found a job as an apprentice clerk with the Indian Agency. The work was pretty boring except when it came time to pay treaty money to the Indians. Norman's job was to sit in the centre of an 8-man canoe with a large, heavy steel box strapped around his neck. The box contained the treaty money. The theory was that if the canoe capsized in the rapids the boy's body would float up and that meant that the cash box was just underneath, at the bottom of the river. Luckily Norman never had to prove this theory.

After some time Norman decided to try his luck in the Cariboo gold fields and so he headed west. Like many young men, Norman had heard stories all his life about the gold fields and thought he might be one of the lucky ones. Actually gold had been found in the area back in 1858 so by the time Norman headed out the Gold Rush was pretty much over. Now seventeen, Norman made his way to Calgary where he talked himself into a job at the *Calgary Herald*. The little paper was run by J.J. Young (owner and proprietor) and Tom Braden (founder). They had told Norman that if he could collect on some long-unpaid bills that they would hire him. Norman found the largest outstanding bill on file, a bill worth several hundred dollars, already two years overdue. To the utter amusement of the two newspaper men, Norman announced that he would collect that one first. Norman found his way to the Empire Hotel where he located the debtor, a Mr. Jack Donahue, who happened to be the proprietor of the hotel. Jack was a clean-shaven, dapper-looking man in tailcoat, top hat, and patent leather shoes. Norman introduced himself and invited Jack for a drink. They sat, ate, and talked until closing time and when Norman asked for the money owing, his new friend removed a roll of bank notes and paid the outstanding bill in full. Braden and Young were good on their word and hired the lad as a delivery boy. When business was slow Norman would sell brand books, which the *Herald* was printing at the time.

Norman worked as reporter, typesetter, editor, and manager, depending on who was away at the time. When times were tough and the *Herald* could not pay for the wire service they would send Norman down to meet the train arriving from the East. After sneaking on board, all the current newspapers would be collected and then Norman would race back to the office and print the stories from the eastern papers. Often Braden and Young were away on business and left Norman to come up with an editorial. Usually in a panic the lad would run upstairs to the office of famed lawyer Paddy C. Nolan and ask for his help. The two became fast friends. After the paper was off the press, Norman would return upstairs to join Paddy for a drink or a cigar. An active member of the little newspaper, Norman took part in the *Calgary Herald Bicycle Race* in 1896.

While Norman was working in Calgary a scandal broke out at the *Winnipeg Free Press.* Norman's dad was fired. William had wanted to expand and to raise money he sold shares in his newspaper business. It was 1890 and William decided to borrow money from CPR director Donald Smith (later Lord Strathcona). The funds were to help finance the takeover of a Tory paper known as *The Call,* later renamed the *Telegram.* He borrowed again to buy out the *Winnipeg Sun* with the promise that the CPR would leave him alone and let him continue to write as before. The CPR agreed but soon broke their word and began to dictate what he could and could not write which was against everything he stood for. William could no longer continue to put down the Tories and his editorials were no longer welcome. In September of 1893, William Luxton was fired from his own paper by the CPR. Because the CPR now owned most of the shares they effectively owned the paper. William, after 21 years, was left penniless. Utterly disgusted, William moved his family to St. Paul, Minnesota and began work as business manager for the *St. Paul Globe.* He worked hard and soon became editor and general manager. In August 1897, the *Winnipeg Free Press,* trying to boost their now-tarnished reputation, offered William a job "doing nothing" for the salary of $30 a week. The offer was simply so that his name could still be associated with the paper. He was told it was an offering of goodwill. Although $30 was still more than he was making in St. Paul it was an insult. He believed that it was contemptible that they thought he would sink to that level. He quickly wrote a letter of reply to their offer of employment.

"Think you that I am such a "thing" that I would be voluntarily even associated with, not to say subordinated to you, even to escape the misery my family and myself are enduring, in the light of your base ingratitude, black hearted treachery and cunning duplicity to me in the past?"

William remained in St. Paul until late in 1901 when he returned to Winnipeg. The boys from the *St. Paul Globe* got together and gave him a going-away gift of a diamond ring, valued at $150. He left his family in St. Paul until he could find work and get settled. William was hired by the Government Public Works Department in Winnipeg and given the job of inspector of public buildings for the province.

Norman's sister Nellie had married Fred Foster on August 5, 1896 and had moved back to Winnipeg. The rest of the family stayed in St. Paul, waiting for William to send for them. The older brothers were already out working with lives of their own. Norman's younger brother George had worked for his Dad as a roving "cub reporter" back in the days of the Free Press so he was able to find a job with the St Paul Globe. He started as a $4-a-week counter boy in the classified advertising department in 1898. Six months later he took his savings of $5 and bought himself a $3 camera. His pictures of a spectacular St. Paul fire landed on the newspaper's front page and he was promoted to photographic journalist for the Globe.

Norman enjoyed his work at the Calgary Herald but it seemed to him that something was missing in his life. It was time to go and find his true calling. After eight years with the Calgary Herald, Norman handed in his resignation. Friends gathered to say goodbye as Norman left for a new life in Vancouver, British Columbia.

THREE

The Tilikum

Norman, now 24, was a handsome man with movie-idol good looks. He was only 5-feet 7-inches but the local girls all seemed to harbour a crush on the dashing young man. He made friends easily and upon arriving in Vancouver he soon made the acquaintance of Frank Burd. Together they decided to start up a little gossip sheet they called *Town Topics*. The two of them gathered the news, wrote the articles, printed the paper, and sold it. The little paper caused quite a stir when the two young lads took on the local clergy and condemned them for not cleaning up the city of its hoodlums and gambling. The paper soon failed and Norman got a job with the *Vancouver Sun* also known as the *Vancouver News Advisor*, while Frank went over to the *Vancouver Province*.

Norman could see that working for the Vancouver paper was no different than working for the *Herald* so he packed up his things again and moved to Victoria, British Columbia. Upon his arrival he looked up his old friend Henry Copeland. Henry and Norman were the same age and had grown up together in Winnipeg. The old friends agreed to become roommates and went in search of work. Victoria harbor was full of sealing ships and both men soon got jobs in the sealing industry. Norman sailed twice up to the Bering Sea working on a sealing ship. It was in Victoria that Norman made the acquaintance of a local hotel proprietor by the name of Captain John Voss. They had enormous respect for each other and Norman loved hearing Voss's stories about his past adventures at sea. Voss was currently the owner of three hotels including the Chemainus Hotel in the town of Chemainus, the Queen's Hotel (corner of Store & Johnson Streets in Victoria) and the Victoria Hotel (1400 Government Street, Victoria). Voss also owned the butcher shop in Chemainus.

John Claus Voss was born in Moordiek, Germany on August 6, 1858, to Hinrich and Abel Voss (Gerdt). At the time of his birth Moordiek was still a part of Denmark so John was actually Danish by birth. John was one of five children with three brothers (Heinrich, Hermann, and Peter) and one sister (Anna). John's father had been a restaurateur and later became administrator of the monastery estate in Horst. Like Norman's father, Hinrich had run for mayor but unlike William Luxton, Hinrich won the election.

Voss was a short and stocky man who stood 5-feet 4-inches but made up for his short stature by being tough, hard working, and dedicated to his passion for the sea and adventure. Voss had much in common with his new friend Norman in that as a child he too hated school and studying. The young Voss preferred to be outdoors and his passion was ice-skating at which he was very proficient. He also never said no to a good fight. After leaving school he learned how to become a boat carpenter and by 16 had already been to sea. At the age of 19, Voss sailed on the *Prussia*. Through the years Voss had worked aboard many ships and eventually found his way to California where he met and married Lillie Baumann in San Francisco in 1886. His daughter Caroline was born in 1888 followed by two sons, Harry and John.

Voss surely had salt water running through his veins and felt far more comfortable on water than on land. He had sailed every sea and had wound up on Vancouver Island after commencing on a trip that took him from Paris, France, down around South America and up the west coast of the Americas, finally arriving in Victoria. Unfortunately on that last voyage, four of his shipmates were stricken with yellow fever and two of them died in South America.

With a family to support John had decided to try working on dry land and settled with his family in Victoria in 1895. He started his first hotel in Chemainus and by 1897 also owned and operated the Queen's Hotel in Victoria. The Queen's Hotel boasted electric lights, hot and cold water, and tram cars that passed right by the front door. The hotel was a success and in 1899 Voss had purchased his second hotel, the Victoria.

Although Voss was successful in the hotel business, he wouldn't be able to keep his feet dry for long. He had quite a reputation as a troublemaker and often found himself on the wrong side of the law. There was no mistake—the little Danish man was happiest while sailing the ocean waves. At the time Voss was still considered to be one of the greatest small-craft sea captains in the world. His life was about to take a turn and fate had arrived in the form of Norman. The two men would soon embark on one of the greatest seagoing adventures of all time.

Voss and Norman often met at the hotel bar and over a few drinks would get to talking, often to discuss the failing sealing business in Victoria. Most of the sealing fleet now lay dormant in Victoria's harbour and Norman thought that perhaps they could buy a vessel for next to nothing and sail it around the world. Voss thought the idea pointless as no one would finance or be interested in such a trip. The news was already full of the recent circumnavigation by Joshua Slocum who had completed a solo trip around the globe. Slocum had gone alone and had sailed in the smallest vessel to date. The *Spray* measured only 36 feet 9 inches long. It had departed on April 24, , from Nova Scotia, Canada and arrived back in Nova Scotia on June 27, 1898. If Norman wanted to make history, the vessel would have to be even smaller than Slocum's. Better yet, why not do the voyage in a canoe? If they could find an old Indian dugout war canoe, smaller than the *Spray,* then they would have a story that was newsworthy—a circumnavigation in a canoe in the world's smallest vessel to date. Norman had already been looking into the financing of such a voyage. He had talked to his old employer, the *Vancouver News Advisor,* who had agreed to put up $5,000 on the condition they would have exclusive rights to print the story. Norman would serve as writer, photographer, illustrator, and publisher. Voss would be captain of and be responsible for the boat.

This adventure certainly appealed to Voss whose only worry was in Norman's ability to sail. A few canoe trips on the rivers of Manitoba and two jobs on a sealing vessel could hardly be counted as sailing experience. Norman was not deterred, he convinced Voss he could manage, and soon the two men were set off in search of the perfect canoe.

Excitedly Norman wrote his parents about his plan, much to their dismay. William decided that Norman had completely lost his mind and Sarah was horrified. William and Sarah convinced their son George to go and talk Norman out of such foolishness. George was quickly packed off to Victoria to save his older brother. Norman was thrilled to see George, and the two brothers were soon part of a group of young people who could often be found at the local dances or playing tennis. George got himself a job with a young man named Oliver B. Ormond, better known to his friends as Ollie. He ran a little bookstore at 92 Government Street in Victoria called O.B. Ormond Bookseller and Stationer. Together Ollie and George ran the little shop. It was a busy store selling everything from books to school and office supplies, novelties, souvenirs, and stationery. Ollie was soon introduced to Norman and they became best friends. Ollie joined Norman's group of friends and they soon became inseparable.

Norman always had a group of girls trailing after him, expressing their undying love. Ollie would just look on and shake his head. The little group included a lovely woman named Dolly and a very young girl of 15 years named Marjorie Kent. Ollie always thought the young Norman should move to Utah and become a Mormon so he could marry all these doting females. As for himself, Ollie had no intention of getting married and had neither the money nor the desire. Of all the young ladies it was Marjorie who was most smitten by Norman and she insisted that she would wait forever as long as he married her. Well she'd wait until she was 16 anyway, that was an awfully long time. Norman loved all the attention but there was work to do.

Norman had put away $800 from a short stint in the stockbroker business to help him finance his portion of the voyage and give him some spending money. Norman and Voss were still on the lookout for the perfect boat.

Voss had been searching the many islands and inlets of the British Columbia coast when in April of 1901 he at last found what he was looking for. Near Cowichan Bay there stood a little Indian village and on the beach lay an old Indian dugout canoe. Voss guessed it to be around 50 years old and it was a true dugout, which means it was literally dug out of one cedar tree. After some quick measurements, Voss knew it was just the boat they had been looking for. It was smaller than the *Spray* and it was a real Indian canoe. They would make history. Now the only problem was talking the owner into selling it. Voss knew the Indians couldn't say "No" to a bit of whisky so he met with the owner of the boat and offered her a sip of rye from his flask and $80 in silver. The owner agreed to the sale and offered Voss a skull she claimed was her fathers who, she said, had originally built the canoe. Voss didn't care if it was true—he suspected it wasn't— but accepted the offering, thinking it might make a nice souvenir. A member of the tribe later said that the canoe had been paddled over from Ahousat by three Indians from that area. They had been suffering from smallpox and died shortly after arriving at Cowichan. The canoe had then been beached and remained unused for years as the natives worried that they too might catch the dreaded disease.

Voss had the canoe loaded onto logs and towed it away. It was taken to a small cove on Galiano Island, and was worked on by shipwright Harry Volmers. Harry owned a small boatworks and agreed to help Voss build up the 30-foot canoe. Between them they built up the sides, added a tiny watertight bulkhead, a tiny cockpit from which they could steer, and a watertight, 5-by 8-foot cabin. Mrs. Volmers got busy sewing the first suit of sails for the now- three-masted schooner. The sails contained 225 square feet of canvass. Two large water tanks were added that held some 80 gallons of water, and 600 pounds of ballast were put beneath the floorboards. The figurehead resembled a cross between a sea serpent and a bird with a mouth that looked like it held the heads of dead mice. The total length including the figurehead was now 38 feet. The total cost to outfit the little canoe came in at $1,000. Voss and Norman decided on a name for the canoe and they called her *Tilikum*, an old coastal Indian word meaning "friend."

While Voss was busy outfitting the canoe it was Norman's job, as journalist, to take care of the photographic supplies. Norman called up his friend Ollie and the two of them left for Seattle to purchase supplies. Between cameras, photographic plates, and film, the two boys were so loaded down with equipment that Ollie felt certain they would pull their arms off trying to lug it all home. Ollie felt sure the weight of the equipment alone would sink the little canoe.

Voss and Norman had found a wonderful old Spanish cannon while digging in the sand one day and she was put onboard. Provisions were bought, enough to last for three months at sea. The *Tilikum* was soon loaded with canned goods of every variety, hard tack, a few vegetables, pots, plates and cooking implements, a medicine chest, and a small stove with wood for burning. Along with the food and medicines, the *Tilikum* also held a .44 Winchester rifle, the .22 Stevens pistol, one 16-bore shotgun, a camera, 12 dozen photographic plates, a sextant, a spirit compass, a Waltham watch, a Bible, and a complete set of books by Rudyard Kipling.

Norman had added his artistic touch to the *Tilikum* by carving the figurehead for the canoe. The design was a combination of sea serpent and bird which carried in its beak the head of dead men on which to feed.

At last the *Tilikum* was finished and Norman, Voss and Harry Volmers sailed her from Galiano Island to Oak Bay near Victoria. Once in Victoria they paid Harry for his work. Everything was set and Norman and Voss were ready to go. The two men had no doubt they could make the journey but letters from friends and family were not so encouraging or supportive. Norman's sister Ollie thought it was a dreadfully long trip. And what of the torture and suspense to his family while waiting for his letters? Why go on such a horribly dangerous trip in an old Indian canoe? Certainly it was a large canoe but two men in such a small space, how would they ever manage? Ollie's friend Bill Hoskings didn't help matters any. He figured Norman's odds of coming out of it alive were one in a million. Sure, adventure was all fine and well, but Norman's crazy scheme was crazier than anything Bill had ever heard of. He told Norman to cancel the whole deal—he'd never make it around the world in some darned old Siwash canoe.

Before the day of departure, a photograph was taken of the *Tilikum* with a few family members and friends onboard. Those in the photo included John and Mrs. Voss (Lillie), Voss's children Caroline, John and Harry, George Luxton, and Norman's good friend Oliver Ormond. Ollie had been allowed his own little *Tilikum* voyage when Norman let him ride along on a trip from Oak Bay into Victoria Harbour. The little trip had taken an entire day and Ollie knew that in a "good" launch the same trip would have been only 30 minutes.

The evening of May 20, 1901, Norman was going to a send off party at the Dallas Hotel. Ollie and Norman dressed up in their best clothes and met up with friends for an evening of drinking and dancing. The plan was to set sail at 7:00 am so the party broke up around 5:00 am and Norman headed off to Oak Bay. Ollie wanted to slip home quickly to change from his formal wear but promised Norman he would be back at Oak Bay by 7:00 am to see him off. Returning home, Ollie sat down on his bed for just a second to slip off his evening clothes and fell fast asleep. He awoke with a start and after a quick glance at his watch was horrified to find it was now 7:30 am. Grabbing some clothes, he raced off to Oak Bay but it was too late. The *Tilikum* was gone. He ran down to the beach as far as Bowkers and then started around to Beacon Hill Park hoping to catch a glimpse of the boat. Far off in the distance he could just make out the tiny vessel but he knew there was no hope of Norman seeing him. Ollie was devastated knowing that he had missed Norman. It was very possibly his last chance to see his friend alive. What Ollie didn't know was at that very moment Norman, being rather drunk from the night before, was fast asleep in the *Tilikum's* tiny cabin.

The departure of the *Tilikum* on that early morning of May 21, 1901 was done with much secrecy. Voss had registered the canoe under the name *Pelican*. In the *Victoria Daily Times* of May 22, there was only a small picture of the *Pelican* with a note that read, "Messrs. J.C. Voss and N.K. Luxton sailed yesterday morning on a voyage around the world." No other mention of the journey was found. Of course no one really thought they had any sort of chance, and bets were placed that they would not likely even reach Cape Flattery, a small point on the northwestern coast of the state of Washington. Many admired them for their audacity but no one expected them to reach Samoa, much less the planned destination of London, England.

So the tiny canoe departed. Meanwhile the U.S. Coast Guard had been keeping a close eye on the proposed voyage. Voss had a history of smuggling in the United States, often bringing Chinese illegally into California. It was an extremely lucrative business and if the American officials did try to board the craft one would simply toss the Chinese overboard in potato sacks. The weight of the potatoes placed around and on top of the immigrants would sink them to the bottom of the ocean like a stone. Many believed that Voss was one of 19 men who had escaped from a California prison years earlier after being convicted of smuggling. Certainly it seemed the U.S. Navy thought so and the American cutter, *The Grant*, was sent to pursue Voss. They tried to catch the *Tilikum* and did spot her 20 miles off Victoria but couldn't catch her. For 30 days the American ship searched the Straits of Juan de Fuca until finally they piled into some rocks. The *Grant* didn't sink immediately and much to George Luxton's delight he was able to watch when the *Grant* was towed into Victoria Harbour where she eventually sank. This little venture cost the U.S. Navy over $10,000. George took a snapshot of *The Grant* and although he knew the *Tilikum* was not being used for smuggling he had a hard time convincing his father of their innocence.

George wanted to set the story straight and along with a photo he sent the real story of the *Tilikum* and its intentions to several newspapers including the *Hearts of Chicago*, the *New York Journal,* the *San Francisco Examiner* and the *Toronto Globe*. George was going to serve as the publicist for the journey and would report the *Tilikum's* progress to papers around the world.

Back onboard the *Tilikum*, the weather had taken a rather nasty turn and Voss and Luxton were forced back to Vancouver Island and the port of San Juan, near Port Renfrew, approximately 107 kilometres west of Victoria. Norman got a chance to visit another old friend from Winnipeg, a Mr. John Baird now living in San Juan. Voss dropped anchor beside the Alberni Inlet while the rough seas subsided. The voyage was now on hold as the worst weather in the history of these waters descended upon them. They decided to remain at the Alberni Inlet until July 6. Word soon got back to Victoria that the *Tilikum* had not yet set sail across the Pacific. Norman's friend, Henry Copeland, decided he had one last chance to save Norman from certain death. He hitched a ride on the *Sadie Turpel*, a sealing schooner, which was due to reach Alberni Inlet in late June. Upon arriving at the Inlet, Henry tried to convince Norman to abandon the voyage. Henry had been talking with Ollie Ormond and they had come up with the rescue plan to save Norman. Henry begged

Norman to think about his mother, his family, and to give up this crazy idea but his pleas met with no success. In a last desperate attempt, Henry invited Norman to dinner on the *Sadie Turpel*. Once aboard, Henry locked Norman in one of the cabins. Unbeknownst to Henry, Norman was carrying a large knife and with it managed to remove the door panel and by 2:00 am had made his escape. The following morning, Henry, undaunted, gathered up some of his fellow crew and rowed over to the *Tilikum*. Norman greeted them with the barrel of his loaded shotgun and they finally gave up and returned to their ship.

At last the *Tilikum* headed out to sea enroute to Pitcairn Island, made famous by Captain Blye and the famous Mutiny on the Bounty. Unfortunately the wind was not in their favour and they would not reach Fletcher Christian's Island. In fact it would be 56 days before Norman and Voss would see land again.

Back in Victoria, George Luxton had a received an urgent cable from his father telling him to return home immediately. George was very upset and worried that someone was sick in the family. Immediately he packed up his things and resigned from his job at Ollie's bookstore. On his arrival in Minneapolis, George discovered that no one was ill but that his father was worried that George might also get it in his mind to go off on some crazy adventure. William didn't want to lose two sons and figured that home was the best place for George to be so he had sent the bogus telegram.

All went quiet as the little canoe crossed the waters of the Pacific. On July 11, the *Tilikum* was spotted by the three-masted schooner *Excelsior* of Vancouver. Norman took a couple of photographs of her. On July 14, the *Tilikum* passed the *Mary Winkelman* which was sailing from Honolulu to San Francisco. Voss got up close enough to her to inquire as to their location from the Captain. He reported that they were near 129 degrees and 11 longitude. The ocean waves were too large to permit Norman or Voss to board the ship. The *Mary Winkelman* reported her sighting of the *Tilikum* upon her arrival in San Francisco. From this report the interest in the *Tilikum* grew rapidly and William Luxton was astounded at the publicity that Norman's voyage was suddenly getting.

Norman kept a daily record of the journey in his diary in anticipation that he would one day write a book ("*Luxton's Pacific Crossing*" - 1971). Voss kept all his stories in his head and at the time agreed Norman would write their story; Voss eventually changed his mind and wrote his own account ("*Venturesome Voyages of Captain Voss*" - 1913).

Again all got quiet with no reported sightings, and the folks at home were starting to worry. July turned to August and nothing was heard of the *Tilikum* or her two mates.

On August 23, the *Tilikum* had just passed the equator. Four days later Voss announced that they are were about three days from Penrhyn Island. That was good news as they were running low on food and had not even one gallon of water left. Norman hoped for a rainstorm to increase their water supply. Voss had considered skipping Penryhn Island, he had heard stories of man eating savages there, but Norman was adamant they would stop. He wanted to step onto some land and they were just about out of provisions anyway. Three days passed but when there was still no sign of the Island, Norman began to worry. It was on the fifth day Voss yelled out, "Land ahead!"

"Yes," muttered Norman, "so is the South Pole."

But Penhryn it was and they could clearly see palm trees growing right out of the water. Voss sailed up and down the coast but could see no signs of life. It was decided they would sail through the entrance to the lagoon and they soon came across a beach filled with dozens of canoes, and a couple of nice sailboats. Above them were all kinds of lovely houses, chickens, and pigs, but still no people. Voss pointed out a beautiful two-mastered schooner flying the flag of the Republic of France and the *Tilikum* pulled up alongside. The captain of the boat saw them approach and once they were within earshot inquired where Voss and Luxton were from. They replied,

"Victoria, British Columbia!"

The captain's name was Winchester, an Englishman from Liverpool. He was shocked that they had come all the way from Vancouver Island. Along with Winchester was Captain Dexter who was half Tahitian and a graduate of a University in California. Later Norman met Mrs. Winchester and was so taken with the friendship and generosity they offered that he remained friends with them for many years. As a gift Mrs. Winchester made Norman a lovely shirt patterned with bright red roses. It came with instructions to wear it until Norman "danced on the outer beach," meaning until he passed away.

The time spent on Penrhyn was a joy with new friendships, dancing, and wonderful food. The decision to leave paradise and continue on the journey was a difficult one. When at last the time came to depart the locals had secretly filled the *Tilikum* with fresh provisions and canned food that had come from the island store. Norman was moved beyond words and his simple thank you hardly expressed his gratitude. Everyone hugged each other tightly and Norman held back the tears as best he could. All Norman had to give was his collection of Rudyard Kipling books which he presented to Captain Winchester before leaving. It was now September 20, and as they waved goodbye the anchor was raised and the *Tilikum* sailed away.

The next stop scheduled were the Danger Islands, about 300 miles away. The *Tilikum* arrived without incident and the voyage continued on to Samoa. It was while on this leg of the journey that Voss and Luxton came to blows and the mutiny unfolded. Voss didn't understand why Norman continued to disobey his orders but Norman had reasons. It all started one evening while Norman was at the helm back in August, when an apparition appeared on the deck of the *Tilikum*. Norman was awake and rational and yet clearly standing before him was an old childhood friend from Winnipeg by the name of George Grieves. This ethereal friend had very strict instructions and his words to Norman were, "Make sail at once!" They had been stuck in the doldrums and after the strange command the wind suddenly came up. Norman hoisted everything he could to the masts to make extra sails including shirts and towels. With everything hoisted their time improved and the *Tilikum* made up to 170 miles per day. Voss, however, was not impressed and advised Norman that the *Tilikum* could simply not go at such a speed and that if he continued they would both be killed. Repeatedly he warned Norman to stop but with no effect; Luxton continued to tie everything to the masts. This practice continued, on and off, until that fateful day on September 29. Voss was cooking in the cabin and Norman was at it again with the shirts and towels. The *Tilikum* was making such speed that Voss was literally thrown around the cabin and could not even hold onto the pots and pans. He had finally had enough and burst from the cabin, with a roar Voss grabbed Norman by the back of the neck, tearing Norman's shirt part way off. He shoved Norman headfirst through the hatch. Voss was yelling at Norman that from now on he would sail the boat the way he was told or he would throw him overboard, kill him, and simply report him missing at the next port.

Norman knew he must take back some control and the thought of mutiny unfolded in his mind. After the mutiny, Voss and Norman reached Samoa and soon word reached the world that the *Tilikum* had at last arrived. Back at home, unaware of the recent events, family and friends were overjoyed to hear of the *Tilikum's* safe arrival in Apia, Samoa. They soon began dispatching letters to Norman.

It was now October and the young Marjorie Kent had been desperately missing her boyfriend and immediately sent off a letter to her beloved Norman.

"My dear Mister Luxton,

I was so glad when I heard of your reaching Samoa. I wish you were back in Victoria. I got your letter and the picture. I am sending you a picture of our house as it was decorated when the Duke of York was here.

Dear Norman don't you be the least bit afraid of my forgetting you. I love you very much better than I do Harry Fuller and will be true to you until I am sixteen years old. If you do not come back by then I shall marry some other fellow. I am tired now.

With fondest love,

Your little sweetheart Marjorie Kent

XXXXXXXXXXXXXXXXXXXXXXXXXXXXXXXXXXXXXXXXXXX

Norman had thoughts other than love and marriage on his mind; he was still trying to circumnavigate the globe. Norman enjoyed many wonderful days of sightseeing in Samoa but it soon came time to ready the canoe and leave. They men sailed away on October 10 bound for Suva.

In Victoria, young Marjorie was making plans of her own. She was not content to wait for Norman and decided to meet up with her young man in Australia. She convinced her family to come along and so the Kent family sailed off to Manley, Australia. Little did Marjorie know that Norman had left the *Tilikum* and was on another ship bound for Australia. He had left Suva by steamer hoping to recuperate from the injuries he had suffered on the coral reef. His plan was to meet up with Voss in Australia and continue on with the journey. Or so he had led Voss to believe.

FOUR

Australia

Norman arrived in Sydney, Australia, in late October and found accommodation in a hotel in Manley, an exclusive area just across the bay from Sydney. He spent his days on the porch basking in the warm summer sunshine. Although 40 pounds lighter than the day he had left Oak Bay on his great adventure, his health continued to improve. Norman spent his days publicizing the arrival of the *Tilikum*. On October 31, a reporter from the *Sydney Morning Herald* met with Norman to get the story of the *Tilikum*. There was no doubt the *Tilikum* would arrive safely and the Sydney papers were soon full of the canoe's pending arrival. Norman kept busy writing letters back to his family and planning the *Tilikum* tour of Australia. The tour would help to raise money to continue the voyage. The *Tilikum* would be taken by sea and over land and shown to the public.

Everything was ready and Voss's arrival was imminent. The people of Sydney were excited and anxiously awaited the *Tilikum*. On the intended arrival date of November 10, huge crowds gathered in Sydney Harbour. As the hours passed the crowds began to thin as people returned to their homes. As evening approached there was still no sign of Voss or the *Tilikum*. Norman was not overly worried as bad weather could certainly have put Voss back a couple of days. Norman remembered how rough his steamer ride was, so certainly Voss would have encountered the same rough seas.

Over the next few days people still gathered but after a week all hope was abandoned. The disappointed crowds returned to their homes. Norman continued to check three times a day with the Sydney Harbour master for any word. There was none. The papers officially reported the *Tilikum* as missing. By the tenth day even Norman had all but given up and felt badly that perhaps both Voss and the young Begent had perished. Little did Norman know that just over in Sydney Harbor the little canoe was making her way through the entrance to Sydney's harbour, the most beautiful harbour in the world, so Voss thought. Voss knew he could check at the post office to find out where Norman was staying and hopped the first ferry over to Manley, some seven miles away. He soon found his young friend on the hotel verandah. Norman was shocked but extremely glad that Voss was safe.

The arrival of Voss was bittersweet as Norman soon learned of the loss of Louis Begent. Norman was horrified and believed it was no accident. It was more likely that Voss had gotten drunk and in a rage, thrown the young man overboard. There was no proof and Norman blamed himself as much as Voss. Had he not come up with this crazy idea to travel around the world then Begent would still be alive. He would have much preferred to take the chance on his own life then to have someone die for him. Norman was devastated and immediately decided that the voyage should be cancelled. He had all but decided to discontinue the journey after leaving Suva anyway and had written his brother of his intentions but hadn't mentioned it to Voss. Now with the loss of Begent, Norman insisted that Voss abandon the trip. He did not want any other men to die in his place. He pleaded with Voss to give up the idea, sell the *Tilikum*, and they could both return to Victoria. Voss would have none of it. If Norman wanted out that was just fine but Voss knew in his heart that Louis Begent had fallen overboard and that he alone had found Australia without so much as a compass. He was now confident that with or without Norman he could complete the journey but it would be his journey now. Still there was the problem of money and Norman was committed to, at the very least, raising money so the journey could be completed.

The Sydney papers, upon hearing of the death of Mr. Begent, decided to drop the story of the *Tilikum*. It did not seem proper to celebrate the arrival of the *Tilikum* when it involved such a tragic loss of life. Still that didn't mean the interest was not there and the public came out, paid their 6 pennies and stepped aboard the Indian canoe. Posters had been put up around town advertising the wonderful treasures you could see onboard. The list of curios onboard were very intriguing.

There was the deep sea anchor, chart of North and South Pacific Ocean, Indian flat heads, skulls and bones of the Indians of Puget Sound, whaling harpoon of the Indians, Indian tools used in making the canoe, models of Indian canoes, Indian paddles, Indian water nottles, Indian basket work, Indian anklets (used in dancing), implements for basket work, papoose carrier, Indian fishing basket, pearl shells from Penrhyn Island, native hats of Humphrey Island made from sugar cane, coconut, sweetgrasses, fans from Penrhyn, Humphrey, Danger, and Samoa Island, Bible baskets used by South Sea Islanders to carry their Bibles, South sea island mats, pandanus strips used in making hats, mats, baskets etc;

model of South Sea Island Canoe known as the catamaran, tappa cloth made by natives out of bark known as "Masi," a Samoan mat made out of the bark of trees, native rope - made from coconut fibre, tobacco grown by South Sea Islanders, and a pearl fish hook.

So Voss and Norman took the *Tilikum* all around Australia, told tales of their journey, and showed off the many souvenirs they had acquired.

Marjorie Kent had arrived in Manley but was not able to see Norman as much as she had hoped. Still they did manage to spend quite some time together and Norman eventually proposed. Marjorie was thrilled and while Norman was away touring the country with Voss she would spend her days planning their future together. They agreed to return to Canada and move to Calgary where they would buy a house. Norman thought perhaps he could get back on with the *Calgary Herald* and he wrote them a letter requesting a position. Things at the *Herald* were not so good and J.J. Young replied to Norman's request. They were happy to hear about his trip and it certainly sounded very exciting. They were equally glad he'd abandoned the idea to continue. Unfortunately, the *Herald's* business department was currently run by Tomlinson and Braden and there wasn't room for a third position. He couldn't see letting either one of them go to give Norman a job.

As the days and months wore on Marjorie got upset that she'd come all that way and hardly ever got to see Norman. By the end of January she got a letter from her fiancé saying he would be back in Manley soon. Marjorie was looking forward to going back to Calgary and starting her life as Mrs. Norman Luxton; she especially liked it when Norman called her by that name.

Back in St. Paul, Minnesota the Luxton family was thrilled to hear that Norman was ending his trip. They had all got his letters written while he was on the steamer after leaving Suva. They in turn wrote Norman back with news that his brother Lou, who had been quite bashful, had turned into quite the lady's man and currently had about five girlfriends. His sister Ollie had become engaged to a Mr. Ed Hoskings, much to her father William Luxton's dismay, and William had actually returned to Winnipeg and would be sending for his family shortly. George was not pleased with Ollie's plan to marry Ed and had written Norman that no marriage would take place if he could help it. Ed had been quite wild although it appeared Ollie had calmed him down. Even so George didn't trust Ed would stay that way. Poor George could do nothing though and before Norman had left Australia the young Ollie and Ed were married.

All friends and family supported Norman's decision to quit the journey except one. Ollie Ormond, Norman's best friend back in Victoria, felt that perhaps the worst was over and he wrote Norman. In the letter he encouraged Norman to finish the trip and that he wished he was in Australia with him. Ollie was still running the book and stationery store where George had worked and it had been very busy over Christmas. He was always trying to convince George to return to Victoria but George had not liked Marie Catterall, the new girl that Ollie had hired. He refused to return as long as Marie worked there but did not give the real reason to Ollie. He felt that Marie was using Ollie and did not have the best interests of the store at heart. Ollie was losing money despite the fact the store had been so busy. Even after the Christmas rush, poor Ollie was still $500 in the red. George figured Ollie must be in love to be so blind as to not see what Marie was up to. Ollie insisted that was not true; he was never getting married as he had neither the price nor the desire. He wished instead that he could have been like Norman and gone off on a grand adventure.

Norman was desperately searching for a buyer for his portion of the *Tilikum* but without any luck. The deal he had with the *Vancouver News Advisor* was off now that he had abandoned the voyage. Neither Voss nor himself would receive the $2,500 each that they were hoping for. Voss had to find a new mate so he put out an advertisement. Many men applied along with one woman. Voss found a new mate and on February 10, 1902, the *Tilikum* set sail without Norman.

It was now time to return to Canada and Norman found passage on a steamer called the *Aorangi*, a 4,163-ton vessel built in 1883 which belonged to the New Zealand Shipping Company. It carried some 160 passengers and sailed regularly between Sydney and Vancouver. Marjorie planned to follow Norman but had decided to remain in Manley for awhile; it would give Norman a chance to find work and a house before Marjorie returned. Marjorie already referred to herself as Mrs. Luxton and she was excited about starting her life together with Norman.

So while Norman ventured once more across the Pacific, Marjorie spent many nights attending parties and dances with friends. One night Marjorie set out with her friends but promised to be back at a respectable hour. That night her mother waited up for her and two hours after her promised return she waltzed in, without a care in the world. She had been having such a good time at the dance she had lost track of the time. Mrs. Kent was enraged and called the girl a whore, just like her mother. Marjorie was stunned, what was her mother talking about? Mrs. Kent then told Marjorie that she was a bastard child, that she was not her real daughter and that she had acquired her some two hours after she had been born. Mrs. Kent informed Marjorie that she did not know who her "real" mother was but that she was a child with no name—a worthless woman who no man would want. Marjorie was devastated; it meant the end of all her hopes and dreams. She could hardly marry Norman now as she was nothing; she could not even offer him her good name. Norman had made a name for himself and should she marry him now she would bring disgrace to the Luxton name. Marjorie knew that Norman would never marry her now but she wrote him a long letter anyway hoping, that by some miracle, he might love her enough not to care. Her letter to Norman was full of despair. How very horrible and wicked it was to love him so much when she now had no name. How could he be proud of her now? A girl without parents and without a name. Why in God's name had she been born? She begged Norman to forget he ever met her and invited him to break their engagement before it was too late. At the same time she hoped that he would marry her anyway. If he chose to break the engagement she would enter a convent. If she coudn't be with Norman then she didn't want to be with any man. She knew she was a "bastard" but it wasn't her fault—she was not like her real mother and she promised she would keep herself virtuous.

Norman arrived in Vancouver and hoped with his new-found fame, but severe lack of money, that the Canadian Pacific Railway might give him free passage to Calgary. He was wrong and they didn't even offer a discount. Norman made his way west to Calgary and looked up some old friends. He had not yet received Marjorie's letter and was hoping to find work in the city but his friends had other ideas. Although Norman felt much better he still looked very thin and very ill to his friends and they convinced him that the best place to recuperate was at the Brett Sanatorium in Banff.

FIVE

Arrival in Banff

It was early April, 1902, when Norman arrived in Banff, a little town nestled in the Rockie Mountains west of Calgary. His family had written him to please come home and recuperate in Minnesota. They were concerned after receiving a disturbing letter from Norman's friend Ollie Ormond. Ollie had told them that their son had lost so much weight and looked so sickly that he scarcely recognized him. When Norman initially arrived in Vancouver, Ollie had managed a quick visit with Norman. The Luxton's pleas fell on deaf ears as Norman had decided that Banff was the place to be. Natural sulphur hot springs had been discovered in the area in the mid-1880's and the town of Banff had grown nearby to support the many tourists that had started to arrive for the healing waters. Banff was thriving and by 1888 the population numbered more than 5,000 people. Among the town's early residents was Dr. Robert G. Brett, chief surgeon for the Canadian Pacific Railway. He practiced medicine at the collieries of Canmore, Anthracite, and Bankhead. In 1886 Dr. Brett had applied for a license to build a couple of bath houses, the average temperature of which was 106-107°F. The bathhouse was nothing more than a 4- X 6-foot pit dug into the ground. Pine boughs were arranged over the top of the bathing pit and next to it a log shack. This "bathing house" was built and divided into two rooms, one for the ladies and one for the men. By the fall the doctor had turned the shack into a three-story hotel and sanatorium he called "The Grand View Villa." The Grand View lived up to its name with a spectacular view looking north over the river towards the Cascade Mountain.

It was to this sanatorium that Norman was headed in that early April of 1902. The warm waters and fresh mountain air might just be the cure he needed after his long journey on the *Tilikum* and subsequent coral fever. With no money, he needed to find work and soon got on with the local haberdashery as a sales agent. Just days after landing this job he stumbled across a little shack on Banff Avenue. Inside was the old office that had been home to the local paper, the *Crag and Canyon*. It was obvious the paper was no longer being published but there, sitting on a table, was a small water-powered Gordon Press. Norman knew that printing press well, as his father had run one just the same in Winnipeg.

Near the table sat all the type for the press, carefully stored in cigar boxes and coffee tins. Norman felt his excitement rise. He knew all about newspapers and printing presses; perhaps this was just the opportunity he needed. Norman set out to track down the owner of the printing press which was none other than Dr. Brett himself. The newspaper industry in Banff had not been successful in the past.

Many entrepreneurs had tried their hand at publishing—all had failed. It started in 1887 with a little newspaper called the "*Hot Springs Gazette.*" It was printed in Winnipeg and only two copies were ever printed. In 1888, Mr. McAlpine bought the press and published "*National Park Life*" but after a few copies it too disappeared. Next up to bat were Bowne & May who were photographers in Calgary. They called the new paper "*Banff Breezes*" and then changed the name again by 1893 to the "*Mountain Echo's.*" They were printing the paper in Calgary in 1889 with the help of John Inness, an artist living in Banff. John was the first cowboy artist in Western Canada. The paper changed hands again in 1900, when it became the "*National Park Gazette*", published by Ike Byers. It was Byers who renamed the paper the *Crag and Canyon*. Mr. Byers ran his last issue on December 25, 1901.

Norman took over the now-defunct paper, kept the name, and soon had presses rolling again. Norman printed his first paper on Saturday, May 8, 1902. The little gazette would be printed once a month starting in May and ending in October. The paper boasted that it was published at the highest altitude in British America and retailed for a mere .10¢ a copy. Norman hired an editor, R.J. Burdle, but the deal was that anytime Norman was in the mood to write an editorial he could. Although some locals complained the paper was not a "news" paper, that was exactly what Norman intended. He advised his customers that world news would be old news by the time he printed it and that what he aimed for was a paper that addressed local issues only. It would also benefit the many tourists and the front page of each edition would carry a story on a local destination to entice the tourists to visit there. The "*Crag*" would cover various dances, birthdays, marriages, and the names of those visiting town. Inside the paper would be local "news" pertaining to Banff, Bankhead, Anthracite, Canmore, and Laggan (Lake Louise). As for advertising, Norman was adamant that the only advertisements he would allow would be legitimate businesses operating in Banff. The *Crag and Canyon* would not be the paper that ran ads on magic elixirs and medical cures; in fact, it rarely ran any product advertising at all. Norman's goal was to promote local businesses to the tourists.

On rare occasions, Norman did allow news of the world in his paper when he thought it particularly important. In the June 14, 1902, issue there ran a story on the coronation of King Edward VII which was scheduled for June 26 of that year. It spoke of the many plans that would take place that day. Some 20,000 police were assigned to control crowds and a choir of 400 voices would take part. There would be a band with 80 instruments and 12 trumpeters would blow fanfares. Along the proposed route, there were placed 2,000 little girls dressed in white and they would strew flowers along the coronation path.

Norman enjoyed tossing little scraps of humour in his paper. The little quotes and poems could often be found along with other news. Perhaps a little recipe for an onion salad might come in handy, providing you didn't take it too seriously.

"How to Make an Onion Salad:

Get one good strong, healthy onion and kill it. Get a hammer and a nail and drive the smell out of it. Soak it in kerosene oil two seconds, boil the onion in the oven, pour the salad over the onion until it resolves."

(Crag and Canyon, August 2, 1902)

As Banff expanded there were stories about the latest businesses operating in town. Just that summer Mr. George Paris had built a house and barber shop on Banff Avenue. He had plans to build a summer tea house and ice-cream parlour which he hoped would be open in time for the tourists in 1903. The Banff Springs Hotel had also been busy installing the latest innovation, the telephone. Every room would have one and they would all be connected to the main office so any guest could reach the front desk at any time.

There was a lot of work that first summer but Norman still managed to climb to the top of Sulphur Mountain with Mr. & Mrs. Sibbald. They didn't actually climb, as there was a new bridle path in the works. Though it was not quite finished the new path was far enough along that the three friends took ponies up, thereby being the first to arrive atop the mountain on horseback. They were very impressed and remarked that it was easily the grandest view of the park.

As word spread around the world of the beauty of Banff and the Rockies, many famous and wealthy people began to arrive. Names like Thomas Edison and W. Rothschild were common. In fact when Rothschild arrived he had a letter of credit for $25,000 ready to be spent on his mountain holiday.

The town of Banff was the best possible place for a man like Norman. It afforded multiple opportunities to be a part of the development of a world-renowned tourist attraction and allowed Norman the ability to enjoy some of his own favourite activities. He loved owning the little paper as he could carry on the newspaper tradition that his father had started so many years before. It also left him time to pursue other interests.

In the fall, after the tourists had left, Norman always went away on an extended hunting trip. This would become an annual event and if he didn't hunt he would canoe instead. After hunting season Norman turned his attention to taxidermy. It was a great hobby and soon it would turn into a very lucrative business.

Over the winter of 1902, Norman built a small combination trading post, taxidermy shop, and museum which he called "The Sign of the Goat Curio Shop." It was located just north of the Bow River on the east side of Banff Avenue (located on the site where the Banff Legion now sits). The "Sign of the Goat" was an authentic trading post. Along with mounted specimens of local animals, Norman also sold furs and Stoney Indian handicrafts. He traded with the Stoney Indians for their furs and beadwork. Soon he put them to work making moccasins, purses, and whatever else the tourists seemed eager to buy. The tourists loved to buy locally made souvenirs.

The "Sign of the Goat" was indeed a store but Norman promoted it as a free museum which, of course, just happened to sell things. It was a shrewd business move as no one would feel compelled to buy anything but would come in to look around. Many local Rocky Mountain animals were mounted on the walls and numerous Indian artifacts were displayed around the store. Along with the furs and Indian handicrafts one could also find fishing poles for 25¢ and fishing tackle, books, ladies footwear, postcards, calendars, and a wide assortment of souvenirs made in Japan. The new taxidermy business kept Norman busy and he soon hired Mr. C.F Hine of Winnipeg to assist him. Mr. Hine was world-renowned, having won the highest award for taxidermy at the Chicago World's Fair in 1893. His customers already included many members of the royal family including the Emperor of Germany, the Prince of Monte Carlo, the Dukes of Cornwall and York, and the Duke of Connaught. Norman always believed that you should never do anything small, and to hire the best if you couldn't do the job by yourself.

Norman's primary concern was how to bring more visitors to Banff. The curio shop and taxidermy business relied on customers so how could he get more people to visit the little town in the Rockies? If anyone ever believed in the motto, "If you build it they will come," it was Norman.

Busy running the paper and his shop, Norman was forever looking for ideas and it wasn't long until he heard the story about the great flooding of 1897.

It had been very hot that June of 1897, and with the heat came the rain and lots of it. There was so much rain, in fact, that every wooden bridge over the Bow River from Keith (now part of Calgary) to some 175 miles west had been washed out. The flooding trapped two passenger trains on their way to Calgary. One train was stranded in Banff and the other in the town of Field, B.C. The CPR soon got the passengers out and provided many with rooms in the hotels in Banff or in their own Pullman sleeping cars. There wasn't much to do in Banff in 1897 other than swim in the hot springs and soon the visitors got bored.

Among the trapped passengers was George K. Leeson of Calgary. He was one of the most well-known men in the west and operated several stagecoach lines along with a large horse ranch in Morley. Robert E. Campbell of Banff and his friend Tom Wilson, the local outfitter, went up to meet George at one of the hotels. They soon found him in conversation with a Mr. John Redpath, a very wealthy businessman who operated the largest sugar refinery in Montreal. He was affectionately known as the "Sugar King of Canada." They all got down to talking and John mentioned that on his travels around Banff he had often noticed several Indian teepees. He wondered aloud if perhaps the Indians might consider running some races to amuse the stranded tourists. Tom thought that if cash prizes were offered that the Indians would definitely be interested and with that John reached into his wallet and pulled out fifty dollars. Perhaps the $50 would cover the cost of one sports day. Tom knew better and figured they'd get a week for that price so off he went. By the following afternoon a race was set up at the Banff Springs Hotel. Tom would be the judge and his friend, Mr. Grainger, who ran the tally-ho for the CPR, would act as starter. Tom had also found a lovely Indian woman by the name of Amelia, who spoke fluent English, and she agreed to assist him.

The races began with footraces for the male adults and children and the Indian women, known as squaws, would race in the three-legged race and sack races. Indian women didn't run in regular races as they were very demure and did not wish to raise their dresses above their ankles. The prize money for adults was 50¢, 25¢ and 15¢ and for the children it was 25¢, 15¢ and 5¢. Many onlookers gathered, placing side bets, and the event was a complete success.

The Indian Days never ran again after 1897 until Norman heard the story of the first-ever Banff Indian Days. He knew a great idea when he heard one and thought that they should bring these races back. It would be just the thing to lure the tourists to Banff. The races would run on Dominion Day (July 1) as part of the local celebrations. Norman arranged for the Stoney Indians to arrive by train from Morley with some coming on horseback. Norman organized the races and ensured there was money available to feed the participants and offer prize money. Norman rounded up a group of volunteers including Howard Johnson, Tom Wilson, William Brewster, Jim Brewster, and John Walker. Norman could not have been happier as he had at last found a way to bring his love of the Indians, their culture, and traditions into his life again. He had always respected the Indians since his days in Winnipeg and after meeting Louis Riel as a child this was his way to bring the white people and the Indians together. The extra tourists wouldn't hurt the local business community either.

Norman was suddenly a very busy man and soon the *Tilikum* and his planned book took a backseat to his current work. He didn't even have time to send off letters to his family and friends. He had received letters from his fiancée Marjorie Kent expressing sadness over not hearing from him since he left Australia. She had written in the middle of May expressing concern over hearing no word from Norman about their future or lack thereof together. Ollie had also sent Norman a letter.

"*Dear Norm,*

What under the sun is the matter with you? I have been looking and waiting for a letter from you for an age. If I don't hear from you very soon I will have a summons out for criminal negligence."

Ollie had done his best to get mail through to Norman but didn't seem quite certain where he was. He sent off two letters to Calgary thinking Norman might be there and finally sent a third letter to Banff upon hearing a rumour that Norman had moved there. In answer to Ollie's letter, Norman sent off a copy of the *Crag and Canyon* to his friend. Ollie wrote back with a story he thought Norman might find a bit of fun. Seems the rage of the day was to write a tiny message on a pingpong ball, stamp it, and post it.

Norman's good friend Dolly, from his Victoria days, was now living in San Diego, California, and she too was complaining that Norman never wrote her either. Poor Norman! Well, he had things to do and true love was waiting just around the corner.

SIX

Georgiana McDougall

For a man like Norman, who held the native Indian in such high esteem, there could only be one perfect woman. Raised on the Morley reservation, she had spent her life living among the Stoney Indians. She was the daughter of the famous trader, David McDougall. Norman was immediately taken with the beautiful Georgie. Her delicate white skin and gentle, fawn-like eyes warmed his heart. She had been the first white child born in what is now Alberta. Georgie McDougall worked at her father's store, the Trading Post in Morley. Life was full and she felt at home among her Native friends and neighbours. The McDougall family was highly respected among all Indians. Most of the week was taken up running the store while Sundays found Georgie at the Morley church playing the organ during the four services held there every Sunday—two services for the Indians and two more for the white people in the area. Her uncle, John McDougall, was the pastor.

It was at the Morley Trading Post that Norman first met her. Georgie was almost 30 but age was not an issue, Norman had found his soul mate. She was the love of his life. He would often tell her that she was the one thing he lived for, that before he met her, life was but an existence. Life had meant nothing until the day he met her. He would compare her to a night he spent on the Pacific Ocean while onboard the *Tilikum*. On that night there was a magnificent storm with fierce winds that howled through the roaring thunder. Lightning lit up the skies and the waves were as high as a mountain. The cold pierced through his body and it seemed surely that survival was unlikely. Then Norman had lifted his head, if but for an instant, and saw a speck of light over the bow. It was a lighthouse and the glow of its light brought hope and life. Georgie was that light in Norman's life, his hope in the storm. The day he had met her he had felt every nerve and fibre of his body come alive. He knew in that moment she was the woman he would be with for the rest of his life.

Georgie would teach Norman many of the Indian ways and beliefs. He studied her life intently and saw that life was about giving to others. It was a way of life he had not experienced and he felt ashamed that he had been so shallow and self-centered. Together they would build their lives for others as well as for themselves.

Georgiana McDougall was born in the late fall of 1872, in Fort Edmonton, to David and Annie McDougall. David would often leave on buying trips to obtain the supplies while Annie stayed behind to run their Trading Post inside Fort Edmonton. David's brother John was a missionary and had recently been posted to Morley. The two brothers had been in Morley for much of the year, building a fort, the mission house, and a supply house. With the store to run and a new baby, Annie had taken on a nanny. Her name was Mary and she was a native Cree Indian. Mary was invaluable and soon became a member of the family. Mary felt in her heart that Georgie was more her child and she loved the child as if she were her own.

David returned to Fort Edmonton in January 1874 and announced to the family that it was time to move to the new mission. Belongings were soon packed into the wagon and on a frigid winter's day David, Annie, Mary, and little Georgie left Fort Edmonton. They took along an Indian lad to help them with their supplies and just enough food to last for the 5-day journey.

The McDougall party left the Fort and had only been travelling for about half a day when the blizzard hit. The temperature soon plummeted to -50°F and the family was forced to make camp in the woods. The snow continued to fall and almost a foot of snow had already accumulated on the ground. It was unbearably cold and the wind was picking up, making it seem even colder. Annie had never known such a storm and the Indian, who was accustomed to the winters, found this more than even he could bare. The little group decided to try and continue but the Indian boy suddenly laid down in the snow and announced that he wanted to die. It would be over quickly at this temperature, hypothermia would soon set in. David forced him to get up and keep going but every time he turned his back the Indian would again lay down in a snow drift. Each time he laid down in the snow he begged David to let him die but David was not about to lose anyone on the trip. The snow continued and the drifts grew deeper and deeper. With the frigid temperatures, a sharp crust formed on top of the snow, cutting through their feet where the snowshoes met their moccasins. The only one not complaining was little Georgie who had been bundled very tightly and placed in a carry-all. As night fell they found a spot and cleared the snow from the ground. Pine boughs were cut and placed on the ground to serve as a mattress and then robes and furs were piled high atop the group, who nestled together for warmth. On either side of the bed area, two fires were built in the hopes of providing enough heat for those sleeping. The days passed and often, upon awakening, the little group would come out from under the furs to find themselves buried under six inches of snow.

With the increasingly difficult travelling conditions it soon became apparent that they would not reach their destination in the anticipated time. The 5-day supply of food was now gone and still the blizzard raged on. Travelling from dawn to dusk, the little group tried to make as much distance as they could but with the bad weather it was difficult. One day David had wrapped up his daughter extra tight to keep her as warm as possible but when Annie went to unwrap her some hours later, she gasped in horror. The little girl had turned blue. David had wrapped the infant too tightly and the girl was suffocating from lack of oxygen. Annie quickly unwrapped the child and to their immense relief little Georgie began breathing again. Georgie's cheeks soon went from blue to pink and the party carried on. It took the McDougalls 14 days to reach Morley. They were forced to stop along the way to go on a quick hunting expedition. A few rabbits were snared, providing enough food to keep them alive until they reached their new home in Morley.

The Stoney Indians welcomed the new missionary and trader to their land and found the McDougalls to be the most generous, kind, and caring people they had ever met. Annie always had food if they were hungry and she gave them sugared tea, their favorite thing of all. David had always been a great friend to the Stoneys and also had befriended Chief Crowfoot of the Blackfoot Indians. The Blackfoot honoured him with the name "Chief Kiachinakai" which meant "Man with the Tooth Out." David had lost two teeth one day while working with a crowbar.

Spring arrived and David was off again on a trading trip to Fort Benton. He bade farewell to Annie and Georgie and they found themselves alone again. Annie knew there was always a danger from the many warring Indians but she also knew that David understood the Indians and was always able to reason with them. As her husband left with his Red River Cart, Annie was comforted to hear the screeching of the cart long after David had left home. John McDougall had also left the settlement, having left for the East on a lecturing tour. John was a widower and his sister, Lizzie, cared for him and his children. She remained with Annie and the two women and their children were on their own that first summer. Annie ran the house and the store while Mary took care of Georgie. David missed the birth of his second child, a little sister for Georgie named Jean Helen McDougall, born June 21, 1874.

It was a nice summer as Annie had her two girls and Lizzie had John's two daughters, Flora and Ruth. The girls played with each other as well as with the Indian children. Mary served as nanny to the girls and taught them to speak Cree along with English so they were fluent in both languages at a very early age. The children loved going berry picking with Annie and the fields were covered in strawberries and raspberries. One day Annie decided it would be fun to go on a picnic. Annie loaded Lizzie and the girls in the ox cart, and headed off to Jacobs Creek. A perfect picnic spot was found, and Annie soon had a campfire blazing. The girls were off picking flowers when a spark from the campfire spit out on to the dry grass. Annie ran quickly to put it out when a gust of wind turned the little spark into a roaring grass fire. The fire spread quickly through the dry grass and Annie looked on helplessly. She turned and yelled for the girls to come quickly and soon everyone was on the cart but it was already too late. They were trapped now by the fire, with no way out. There was only a slim chance of survival but it was all they had. They put the cart in the creek and prayed that the little bit of water was enough to save their lives. Even with the cart in the creek the ox refused to step into the water. Annie pushed and shoved, but the ornery old animal simply refused to enter the creek. It was not until the ox's tail and underbelly were singed, that he finally relented. As the fire raged around them, the little creek kept the flames away from the terrified women. The fire had quickly swept across the prairie toward the mountains. Half an hour passed and left nothing around the creek but a smoldering mass of burning embers. At last it was safe to pull the cart out of the creek. The children, unaware of the danger, had thought it was all just a bit of fun but Annie knew better. Even with the immediate danger from the fire now gone, Annie knew that was but a small part of the problem. The Indians, upon seeing the blazing prairie, would believe another tribe had started the fire as an act of war. She had to get the word out and fast. It had not been a declaration of war but simply an accident. Perhaps even worse for her was how she was going to explain to David how she had burned down the entire prairie from Morley to the mountains.

The Indians got the message in time to avert a war and David was just happy that his family was safe. Over the next few years a new parsonage was built for John just up the hill, overlooking the Bow River, near Jacobs Creek. It was large enough to accommodate John and Lizzie, who lived upstairs, while David and his family lived downstairs. David then built his store and a house for himself. David's new home sat atop a hill with the store at the front and a room at the back where his family could live. There was one bedroom built above the living area.

John's original house had become an orphanage although technically the Indians had no such word. Any child whose parents were dead were immediately raised by other members of the tribe, to them everyone was family. Still many children were left alone when the parents were away on the hunt so during that time they moved into the orphanage temporarily. The original log church had now been turned into a day school and a new church was erected. Prior to the new school David had educated his children by means of a governess—Miss Adams.

Over the next few years, David continued to add on to the house. By the time he was finished building, the home consisted of some 14 rooms. It was considered extravagant and included a dining room, living room, upstairs den, and several more bedrooms. With the upstairs addition the stairway had to be altered and poor Georgie managed to fall down the stairs and break her nose. Annie set her daughter's nose herself and it healed up very well.

The Trading Post at Morley did very well as the Indians loved to buy beads and the wonderful coloured fabrics that David always carried. They also had a sweet tooth and often purchased dried fruit, apples, prunes, apricots, raisins, and currants. Occasionally there was even chocolate but it was a luxury and very rare. Sugared tea was still the favourite drink, but it too remained difficult to get. Along with food, David's shop carried candles, lanterns, coal oil, horseshoes, saws, hammers, pots and pans, dishes, saddles, and horse blankets. Later David brought in all sorts of hats from peaked caps to sombreros and the Indians loved to wear the many silly hats.

On Treaty Day the Indians always had lots of money and David made certain that his store was fully stocked. It was like a holiday and the store remained open until midnight. All the Indians would crowd into the store at once but nothing ever was stolen. The Stoneys were always honest and David trusted them. While the parents shopped the children played in the fields, the young braves racing their horses, placing bets on which one could run the fastest. David had a good business but he never overcharged and always gave the Indians the best deal he could. He believed their land had been stolen from them and he and his family did their best to be as generous as they could.

It was 1879 and the buffalo were almost all gone. It was decided that there would be one last great buffalo hunt. This would be a historic occasion and Annie decided she wanted to be a part of it. She would take her little daughters, Georgie and Jean, in a separate wagon and watch the last great hunt as it would unfold before her. David would actually take part in the hunt while his family watched safely from their buckboard.

The day of the great hunt dawned bright and sunny and Annie was looking forward to an exciting day with the children. The girls were put in the back of the buckboard and Annie, now eight months along with her third child, climbed aboard and took hold of the reins. They could see the stampeding buffalo and found a place where they would be out of the way. No sooner had they got settled when, without warning, Annie's horses clamped down on their bits and bolted, dragging the buckboard along behind them. The horses began to race off toward the storming herd. Annie pulled hard on the reins but her efforts were ignored and with horror she realized that the horses attached to her buckboard must have been old buffalo runners and her team thought they were part of the chase. With the horses in full run, the buckboard bumped dangerously on behind and Annie grabbed her two girls and pushed them under her feet. Again she pulled back hard on the reins but the horses refused to obey and continued amid the thundering herd now racing towards the steep embankment ahead. It seemed certain they were going to follow the buffalo over the cliff and plunge to their deaths and there was nothing Annie could do. Even if the horses could stop in time, at this speed they were sure to tip the wagon or lose a wheel and then they would be trampled to death. The stampeding buffalo continually bumped up against the wagon and Annie searched in vain for a glimpse of David, somewhere in all the dust and buffalo. She wanted to just see her husband one last time, if only for a second, before she died. The ground shook with the weight of 2,000 stampeding buffalo, many of which weighed in excess of 3,000 pounds each. Even with death staring Annie in the face the worst thing of all was the smell. Between the stench, the great hairy bodies and dust so thick you couldn't see through it there was really no hope of seeing her beloved David again. Annie continued to pull hard on the reins but she no longer had any strength left.

David, now up ahead, was completely oblivious to the terrible plight of his family. He wondered how his wife and girls were enjoying the spectacle. He turned around to check on them. Peering through the dust he looked back towards the location where he had left them but the wagon was gone. After searching the landscape he began to worry when he could not spot them anywhere. Annie wouldn't have left, he knew that. Something had to be wrong. For just a second he turned his attention back to the buffalo when suddenly, right in the middle of the herd, he caught a glimpse of his wife's head, her hair blowing back in the breeze. Without a thought for his own safety, David raced towards Annie, pushing his horse through the thundering herd. Could he possibly reach her in time? The buffalo were now in a frenzy and trying to get through them was likely impossible. Even if he did reach her could he stop the team of horses? All he knew is that he had to try because if he didn't they would all be killed.

Annie was now in shock and no longer had any control of her wagon. She thought she must surely be dreaming when David suddenly appeared alongside her racing horses. It seemed as if he was guiding them and from somewhere deep in her mind she realized that she must help him control the horses. With her last bit of strength she pulled hard on the reins and between them David got the horses and cart back to safety.

Once the wagon came to rest, David helped his very pregnant wife down to the ground. She was in a daze and did not seem to notice that her other children were still in the buckboard. David got them out as well and Annie seemed a little surprised to see them. The only thought in her mind was that she had ever doubted that David would come and save them. He always seemed to appear like magic whenever she needed him.

Annie soon recovered and the little girls, never realizing their danger, had enjoyed the immense thrill of the racing wagon. The little baby inside Annie was born on schedule, a son they named David Hardisty McDougall.

Little Georgie soon had two more sisters to play with. May was born August 1881 and Annie Jr. came along in March of 1884. The McDougalls had hired a nanny for their daughters by the name of Miss Augusta Adams from Toronto. Annie and David had agreed that it was best to send the girls off to finishing school in the East and so Georgie was the first one to go. They chose to send her to Hamilton Ladies' College in Montreal. That fall, David and Annie took their eldest daughter to Calgary where she boarded the train. She would be accompanied by their good friend Sam Livingstone was also travelling East at the time. He would travel all the way to Montreal with Georgie. Little Georgie, now aged 12, arrived to find that she was the youngest girl in the school.

Georgie would be away for 4 years during which time her Mother would win first place at the First Alberta Agricultural Fair in Calgary. The fair had been the dream of Colonel James Walker who wanted it to be the grandest fair in the West. He had raised over $900 in prize money. On October 20, 1886, Annie was awarded first prize for her Cinnamon Bear Rug.

Georgie returned home in 1888 and made plans to accompany her father on a trip to the Red Deer River. Father and daughter had decided to camp overnight at a place then known as Atkinson. The next morning David lifted the buckboard to turn it around when suddenly a searing pain shot through his abdomen. The pain was so intense that David could not even walk and Georgie knew something terrible had happened to her father. She managed to lift her father into the buckboard and hitched her saddle horse to the team, driving the three horses back to Morley just as fast as she could. Upon reaching the Morley Trading Post she jumped form the wagon. Annie was already running out to meet her. Georgie explained to her mother that David had somehow seriously hurt himself while lifting the wagon. No men were around to help so the women got David out of the cart, into the house, and into bed. Georgie then got back on her horse and rode to the station to send an urgent telegram to Dr. James Lafferty in Calgary. Luckily, Lafferty was able to get on the morning train to Morley and he remained at David's side for several days. David had ruptured his gall bladder and Dr. Lafferty set about repairing the damage as best he could. Annie served as his nurse. It took David a full year to get over his injury but he would never again be the rugged man he once was. Georgie and Mary now had to assist in the running of their father's ranch in Red Deer. Georgie also spent a great deal of time running her father's trading post, a position she kept for some 17 years.

It was while working at the trading post that she met Norman Luxton. She also ran a wood supply business along with 30 natives who were employed to cut rails, fence posts, logs, and firewood. Georgie was a highly respected businesswoman and although very firm with her Indian employees she was also known for her kindness. In her spare time she enjoyed writing and painting.

It didn't take Norman long to know that Georgie was the right woman for him. The couple married in David's home at Morley in November of 1904. The ceremony was performed by her uncle, the Reverend John McDougall. After the marriage, the couple travelled to Winnipeg and Minnesota so Norman could introduce his new bride to his family.

SEVEN

The Hotel King Edward

By October, all the tourists had left Banff for the season and the locals were all hard at work. It was early winter of 1903 and Norman had decided to build himself a hotel. With King Edward VII currently on the throne, it was decided that the hotel would be named the Hotel King Edward. Construction began on the southwest corner of Banff Avenue and Caribou Street. The CPR had the grand Banff Springs Hotel up by the hot springs but Norman decided that a modest-priced hotel, located right downtown, was very much in need. It would be the only all-season hotel in the town besides Dr. Brett's facility. Norman set his mind on finding ways to bring tourists to Banff over the winter. With only seven short months until the tourists returned there was much work to be done. The new hotel was furnished with the latest conveniences and was ideally located, just a 10-minute walk from the train station and a 15-minute walk to the hot sulphur water. A livery was attached to the hotel with saddle ponies for hire.

It became apparent that Norman was going to need help and he sent off a letter to Minnesota, home to his brother George, begging him to come out to Banff to work for him. He remembered the great times he and George had shared in Victoria and looked forward to continuing their friendship in Banff. There was just one little problem. George had fallen in love with his new city of St. Paul and so he chose to stay. He did pass along the letter to his older brother Louis. This was just the sort of opportunity that "Lou" had been looking for—he was ready for a change and quickly replied to Norman's letter asking if he could substitute for George.

The Hotel King Edward was decorated with various mounted heads of local animals and a dining room was now in full operation. Norman had hired himself a manager by the name of William "Billy" Potts. Now that the hotel was all furnished there was the matter of insurance policies and various licences to contend with. In order to even get a liquor license the hotel had to have at least 10 bedrooms, 2 public sitting rooms plus accommodation for family and staff. These rules were strictly enforced with inspections that would be carried out yearly.

Although not the best businessman when it came to financial affairs, Norman was always cost-conscious and did his utmost to get the best prices he could. It was difficult as very little was available locally. Toilets came from the Standard Sanitary Manufacturing Company of Pittsburgh. The iron bowls which were enameled throughout cost some $38 each although one could buy the cheaper earthenware variety at a mere $22. The washroom fittings were referred to as water closets as they came complete with bowls, tanks, and fittings. Even the soap came from as far away as the Liquozone Company, the nearest outlet being in Winnipeg.

Employees for the hotel were required immediately and ads were placed for a bartender ($75 per month), chef ($75 per month), and an office girl ($25 per month). That was the full summer pay although off-season the pay would be somewhat less.

With staff in place, the new manager was running about trying desperately to get the hotel ready for its grand opening. Many new buildings and businesses were ready to be opened in time for the new season. Across the street, Mr. Paris had opened a tearoom with his wife acting as manager. She was assisted by Miss Ada Thompson and the little restaurant served up afternoon tea with cream, ice cream, cakes, and light refreshments. The Canadian government was putting the final touches on their new museum, which stood just north of the Bow Bridge, opposite the Sign of the Goat. It was due to open in July. The Brewsters had a new stagecoach running from Banff to Bankhead and up the road the new basin was opening at the Cave, making it four times larger than the original. Even the Upper Hot Springs had new dressing rooms installed. Around town many new cottages and homes had sprung up which offered accommodation to tourists who preferred to stay in self-catering cottages rather than hotel rooms. These days it was impossible to find a lot to build on that was closer than a half mile from the post office.

The hotel was just about ready, everything was spotless. The dining room was particularly well-thought-out and everything necessary was provided for the guests. The livery and feed stables were well stocked and the bar room was equal to any in the Northwest.

At last she was ready and the Hotel King Edward held its grand opening on May 29, 1904. An all-season hotel meant that the doors would never close, so it was with great ceremony that Norman announced that, since the doors would never be locked, there was no need for a key. With that he held the keys aloft and then tossed them into a nearby snowbank.

Next door to the King Edward was the Dominion Store which sold groceries, gentlemen's clothing and accessories, stationery, tobacco, fruit, and confections. Bill Potts had opened the hotel but the actual running of the establishment would be left to the new manager, Mr. Olaf Millar. Norman kept busy down at the Sign of the Goat Curio Shop.

The Sign of the Goat was a busy little place now selling clothing, furs, rugs, native beadwork, souvenirs of all descriptions all from a 150-mile radius, tobacco, pipes, cigars, and cigarettes. The store also featured many exhibits including life-size animals and mounted game heads. Displays included the smallest grizzly ever captured in the area, one of only three mountain goats in captivity, two mountain lions, a black bear, bob cat, wolverine, wood martin, mountain rat, prairie wolf, prairie antelope, and a sheep with 17-inch horns. It really was a curio shop in the best Victorian tradition.

The Stoney Indians who supplied many of the shop's local souvenirs, had recently been bursting with news of a meteor that tore through the sky near Morley. Of course they didn't know it was a meteor and so told stories of a steel black monster, some 20 feet long, with a head of fire. It had sailed overhead and seemed to be headed directly for Banff. Of course stories of spirits and monsters were a large part of the native culture. Other local spirits or monsters included that of a hideous monster that lived in Lake Minnewanka, just nine miles from Banff. The lake's monster was described as a huge black fish, many yards broad and from its side came a beautifully shaped arm and hand that would try to grab anyone that was out boating on the lake. It seemed to prefer people that were singing and legend said that the monster grabbed a canoe full of Indian women and children. The canoe then tipped over and only one of the passengers made it back to shore. The story of the Minnewanka monster fascinated Norman. He had no reason to disbelieve the legends after having sighted his own monster while on the *Tilikum*. It was on his voyage in early July of 1901 that he spotted some type of large fish or perhaps it was a mammal? Norman described it vividly in his diary. The creature was longer than a sealing ship, about seventy feet in length and the head stood high in the water, higher even than the waves at the time. It did not swim like a dolphin or a whale but moved with ease through the water. The head was set upon a long neck and the animal's colour was a dark grey. Norman assumed that Voss would know the species of animal and quickly woke him to show him the strange beast. He questioned Voss,

"What manner of creature is this?"

Voss was equally mystified. Assuming it was a common sea creature of the South Pacific, Voss assured Norman they would inquire further upon reaching Australia. At various ports further along the journey they questioned locals as to this strange animal but soon found their inquiries were answered by bewilderment, or worse, amusement. Many believed that perhaps the monster was a figment of their imagination and perhaps they had been at sea too long. Voss quickly realized that if people believed that the men had suffered from some sort of hallucination, their entire journey would be less credible. Norman was instructed to simply not speak of it again. Norman agreed, but long after the journey the mystery of the sea creature haunted him. Throughout the years he scoured newspapers hoping to find some mention of what they had seen.

Norman continued as publisher of the *Crag and Canyon* which was doing well. Subscription charges were set at $1.00 per year unless they were shipped to the United States or Britain, in which case subscribers paid an extra 50¢. Advertisement rates were $1.00 a month per inch.

Norman always assisted visitors with finding private cottages to rent in Banff and would match the tourist to the owner. People often wrote to the Curio Shop hoping Norman could help in finding a place to stay.

The summer of 1905 was in full swing with four trains passing through Banff every day. Two on a westerly heading came through at 6:08 pm (No. 1) and 6:25 am (No. 97). Going east they came through at 10:25 am (No. 2) and 10:00 pm (No. 96). There was so much to do now in the little resort town that Norman ran an entire list of possible activities in his paper. Visitors could climb Sulphur Mountain, go bathing in the basin, drive around the Tunnel Mountain loop, visit the Buffalo park, drive up Tunnel Mountain and visit George Fear's Curiosity Store, ride a bucking horse, ride a horse that didn't buck, visit the new government museum, take a drive in one of Walter Fulmer's comfortable rigs, catch a 9-pound trout, go to church, have a bath at the Grand View Villa, have a meal at the Hotel King Edward and, of course, visit the Sign of the Goat Curio Shop. Another wonderful pastime was to take a trip up the river from the Banff Boat House on the *Mountain Belle*. She made two trips daily up the Bow River for some 8 miles. It was a lovely trip with spectacular views of Mt. Edith, Mt. Massive, and the Duke of Wellington.

The Stoney Indians were really having a difficult time making any money and in late July of 1905, a large number of Stoneys left Morley and passed through Banff on their way to the Kootenays, in south eastern British Columbia. They hoped to be better able to support themselves there. The Luxtons and McDougalls had done all they could to help the Stoney's but food was scarce on the reservation.

In other news, Alberta was now, officially, a new province. It was inaugurated on September 2, 1905.

Summer wound to a close and the locals looked forward to another quiet winter. Norman left on his annual hunting and canoe trip before the snow arrived. Winter found Norman busy with the painting, renovating, and restocking of his various businesses. Norman had purchased some new type for the *Crag and Canyon's* printing press and he was pleased with the results. The paper was now much easier to read. In honour of the new type, Norman started printing his paper in April instead of May.

There was much excitement in town as lights had finally been installed in Banff. Not so exciting for the locals was the arrival of the town's first Chinese restaurant. Rumours abounded that Chinese restaurants produced a lot of trouble and the town residents really didn't understand why Banff needed one. They thought it was a pity that any trouble should be brought to the town. The Kwong Lee Restaurant would open for business by Dominion Day, 1906, up on Station Road.

Norman was busy preparing for the Indian races again as this year they were to be held on Victoria Day. Early on the morning of May 24, the town's residents awoke to find six inches of snow but spirits remained high and the Indian races were a go. By 10:00 am the sun had just about melted all the snow just in time for the races to start. Norman had approached the various businesses to raise money for prizes and had collected $150. The local ladies had erected a refreshment tent but it didn't do as well as expected, it was still too chilly to be standing around drinking a cold beverage.

The Hotel King Edward was doing a roaring business and now proudly displayed the new gramophone Norman had purchased. He had also acquired two black bears for the Curio Shop which were kept temporarily at the pheasant house, until some sort of enclosure could be built. As busy as the hotel was, it had become apparent that Olaf was not managing the hotel in the manner Norman expected. Bills were not being paid and the books were in a sad state. Olaf was let go and Norman was forced to manage the hotel himself while trying to also run the Curio Shop and publish his paper. It came as a relief when it was decided that the Dominion Day activities would be held in Canmore that year.

Georgie and Norman now lived in a little house at 206 Beaver Street. Norman had purchased it from Annie McDougall and put it in Georgie's name. Upon entering, the well-kept front sitting area sat over to the left. There was a small sofa and two chairs and the walls were decorated with the mounted heads of deer, bear, wolverine, and mountain goat. Paintings of Indian friends completed the decoration. Off to the right was the living room which contained Georgie's piano and many of her paintings. She loved to paint mountain streams. Annie McDougall's needlepoint also adorned the walls. The rocking chair also had belonged to the McDougall family. Adjacent to the living room was the sitting room, which served as the library where Norman kept part of his book collection. Further on came a small room that served as an office, den, or bedroom, depending on the need at the time. The kitchen was on the left, straight down the hall from the front entry. From the kitchen a set of stairs led up to the two bedrooms.

Georgie always kept the house spotless but her pride and joy was her garden. She loved to entertain her family when they came to town. Just that summer her sister May had come to stay for three weeks. There was always something to do in town and that August, "Arnold Shows Under Canvass" came to Banff. Visitors were invited to see the famous Kober family of aerialists along with dog shows, acrobats, gymnasts, and clowns. The show was held directly across from the King Edward where a large pavilion was erected along with various sideshow tents. The train had arrived too late for them to run a matinée but the evening show was well attended. Later in August another friend of Georgie's, Mrs. Young, came from Edmonton for a visit. Later still came a visit from Georgie's brother, David McDougall, who stayed for several days.

The *Crag and Canyon* was running a story on the famous Dominion Exhibition which was to be held in New Westminster, B.C. that fall. This was Canada's largest show, with $100,000 in prize money and events such as rowing, lacrosse, horse racing, bronco busting, military parades and exercises, plus the Royal Irish Guards and other famous bands. This year boasted a water carnival with Indian war canoes.

Norman had at last hired a new manager for the King Edward by the name of Mr. Rose. It was a relief and it meant the Luxtons could take a break. In late September Georgie headed to Morley as she had promised to assist at Treaty Day where the annual gathering of the Indians would take place. Norman was going to carry on to Gleichen and do some hunting.

Winter came with the usual renovations, parties, dances, curling, and skating. Norman decided that it was time to move his Curio shop and picked a location just across the river, immediately south and west of the Bow Bridge. It was on the way to the Cave and Basin and was only a short walk from town. With the move of the store, Norman hired himself a new taxidermist by the name Charlie Prior of Winnipeg. Mr.Hine had decided to move to Edmonton.

Norman had also moved the *Crag and Canyon* office, which originally sat across from the government building by the Sign of the Goat. He had purchased a new gasoline-powered printer that made life much easier. Norman also took a job as an insurance agent for several companies including Liverpool, London and Globe, Guardian Fire and Life, and Canada West Fire. It was a nice little side income and with all of Norman's local contacts, it seemed a good fit.

That winter major renovations were undertaken at the Hotel King Edward. It was expanded to include more bedrooms and bathrooms. A café and dining room were also built, and the livery was overhauled and expanded. The dining room could now hold 50 guests. A new entranceway had also been added with lovely plate glass entry doors. Unfortunately, the hotel's namesake, King Edward VII, died on May 6, 1907.

The talk of the town was a new cement plant to be built out in Kananaskis for the Western Canada Cement and Coal Company. It would be a huge operation, putting out 1200-1400 barrels of cement per day, at a cost of $1 million. The headquarters would be in Calgary. The company had bought up 1000 acres of land of the highest quality of rock and clay with which to make the cement. They also owned 350 acres of coal land to use for fuel. The plan was to have the new plant up and running by the following August. This would mean that the area known as Exshaw would now be home to the many new plant employees. Norman, never one to miss an opportunity, was already thinking up ideas on how he could make some money on the deal.

Lou Luxton was enjoying the single life and had been invaluable to Norman the previous summer. He had helped run the curio shop but now Norman had a new job for his younger brother. With the opening of the cement plant, Norman acquired some property in Exshaw. He had decided to open a general store and planned to ship all the stock and fixtures of the Banff Clothing Store and send them to Exshaw sometime in July. Lou would be the stores new manager. Norman also was owner of the new Exshaw Laundry.

Georgie was excited as her father and mother had had decided to retire from Morley and move to Banff. David McDougall purchased a house on Beaver Street, close to the Luxtons. He had decided that he too would go into the hotel business and so he purchased the land directly across the street from the King Edward. It would take a full year before his hotel, the Mount Royal, would be ready. In the meantime David opened a livery, and along with his partner Mr. Rattray he ran Bow Livery which offered democrats, 3-seaters, and saddle ponies for hire.

Dominion Day of 1907 was host again to the Indian races. Some 260 Indians would arrive by train and pony for the celebration. Norman was acting as parade marshal and had managed to collect $179 for this year's prize money.

Norman was still adding on to his hotel and was trying to finish the new billiard room along with a shooting gallery. David, across the street, was trying to complete the Mount Royal Hotel in time for a summer opening. Norman had to leave for a quick visit to the coast so he left on May 12 and expected to return by May 20 in time for the Indian races.

Norman returned as expected and was looking forward to the races scheduled for May 24. There wasn't much time to prepare but on Tuesday morning, May 21, a devastating telegram arrived. William F. Luxton was dead. Norman's beloved father had passed away just before midnight the previous evening. He died at the Winnipeg General Hospital at 11:00 pm after suffering a massive stroke. He had been taking a bath at the Commercial Club of Winnipeg when it happened. He was paralyzed and quickly taken to the General Hospital. He never recovered consciousness after being found in the bath. His family was immediately notified and his son Harry arrived at the hospital but was the only one present when he passed. All other family members either lived outside Winnipeg or were away and none were able to reach Winnipeg in time. The service was held on May 24, at the Holy Trinity Church which was filled to capacity. The procession of carriages extended from Donald Street to Main Street on Portage Avenue. The procession attracted crowds of citizens to watch as it passed by. The number of floral tributes was extraordinary and they were lined up along Donald Street on either side. The pallbearers included the premier, and the city's sheriff. William was buried in a plot purchased by the Masons, to which fraternity, William had been a member. The plot was in the churchyard of St. John's. Family had come from all over Canada and the States. Norman had arrived from Banff, George had come from St. Paul, and along with brother, Harry, were the only immediate family able to attend. Norman's namesake, Mr. John Kenny, was also there. Others attending the service included the Lieutenant Governor Sir D. H. McMillan, Premier Greenway, Chief Justice Howell, many members of the school board, fellow Masons, and many friends.

The annual Indian Day, as it was starting to be referred to, went on as scheduled. Norman had raised $150 and this year the entire Stoney band came along with all their papooses and ponies. This year included the usual footraces, boat races, high jump, long jump, and baseball throwing. The races were strictly for the Indians but the other activities were open to all. In order to participate in the other activities a fee had to be paid, except for the children's sports. The fee was always 5% of the total purse, with average prize money between $1 and $5. The children's races were held in the morning, followed by the boat races. The adult Indian races followed in the afternoon.

The Stoneys arrived on Thursday morning in a special car provided by the CPR attached to engine No. 97. Over 300 natives arrived, with 50 more coming on their ponies. The bucks (young warriors) wore wonderful costumes as did the squaws with their beautifully beaded gowns. They all did some shopping before pitching their teepees that evening at the campground. A Powwow was held which was attended by many visitors and locals from town.

Banff Indian Day of 1907 started at 9:30 am with the children's sports at the recreational grounds. The laughter always came from the potato sack races where the entrants were placed in a potato sack and holding the edges of the bag with their hands, did their best to hop their way down to the finish line. They had to be careful because if they went too fast they usually fell in a heap to the ground. After lunch the parade commenced with the braves in full war paint and feathers, a scene almost never to be found elsewhere in America. The afternoon consisted of the adult Indian races followed by music provided by the Bankhead band. After supper the fire brigade gathered, in full gear, for the hose-reel race. The day ended with a Powwow held at 8:30 pm followed by a concert up at the Opera House.

Norman was proud of his Indian Day races. Soon the frontier conditions of the west would disappear along with the picturesque setting of the cowboy and the Indian. He so regretted this passing of history and knew that with the parade that perhaps he could keep some of that history alive for future generations. Always the Indians came dressed in their finery and showed off their homes, culture, and shared their stories. It was a living museum of the soon-to-be distant past and a chance for the visitors from other lands to share in the history of the Canadian West. Norman believed that for many, the chance to see the local Indians was a spectacle—a sight of a lifetime.

That summer the boat business on Lake Minnewanka was in full operation and Norman was running the *Aylmer*. He always offered a full-day trip that departed by stage from his hotel and included a round trip to the lake plus a trip down the lake on his launch. He had received his permit to run the *Aylmer* again and had hired an experienced fisherman from Norway by the name of Ole Dahl to captain the vessel. There was good fishing in the lake with some trout weighing in at up to 40 lbs.

Banff was thriving and down at the Banff boathouse there were now the two passenger launches plus row boats, canoes, and even bicycles to hire. The Opera House, built the previous summer by Sherman Grand, was now a star attraction. All the local tourist cottages were filling up fast. Already over 100 applicants had been refused. Norman had purchased a new rubber tired, horse-drawn bus for the tourists. It was the only bus in town with rubber tires. Plans were underfoot to start up a zoo and one of the locals, Mr. J McRavey, had gone to Chicago to inspect their world-renowned zoo, hoping to get ideas. The zoo was to be located directly behind the government museum.

That summer Banff said goodbye to their party line telephones and the private telephones were connected to the long distance lines in Calgary. Private lines had also been run from the town up to the Hot Springs, the Cave and Basin, Bankhead, and Lake Minnewanka. The new Banff telephone exchange was located in the government building along with the museum and government offices. It operated from 8 am to 10 pm although the hotels were connected all night directly to the train station for the late arrivals. Miss Sibbald had been hired to run the switchboard. The rates to connect to Calgary were 40¢ plus Bell's rates for the actual long distance call.

Although hunting was Norman's passion, his brother Lou preferred mountain climbing and was happiest when he was scrambling up Cascade Mountain yet again. No one climbed Cascade more often than Lou did. The last time Lou had gone up with Ernest Riley of Calgary and Eddie Wilson. They reached the summit in nine hours. That August while Lou was scaling mountains, Norman took his hotel manager Mr. Rose and they went off on a day-long duck hunting trip to Gleichen. The guests at the King Edward let the men know that they expected a fine duck dinner upon their return. The guests were not disappointed when Norman returned with 60 of the little winged animals.

While Lou kept busy planting flags on top of Cascade Mountain, Norman decided that for many non-climbers the only way to see what lay atop the surrounding mountains was by looking through a telescope. Knowing that, he purchased a high-power telescope which came all the way from Paris, France. Upon its arrival it was set upon a platform built on top of the Curio Shop. It was intended for the public's use. Lou had recently scaled Cascade again and beat his previous record. He reached the top in only 7 hours and 45 minutes. Lou had spent the summer running the summer curio shop across from the Banff Springs Hotel.

With the end of summer came the announcement that Norman's good friend Jim Brewster was moving to the B.C. coast. Norman felt abandoned by his friend as did many of the locals. Jim was leaving and that summer business had fallen dramatically. The great depression of 1907 had arrived and businesses were starting to feel the effects. It was a difficult winter financially and soon creditor's letters began to pile up. Norman's answer was simply to ignore them as best he could. Not the best thing to do perhaps but there was very little money coming in. Norman figured things would sort themselves out the following summer and he tried not to worry about it. With what little money he had he added a third storey to his hotel. Trying to raise some capital, he advertised that with his printing press he could do letterheads, billheads, menu cards, and sundries—anything a local business might need. He also decided to inquire about purchasing a new boat for Lake Minnewanka. The boat should hold 125 people and have speeds of up to 22 m.p.h. He would be in direct competition with the *Minnewanka*, another tourist launch that boasted musical and moonlight excursions. In the spring, Jim Brewster decided to return to Banff and Norman was glad to see that his friend had come to his senses.

The big story of 1908 was the pending arrival of the famous Dominion Fair, which was to be held in Calgary that year. It would mean that all the Stoneys would be in Calgary for the fair so the Indian races in Banff were scheduled for May 25 and June 10. Norman contacted the Indians and they replied back saying they would arrive on May 22 if the weather was good. They too had suffered from the depression and desperately needed the money the tourists and games provided. Norman would judge the races this year along with William and Jim Brewster. Norman was in charge of the food rations for the encampment. Always when the Indians visited Banff, they were fed by the local people.

The excitement over Calgary's Dominion Fair was building and Norman had work to do. The CPR was offering excursion tickets return from Banff for $3.30 per person. Norman was planning a huge display to serve as one of the fair's leading attractions. Once all his animal displays were ready, he shipped them by rail to Calgary. The shipment contained a huge grizzly bear and a buffalo bull. The size of the display required an entire train car full of stuffed animals and birds. The Dominion Fair commenced on July 1 with a huge historical parade. The display Norman produced was amazing and the *Calgary Herald* wrote that this collection of wildlife must certainly be the largest ever seen in the West. Georgie was anxious to attend the fair and along with her mother and her friend Mrs. Harmon she boarded the train to Calgary.

Norman's display was an unqualified success and he took home first prize for his collection of birds, first prize for animals, second prize for his game heads, a silver cup for best game heads, and a silver cup for best general exhibit. He missed winning the gold cup for exhibit, by only one point. The event in Calgary was a success although Norman was quick to point out that the races and events were badly organized with long waits between each one. Perhaps they would have done better had they studied the way the Banff Indian Day races were held. Norman was happy that he didn't have to ship his large buffalo bull home. It was purchased by an English tourist and sent off to London, England. The animal filled an entire express car.

The weekend following the Dominion Fair was the busiest time in the history of Banff. When the last train cars arrived in Banff the number of travellers far exceeded available hotel capacity. One hotel had only four rooms left for over 70 people. Another hotel had 35 people and no rooms. Beds were quickly found, cots were put in every corner of every hotel, and even tents were set up. By the end of the night every tourist had some place to sleep.

Earlier that year, at the end of May, a very special visitor had arrived at the Luxtons. Norman's youngest brother Malloch had arrived from Minnesota. He had been there earlier but had left on a trip to the coast. Lou was up to his old tricks again, climbing Cascade Mountain, but heavy snow meant that even by mid-July the snow on the mountain was still 8 to 12 feet deep. Still that didn't deter Lou who managed to reach the summit in 13½ hours, despite the snow. Family had always been important to Norman and soon he would welcome a new member into the little house on Beaver Street.

EIGHT

New Additions

The latest 'employee' at the Curio Shop was a black bear, captured in Golden, B.C. by a trader friend of Norman's who brought him to Banff. The bear was named "Teddy" and his job was to attract tourists as he stood outside the store, attached to a 15-foot-long chain. Both tourists and locals adored the bear and would spend hours visiting and feeding him. He enjoyed the biscuits and candy and seemed to enjoy his new home and the attention he received. One day three young boys arrived to visit Norman's bear. One of the boys was Forrest Oliver Brewster, the youngest boy in the Brewster family, affectionately referred to as "Pat." Twelve-year-old Pat and his friends Stewart Armour and Gordon Reed had been out camping the previous evening when Gordon had hatched a rather cruel plan. Details of the plan he kept secretly to himself. Stewart and Pat were told that all would be revealed the next day.

It was busy that day at the Curio shop and many folks were gathered about outside watching the bear. The three boys had arrived and Pat was busy feeding Teddy the bits of bacon he had saved. Gordon was planning to feed the bear as well and he quietly waited in line. At last it was Gordon's turn and he reached out and handed the bear a bit of chocolate and then quickly turned to leave. Suddenly Teddy reared up on his hind legs and let out a horrifying yelp. He began running in circles growling and it was obvious to all that the animal was extremely distraught. The anxious crowd felt certain that the angry bear was seconds away from breaking free from his chain and in fear they began to run. One lady stumbled up the grass slope in panic, tearing the buttons off her dress as she made a run towards the Bretton Hotel. Another gentleman tore his suit and yet another man jumped over the riverbank to escape the stampeding tourists and sprained both ankles. The mounted police were called and soon understood that the three young boys had most definitely done something to aggravate the poor bear. After questioning the three it was revealed that Gordon had spent the previous evening at camp, lacing the chocolate with red peppers. Pat and Stewart now knew the "secret" that Gordon had kept from them. The Mounties told Norman that he could no longer keep the bear as a tourist attraction and that he must get rid of him. It didn't much matter since after the chocolate incident the bear would only accept food from Norman anyway. A home was found for Teddy with a hotel keeper in Golden, where he lived happily for many years.

Norman missed the old bear but he had much to celebrate. On July 31, 1908, Georgie and Norman had their first and only child. They named her Eleanor. Just nine days after her birth a meteor flashed across the sky, lighting up Banff as it tore past the town and loudly crashed into a nearby mountain. There was much discussion whether it hit Sulphur Mountain or landed somewhere in the Vermillion Lakes area. The meteor was never found.

With the birth of the new baby it was the perfect excuse for George to visit Banff and so in August he arrived from Minnesota to see his new niece and visit his brothers. Norman was busy as always with his curio shop and plans to build a new launch for Lake Minnewanka were in full swing. Money was always tight but with the depression of 1907, Norman's bills were now long overdue. Overdrafts were left unpaid and NSF cheques were now quite common. The creditors had begun to panic when the King Edward Hotel was in overdraft even though it was the busiest time of the year. Was Norman really that low on funds or did he simply not keep his books in shape? Actually, it was a bit of both as when Norman got busy, keeping the books took a backseat to customer service. The money wasn't there to pay either. Norman first ignored the problem but it wasn't long before he was asking for extensions. He tried to find other ways to make money. There was the new boat for Minnewanka that he was having built and he hoped to make some extra money in the curio shop by selling the latest invention. This new product was called the "Thermos" and had just been invented in 1907. A special stand was erected and training material was provided by the new company so that Norman could properly explain the benefits of this new miracle product. There was a huge margin for profit if you could sell the Thermos properly. The Thermos Company assisted their retailers by spending $2,000 a month on magazine, newspaper, and circular advertising. They guaranteed the container would keep your drinks hot for 24 hours, warm for 48 hours, and no liquid would freeze in the Thermos for up to 30 days. This certainly was the greatest invention for people in the mountains who climbed, hiked, or went trail riding.

Along with the Thermos there were the new boxes of chocolates ordered from the Ganong Brothers of Winnipeg with the "Sign of the Goat" emblem on them. Norman tried not to worry about his financial affairs. He would just do the best he could, for now he needed to concentrate on his new passenger boat. The general store at Exshaw had been closed down and that left more time to focus on the new passenger launch. There were many questions from the boat manufacturer such as how many passengers it should carry, what speeds did Norman hope it would attain, and how big an engine was needed. If the trips down the lake were lengthy then he would need a vessel that travelled at least 10 to 12 miles per hour. A proper engineer would be required to run it at a cost of at least $3.50 an hour. Since no experienced ship engineers lived in Banff, there would be travelling expenses to deal with. Onboard there would be storage space necessary for batteries for the ignition system, headlights, a searchlight, air tanks or airtight bulkheads and lifeboats. This was not going to be easy.

Norman had hoped the boat would be completed and in place on the lake in time for the tourist season of 1908. It soon became painfully clear this was not going to happen. The vessel was delayed when the paperwork for the British-built Thorneycroft engines was lost. New papers had to be sent for from England. When the engines did finally arrive there were parts missing which then had to be replaced. Then the government official who was registering the boat went and died thus causing yet another delay. The boat could not be shipped by rail until the official's successor was able to complete the paperwork. This venture had been entered into by Norman and his partner George Manners. If the boat was not going to arrive in time for the 1908 season Norman feared he would have to pull out of the partnership; he simply didn't have the money. The vessel had been named the *Minnewanka*.

The *Minnewanka* arrived the third week of September 1908 and she was quickly moved up to the lake before the winter set in. The other exciting arrival that fall was a certain famous inventor by the name of Thomas Edison who was spending his holiday in Banff.

Winter passed and with it came the building of the new King Edward Livery; the original had had burned down the previous October. It would be rebuilt on Bear Street in plenty of time for the new season. By the spring of 1909 the *Minnewanka* was getting readied for service. The proposed trips would take the passenger some 40 miles on Lake Minnewanka in 4 to 5 hours with a ticket price of $2.50. The stage would pick up passengers at the Hotel King Edward and take them to the lake where they would board the vessel. Her captain was George Manners. Norman was busy fighting with the Marine and Fisheries Department. Over the winter they had decided to change the laws regarding boat operation. The new law stated that all boats carrying passengers would require a certified captain. Norman advised them that due to the nature of his business and the shortness of the season there was no way enough income would be generated to pay for a new captain from the East. He also argued that Lake Minnewanka was not a place where any shipping took place and that his boat was thoroughly safe and equipped with all the latest safety features. He had already paid $5,000 for the boat with the understanding, based on 1908 Marine rules that George could serve as Captain. He requested a special permit be issued to operate the new launch with an "ordinary" man. He also advised the Marine and Fisheries Department that since the lake was enclosed by mountains it did not endure rough waters that might be found on more open areas of water. Norman won and the *Minnewanka* plied the lakes waters throughout the summer of 1909 and for many years thereafter. She was a fast boat with a top speed of 22 miles per hour. Norman did finally leave the operation to George Manners but Norman's little hotel at Lake Minnewanka continued to operate until 1912. The *Minnewanka* would eventually be renamed the *Aylmer* after the original *Aylmer* that had operated on the lake.

Tourist season was soon in full swing and it looked like a busy summer ahead. It was Sunday, June 19, 1909, and Norman was out walking when he saw a team of horses attached to a rig suddenly bolt nearby. The runaway team was in danger of causing serious injury to anyone on the street. Norman jumped to the rescue. Desperately trying to stop the runaway team, Norman was thrown down and the rig turned over on top of him. Norman lay on the road with blood pouring from a deep gash to the face. His knee was so severely wrenched he was unable to walk, and he was carried home. Norman remained in bed for a week, unable to walk or help out at work. Additional rest was ordered before he was allowed to resume his busy life. Letters came in from friends and well-wishers along with letters from his creditors. All were sorry about his accident and most creditors agreed to delay payment on his many loans. He was a hero and had possibly saved many lives.

Banff Indian Days were held the first week of July and Mr. John Kenny, Norman's namesake, had arrived in town for a visit. It was great to see his father's old newspaper partner again. Norman also got great news that the government had listened to his suggestion of bringing a herd of buffalo up to the town of Wainwright and to construct a buffalo park there. One hundred and ninety buffalo were to be brought from Montana to the new buffalo park. The number included one 117 cows. Norman felt very strongly that the buffalo, once the great animal of the plains, should not be extinct from Alberta. It was such a strong part of the province's history.

August of 1909 was an exciting time as the very first automobile arrived in town. Norman Lougheed had arrived using the new Banff Coach Road. Other vehicles followed and they were kept in the garage at the King Edward Hotel. Later that same August, Norman received a wonderful letter praising the virtues of his wonderful hotel. Proudly Norman ran the contents of the letter in the next issue of the *Crag and Canyon*.

"This family not happy paying so much to CPR set out to find breakfast and stopped at a most unpretentious and unassuming little hotel called the "King Edward." Our welcome was right royal. Our rooms were plain but spotlessly clean. The proprietor (Luxton) visited us personally and looked after our comfort. The table was bountiful and well cooked. We were told the service did not pretend to vie or compete with any of the higher priced hotels, but we were assured the best that could be bought in the market was placed upon the table and served in the plainest manner possible.

Our intention to remain for the day only, was changed at the close of the day. So comfortable have we found ourselves that we have stayed on and explored Banff to our heart's content.

J.M. Williams
Newark, N.J.
U.S.A."

For many years, Norman had begged the CPR and the Government of Canada to consider Banff as a winter resort. Year after year they refused but Norman would not give up and in the winter of 1909/10 they finally relented. Norman was thrilled and ran a special edition of the *Crag and Canyon* on February 12, 1910 announcing their decision. Mr. Hayter Reed (head of the CPR Hotels system) and Mr. Howard Douglas (Commissioner of Parks) had relented and even agreed to finance a toboggan slide. It would be from two to three miles in length and building could get underway. The town decided to build a larger skating rink plus a curling rink for visitors. Skiing, ice-boating and a winter trotting track would be available and the CPR would begin advertising Banff as a winter resort. This was wonderful news as Norman's hotel was an all-season hotel whereas the Banff Springs Hotel was still only designed for summer use.

For years locals had already enjoyed ice-boating and Dr. Brett, Jim Brewster, Jack Standly and Walter Spicer already had their own boats. The Banff curling rink was certainly the most picturesque in the west and sleigh rides were hugely popular. Not to mention the Hot Springs which were a real treat on a cold winter's day.

The new decade looked very promising for Banff. Norman's family were doing well and Georgie's folks were thinking about retiring to Calgary. Annie and David McDougall had planned a 3- month holiday to Cuba and invited Georgie and little Eleanor to go with them. Annie's brother, Adam MacKenzie, had moved there and owned six ranches where he raised cattle and hogs. Now cattle and hogs were one thing but Norman had something that Adam certainly did not. Norman had a merman, not a mermaid but a merman, half fish and half man. The story Norman told was that he and brother Lou, had gotten drunk one night and with the various bits from their taxidermy supplies, they had pieced together the strange looking creature. Sometimes the story was that the creature came from Lake Minnewanka. Was it real or was it pieced together from taxidermy scraps in the back of the curio shop? Whatever it was, there was one thing on which everyone agreed—it was ugly! Children loved the strange little creature and certainly it looked real enough to fool the young ones if not many of the older ones.

The merman was actually purchased from J. Cumming of Japan. The merman's original home was at 142C Yamotecho, Yokohama, Japan. It had come across the ocean on the *Empress of Japan* before finding its permanent home at the Sign of the Goat. These mermen were sold primarily to American circus shows and were found in the freak or sideshow tents. They first appeared in 1822 with the first one arriving in America in 1842 as part of P.T. Barnum's shows. Norman's example was kept under glass, preserving it in excellent condition. It would eventually become one of only eight known examples in the world and the only one easily accessible to the viewing public. Other mermen can be found in Albany at the New York State Museum (not on public view), Milwaukee Public Museum (not on view), and the Peabody Museum at Harvard (not on public view). The only one similar to Norman's can be found at the Arkansas Alligator Farm in Hot Springs, Arkansas. Norman's merman, at the Sign of the Goat, is the only known example in Canada.

Norman continued to expand and purchase things but his finances were in ruin. His ability to keep his financial affairs in order had never been his strong suit and with the Depression still on since 1907, Norman soon stopped paying his creditors altogether. It hadn't helped being injured in the runaway rig accident in the summer of 1909. By the fall of 1910 Norman was forced to declare bankruptcy. His entire estate was valued at $11,831.27 and from this the lawyers would pay off his creditors. All of them had agreed to 60% on all monies owed them with the exception of Mr. Standish who had been promised verbally by Norman that he would be paid back in full, eventually. Norman promised to pay all his creditors back eventually even though legally they had agreed to only 60%. Mr. J.P. O'Leary proposed to take over the entire estate and run the hotel, curio shop, fur business, etc. He promised to pay the creditors 12½% of the gross receipts of the hotel and 65% of the gross receipts of the sale of furs, curios and the rest. Mr. O'Leary promised to pay all taxes and insurance plus the interest on the mortgage for the Hotel King Edward. He also promised to cover all costs and repairs on the hotel. Most of the creditors thought this was a good idea and supported Mr. O'Leary, but some did not. The initial meeting of the creditors had been held on February 8, 1910 at 2:30 pm. The estate was currently under the control of lawyer Mark Bennett Peacock.

Even though Norman owed so much money, his creditors admired him and were afraid to offend him. The Hemming Manufacturing Company were staunch Norman supporters and wrote him a long letter on what exactly was going on in regards to the estate. It seemed that although Mark Peacock had taken it over nothing was being done. O'Leary was not popular with some people and perhaps Norman would consider taking on a business partner. If he could find a partner then with that money the creditors could be paid off and Norman could retain control. The partner could also help him with the operation of the various businesses. This had to be better than O'Leary running everything. They also had suggested earlier that Norman look up a Mr. King who was known for getting businesses through their financial troubles. Norman did make a motion to contact Mr. King but never followed up on it. The Hemming Manufacturing Company felt that regardless of what happened the estate should be given back to Norman. O'Leary was a trustee and knew nothing of how to run a hotel, fur trading business or souvenir shop. They commended Norman, saying that they knew of no businessman who worked harder or should be expected to. They knew Norman could be a success and they thought no one deserved it more.

Norman was given back his estate and bills were paid over time. Meanwhile the fight was on with the federal government as Norman wanted to build a hotel up at Lake Louise to compete with the Château Lake Louise of the CPR. The answer from Ottawa was a very emphatic no. They were firm in their belief that,

"The National Parks are dedicated and kept up by the public, for the public, and not to serve the interests of any private individual. It is certain that certain private enterprises are necessary in order that the public may receive due advantage of the beauties of the park and such private enterprise is permitted as the public needs seem to demand."

An earlier letter from Ottawa had stated that the CPR hotel in Lake Louise was sufficient to maintain the beauty of the area and no other hotels would be considered. They had suggested that Norman consider building at Laggan Station (the Lake Louise train station).

Norman knew there was no point in continuing the fight as they wished no further correspondence on the issue. Norman felt it was unfair that the CPR and the Brewsters always seemed to be given all the opportunities. After all, was he not the only one willing to operate hotels through the winter at great cost to himself?

Another Christmas would soon be upon them but the event would be more somber this year. On December 17, 1910, word came of the death of Norman's older brother Harry. A massive heart attack had killed Harry at the young age of 38. Harry had lived in St. Paul where he worked as Chief Deputy Clerk in the office of the Clerk of the District Court. At the time of his death Harry had been living with his brother George while his wife was in Milwaukee taking care of her sick mother. The previous evening, Harry had been taking a shortcut home and that is where they found him the next morning. The doctors believed the heart attack was brought on by the steep ascent up the hill. Harry's heart had always caused him problems ever since he had suffered severe sunstroke while serving in the Philippines. He had served with F Company of the 13th Minnesota Volunteers. On his final evening Harry had fainted at the courthouse but was revived with a little fresh air and thought himself well enough to walk home. It was a walk he would never complete. Harry had served as city editor for the *Winnipeg Free Press* but had spent the last 18 years of his life in St. Paul. He had spent six years as chief sanitary inspector and later got the job at the District Court. The private family funeral was held in St. Paul so his mother Sarah, brother George, sister Ollie Hoskings, and her husband Ed could attend. Ollie's husband Ed was the telegraph editor of the *St. Paul Dispatch*. Harry Luxton was buried at Lakewood cemetery.

In 1911 there was a new king on the throne; King George was crowned June 22, 1911. Banff residents went all out and decorated their shops and homes but no one got a day off. It was tourist season. The

King Edward and the Mount Royal Hotel did their bit by decorating their hotels with flags.

Georgie kept busy that summer and decided to throw a huge picnic for her mother Annie, Mrs. Howard Douglas, Mrs. Paddy Nolan and many others. The picnic was located on the Spray River at the first set of falls. Everyone agreed that this was perhaps the most beautiful scenery in the entire Banff and Canmore area. That and the trout fishing was particularly good and the party returned with a full basket of freshly caught mountain trout. Norman was too busy for picnics as he was building a summer home on Buffalo Street for his good friend Paddy Nolan.

With the rapid increase in tourists and residents in Banff the construction of a dam at Lake Minnewanka was soon underway. The dam was built by the Calgary Power Company and would result in the level of the lake being raised. Before the dam construction began, Norman had been building a chalet on the lake but with the lake level being raised his chalet would be under water instead of on the shore. The power company agreed to move the chalet to the new shoreline. On the evening prior to the lake level being raised Norman's old chalet on the lake was burned down and a party was held to watch the fire. The new chalet that Norman was building would be completed by July 20, 1912 and would stand just north and west of the old chalet. It would a 2-storey log building, 20 by 40 feet, with a 10-foot verandah on the lake front. The dining room measured 20 by 12 feet with a large kitchen and apartments were in behind it. The little chalet also included 4 bedrooms.

Norman's hotel competitor and father-in-law, David McDougall, had decided to retire to Calgary and sold the Mount Royal Hotel to Jim Brewster. The price was $100,000 and the interest rate was quite high but Jim felt it was worth the price. The Mount Royal had 60 rooms plus a dining room and billiard room. Norman was busy across the street with reconstruction on the King Edward Hotel. A new concrete basement and dining room were added.

July of 1912 brought news of an exiting discovery by Bill Peyto. Bill had found a meteor just east of Exshaw, just four miles from the CPR track. It was brought to Banff's Government Museum and put on display for the public. The meteor weighed in at 300 pounds.

Norman decided to move the Banff Indian Days to the last week of July and it was the largest turnout ever. Some 1500 people attended and over $700 was raised in prize money. The newest attraction was a football game.

By the third week of August all the major renovations on the Hotel King Edward were complete. It looked very different now with its red brick walls and 40 large windows looking down onto Caribou Street. The hotel looked much more appealing from Banff Avenue as large glass entrance doors had been installed, opening into a large rotunda. In the lobby sat a large fireplace built of cobblestone where guests could lounge on cold or rainy days. There was now steam heat in every room and the new dining room held 120 guests. From the lobby a staircase led up to the first and second floors which now contained 40 rooms, most of which had their own hot and cold running water. Bathrooms were located on each floor along with a hydrant and hose. Electric lights were featured throughout and most of the furnishings were new and of good quality. The new and enlarged kitchen was first class and was considered to be the best in Banff.

The *Crag and Canyon* was reporting on the first-ever Calgary Stampede which was scheduled for the third week of August. Among the distinguished visitors would be the Duke and Duchess of Connaught. A special train ran from Banff to Calgary return for just $3.50 a person. The train left Banff at 8:30 am and returned at 7:30 pm thus allowing a full day at the Calgary Stampede. Norman heard that the races and shows were poorly organized with long waits between each and he didn't hesitate to mention that perhaps they should have consulted him first. With his years of experience operating Banff Indian Days he could have helped to ensure everything ran on time and that no one ever missed a train or their dinner. Little did Norman know that the man responsible for that first Calgary Stampede would eventually become one of his very best friends.

Directly after the Calgary Stampede the Duke and Duchess of Connaught headed out to Banff and Norman was asked to act as the official town guide to the Duchess and her daughter, Princess Patricia. Just a few days after their arrival, Norman took the ladies up to Lake Minnewanka and for a trip on the *Aylmer*, down to the end of the lake. With the level of the lake raised due to the new dam, all agreed that the scenery at Minnewanka was much improved. Earlier in the week Norman and Georgie, along with Jim Brewster and his wife, had all been invited to lunch with their royal highnesses. The visitors left after a lovely 5-day visit.

Norman had recently got his hands on an old Red River Cart, just like that which had brought his parents to Fort Garry back in the early days.

He added the cart to his expanding list of attractions at the Sign of the Goat.

At long last, the federal government finally built the promised toboggan run on Caribou Street just in time for the winter of 1912. There were also plans for a 5-mile bobsleigh run to be built on Sulphur Mountain. It was to start at the Upper Hot Springs and run all the way down to the Banff Springs Hotel. Blasting was also underway for the new pool up at the Cave and Basin. There were 120 men already hard at work on the new 150- foot length swimming pool.

That winter a new skating rink was opened where one could buy season's tickets that allowed one to skate as often as they liked. It was open afternoons and evenings and both skates and boots could be rented.

Norman was busy trying to make ends meet over the winter and had signed up to be the agent for the People's Home Company Ltd. He was licensed to provide loans over a 7-year period with interest rates of 5%. The *Crag and Canyon* was now running all year round and contained some world news along with funny little quotations and stories. Of course to finance the expanded paper Norman was forced to include those pesky ads for magic elixirs and tonics. The good news was that the locals had year' round news on Banff happenings like the upcoming Banff vs. Bankhead hockey match scheduled for Christmas Day. The December issues contained stories about the beautiful Christmas window displays in the local stores. The attractive displays included lots of Cadbury chocolate, fruits, and candies. The electric lights made the displays look very tempting indeed.

February of 1913 brought sad news for Norman. His good friend Paddy Nolan had died. The popular lawyer had been a good friend of Norman's since those early days working for the *Calgary Herald*. Paddy, a native of Limerick, Ireland, had an amazing career. He had defended some 19 murder cases in his life and only lost 2. He was a brilliant man with a legendary sense of humour and was loved by thousands. There was not a village or town that would not welcome him with open arms. He had died on Monday, February 10, of an internal hemorrhage. It came as a shock since he has only been sick for a week. The funeral was held at St. Mary's church in Calgary on the Wednesday morning and then his body was brought to his beloved Banff where it was buried.

Norman was busy as usual, always with a new business venture up his sleeve. He decided the time was right to open a movie theatre. Norman called his brother George in St. Paul and managed to convince him to leave everything and move to Banff. He would make him manager of the new theatre. George left his job at the *Twin City Press* and said his goodbyes at a large farewell banquet thrown in his honour. George arrived in May along with his new wife Ada and purchased a house on Muskrat Street. The new theatre was named the Lux and it was part of the King Edward block. George was a brilliant photographer and Norman was sure his brother's experience would be an asset in the film business.

The Lux Moving Picture Room, which replaced the old pool hall, was just about complete. New opera house chairs were on order from Chicago but would not arrive in time for the opening so regular chairs would have to make do to start. The Lux name was chosen not as an abbreviated form of Luxton, but rather referred to a "lux" which is a measurement of reflected light. The theatre boasted the newest technology and featured rear projection. Rear projection meant that the projector was located behind the screen. Up until the introduction of rear projection the films had been difficult to watch and actually painful to the eyes. This new system meant the pictures were clear and steady. The Lux Theatre in Banff was the second theatre in Canada to offer rear projection; the other theatre was located in Montreal. The machine house, where the films were operated from, was situated out in the lane some 30 feet away. The machine house was built of solid stone and all openings could be closed with fire doors. In these early days the film was highly flammable and precautions had to be taken.

The new theatre was put to the test with a trial run on Thursday, May 15, 1913. A select group of friends were invited to try out the latest in motion picture technology. Norman had arranged for one of the finest films in history to be shown for the grand opening. The film was Cleopatra, produced by and starring the great Helen Gardner. The actual film was 6,000 feet in length and was considered the finest film ever made. Norman placed huge ads in the *Crag and Canyon* to promote the wonderful film and the new Lux Theatre. A top-notch projectionist had been hired by the name of Sid Blumenthal and admission prices were set at 15¢ for adults and 10¢ for children.

In the summer there was plenty of entertainment in town over and above the swimming, mountain climbing, hiking, or fishing that many enjoyed. In July the "Oklahoma Ranch Wild West Show" was coming to town. It featured Indians from several tribes including the Sioux, Cheyenne, Blackfoot, and Apache. There were also Russian Cossacks. Two performances were held a day featuring expert rifle shots, a staged

Indian attack on an immigrant train, stagecoach holdups, and even the pony express. It promised to be a lot of fun for young and old. Banff Indian Days would follow on July 18 and 19. Both the Wild West show and the Indian Days were an outstanding success. It was the largest gathering of Stoneys so far with over 800 coming out to the celebrations. The prize money passed all previous amounts, coming in at over $2,000. The tourists and locals were out in full force and the attendance climbed to over 5,000 spectators. This year the new bow and arrow competition was added and proved the favourite as 16 competitors were lined up and in unison shot their arrows which glided through the air in a graceful arc.

As summer came to an end the Lux theatre was offering special deals. If adults attended on Thursdays and Fridays their children would be admitted free to the Saturday matinée. In the fall George Luxton installed a $250 Victrola machine to provide music in the one-minute wait between changes of film. There was only one projector so at the end of each reel the first reel was removed and replaced with a new reel. The projector was not automatic so it had to be hand cranked at a rate of 60 feet per minute. George made sure during the film breaks that he played the latest music and songs of the day for his patrons' listening enjoyment. There were new films every week so movie- going became a weekly habit. The only fly in the ointment was the Alberta government, who had decided to put their noses into the movie business. They were going to impose a license on all moving picture theatres to prevent them from running movies on Sundays. Opening your theatre on a Sunday would mean your license would be cancelled and your theatre could be shut down.

The movie projectionists had also formed their own union, Local 302, which operated in Calgary and covered all of southern Alberta.

With the latest films now being shown in Banff it was time the little town starred in one as well. The Universal Film Company of America was due to arrive early in 1914. They would be coming in a special train car full of moving picture artists and their related equipment. The film would be called "Banff the Beautiful."

Tourist season of 1913 was over and Georgie and Eleanor, now nicknamed "Billy," had just returned home from a visit to Morley but were off on a visit to Calgary. It was while in Calgary little Eleanor became ill and a slight operation on her throat was required. She soon returned home and recovered.

Another winter meant it was time again for building and renovations. The theatre was to get a new floor with the floor at the rear being 2 feet higher than the old one. There would be air space between the old floor and the new one, which would result in more comfort for the patrons. It would help keep their feet warmer. Each row of chairs would now be set 4 inches higher than the row in front to provide better viewing and aisle lights were added. The theatre's first official inspection was conducted by A.R. Brooke in December. It was a standard safety inspection and Norman passed with flying colors. Although the requirements sounded easy enough to comply with, many theatres over the years did not fair as well. Norman and his brother always kept the exit lights in working order, the exit doors were unlocked when patrons were in the theatre and all exits were free from obstruction. The theatre was kept clean and tidy with good ventilation. Mr. Brooke couldn't think of any suggestions for improvement. There was another theatre in town called the Harmony Theatre. It was not found in the same condition. Over at the Harmony no red exit lights existed and the exit doors in the rear were found locked. When Brooke did get them opened, one door would only open half way due to frozen earth blocking the door from the outside. Inside there was stage scenery standing in front of one of the exits. The Harmony Theatre was determined to be a dangerous place in case of fire or panic.

With George as manager, the Lux theatre was extremely well run. One evening a woman had left her purse hanging on the back of her chair. After the theatre closed a man sought out Norman in a panic as he desperately needed to recover the purse. The theatre was opened up and the handbag was found hanging from the chair and still contained all of its $2,000 in cash!

At Christmas, the Lux Theatre had become the official post office for Santa Claus. The theatre would remain open over the Christmas season for children to drop off their letters to Santa. That year a total of 104 letters were posted at the little North Pole Post Office and all were answered by the theatre's staff.

At home Norman and his wife celebrated Christmas by having David and Annie McDougall over for Christmas dinner along with Mr. And Mrs. George Ross and several of their local Banff friends. Everyone was looking forward to a wonderful year ahead and there was much to celebrate.

NINE

The End of Innocence

It was 9:00 am on Saturday, February 7, 1914, when the little fire was discovered over the O.K. Electric shop in the King Edward Hotel block. Hotel employees sounded the fire alarm and got busy with the hotel's fire hose but it soon became obvious that outside help would be required. The town's fire bell was sounded which brought Banff's volunteer fire brigade quickly to the rescue along with hundreds of the town's citizens. No one was too concerned as the fire was small and would soon be out. The fire brigade crossed the street and went to attach the hose up to the fire hydrant next to the Mount Royal Hotel. It was frozen solid. Twelve men put all their weight and strength into turning on the hydrant but it wouldn't budge. Quickly they set out in search of other hydrants nearby, all of which were frozen solid. The men scattered in search of a working hydrant and at last found one on the corner of Caribou and Bear Streets. The water flowed for a minute and then stopped abruptly. Sections of the hose were unfit as the couplings froze as soon as the cold water touched them. Had the hoses been stored inside this would not have been a problem but they had been stored outside. The chemical engine was brought to the scene, only it too was useless—the government had neglected to keep the engine charged with the necessary chemicals.

Thirty minutes had now passed still with no active fire hydrants or useable engine. The fire was spreading rapidly. Desperately the firefighters stacked hay and anything they could find that would burn and placed it around the hydrants. The haystacks were set ablaze in the hopes the hydrants could be thawed out in time to save the hotel and surrounding buildings. Another hour passed before the hydrants were functional but now there was no hope in saving the hotel block. The best anyone could hope for was to possibly save the hotel itself. All energy was now focused on that task. Another business now in jeopardy was the Brewster Trading Company store located adjacent to the hotel. The firemen were already exhausted but they refused to give up. The temperature that morning was -20°F and the firefighters were soaked from head to toe. The outer layers of their wet clothing had now turned to ice but they fought on. Some of the men fought the fire from 9:00 am, February 7, until 3:00 am the following morning. That day the brave firemen of Banff proved that they were indeed true heroes.

All the hotel's guests had managed to get out in time and the tailor J.D. Anderson had managed to save the contents of his shop. The Lux theatre's contents were also saved. Total losses from the fire were estimated to be in excess of $62,000. The losses included 50 bedrooms in the hotel, fixtures, all stock of liquor and cigars in the King Edward Bâr and many personal effects of the hotel employees whose rooms were all destroyed. Damage to the hotel was estimated at $47,425 and the Brewster Trading Company loss was $15,000. Only 75% of the total loss was covered by insurance. To make matters worse, looters stole hundreds of dollars' worth of goods from the hotel and the Brewster Company store. Although it was never confirmed, it is believed the fire was the result of defective wiring.

Norman was angered by the inefficiency of all the fire equipment and looked to Ottawa for further compensation. As usual, the government refused to take responsibility. The official fire report was laughable as the following excerpt confirms:

"The Official Fire Report
Dominion Parks Branch - Ottawa
Chief Superintendent
Twenty witnesses were examined on oath before the Inquiry adjourned after five hours.

1) That the fire was started by an overheated stove pipe on the premises of the O.K Electric Co (Carl Alexander Friezen – proprietor) although defective wiring was given by three witnesses as probable cause.

2) That there was considerable delay in sending in a general alarm while an attempt was being made to extinguish the fire with hotel appliances which, although there was ample water, were inadequate.

3) That none of the hydrants were frozen although the screw of the 1st hydrant tried (that outside the Mt. Royal Hotel) was seized with the intense cold which prevailed (-20°F) but was easily turned and gave a copious supply when this screw was slackened by means of a small hay fire.

4) That the hose was generally in good condition except for a few lengths which had been put on the reels in a damp condition and which because the nozzle had been attached before allowing the shell ice to be flushed out became choked and was frozen.

5) That the chemical engine was on the ground a few minutes after the alarm was given but it's condition was not adequate to cope with a fire of the dimensions this one had assumed, that in ordinary circumstances the engine, which should give 120 lbs. pressure, would only give 60 owing to the worn-out conditions for the domes etc, but on this occasion only 10 lbs. pressure were got.

6) All the government employees did respond as quickly as they could with many on duty from 9:30 am on the 7th to 3am on the 8th. No charges of negligence on the part of government employees".

Norman agreed that on the day in question that he could not have asked the firemen to do more; his issue was with all the equipment, none of which had been properly maintained. If "seized with the intense cold" didn't mean frozen, then it was hard to imagine what it did mean. There were those in Ottawa that did feel for Norman but their hands were tied. Norman had even offered to pay for a private lawyer to represent the people who suffered the greatest losses (himself, Brewster and Anderson) so a proper report could be done. He admitted in this same letter to the Hon. Frank Oliver, House of Commons, Ottawa that he was almost completely busted financially but that he would stay and fight against the corruption as best he could. He would also rebuild and he thanked Mr. Oliver for everything he had tried to do on his behalf.

The fire had made headlines in Calgary, Edmonton, and even as far away as Minneapolis where Norman's mother was living. She read of the terrible fire before her son had a chance to call her. She was very worried and quickly sent off a letter to which Norman replied:

"My dear mother,

I received your kind letter and I do not want you to worry. I guess I am used to these setbacks by now and I am not going to lay down on this one. I hope to have another place up within two or three months. George's picture house went with the rest of the building. We have been all week clearing away the burnt places. Louis, George and myself know how to work and I guess the ladies of the house know how to keep their end up which is really the most important. Love to my dear mother and the rest.

Your Norman."

In the following days Lou, George, and Norman Luxton worked non-stop to clear up the debris from the fire and get the lot ready for rebuilding. If finances were bad before, they would get worse. The 25% the insurance didn't cover would have to come from Norman and with no hotel to make money it would mean that Norman's financial affairs would again be in dire straits.

Within 3 weeks of the fire the excavation and rebuilding of the new King Edward Block began. A temporary bar was erected that very week for the hotel and a week later the electrical work was completed. New, coloured exit signs were installed over the fire escape exits. Still there was a lot of work to be done on the hotel even though the actual structure had been saved. It had to be thoroughly cleaned and all traces of fire removed. Every square inch had to be repainted and all the furniture that had been burned or broken was replaced. The office was moved next to the stairway and a beautiful, semi-circular counter enclosed it. New rugs were laid and on March 21, 1914, the hotel reopened for business. The manager was Mr. Lorne C. Orr and he and his staff had worked very hard to get the hotel up and running again.

With no theatre to run, George Luxton decided to take a trip to Minneapolis and stopped briefly in Winnipeg in order to visit friends and family and do a little business. He left in late April but was back in Banff by the end of May.

The contract for the new King Edward block had been given to the Calgary firm of Thomas, Jamieson, McKenzie and Company. The new plans would call for a one-storey building with a second storey to be added the following spring. The structure would be built of brick and concrete with a foundation strong enough to accommodate an additional 4 or 5 storeys. The new ground floor would contain a bar room for the King Edward Hotel, three stores and a modern moving picture theatre.

By April things were looking up and Lou Luxton had finally decided it was time to settle down and married Nellie "Elsie" Manley. She had been born in Devon, England and had arrived in Calgary in May of 1912 but continued on to Banff in July of that same year. The couple married on April 14, 1914, had had three children including Olive (Biel) (1915), Elsie Minota (Olley) (1917) and William F. "Bill"(1919).

With construction well underway a cashier was hired for the new Lux Theatre. Miss Cynthia Price of Sydney, Australia got the job. She had traveled by ship via Auckland, Fiji, and Honolulu and was looking forward to working at the newest theatre in Banff.

Norman was also renovating his curio shop and getting it thoroughly cleaned and stocked in preparation for the summer tourists. The contractors had promised the new King Edward Block would be ready by mid-July and with it a brand-new, state-of-the-art Lux Theatre. Although the contractors were out by a couple of weeks the new theatre opened its doors by the beginning of August. It was an impressive addition to the local entertainment scene. The new auditorium was 40 by

80 feet wide and had a seating capacity of 500 people. The aisles were 8 feet wide and the beautiful interior wood finishings were done in the early English style. The walls were painted an elegant buff and maroon color with four semi-radiant, inverted globes which would provide soft and subdued lighting during the shows. Between films the current was increased to the bulbs to provide four times the lighting. The new building was steam heated and in place of the old steps to accommodate the raised rows of seating there was an inclined floor. This new floor would mean fewer accidents, a common occurrence on the steps of the early theatres. The building was made of brick, tile and cement to be fireproof. Rear projection was again used with the projector now installed in a cement, fireproof booth. Outside the entrance, over the arch, the familiar Lux sign was installed. Ladies rooms were provided to the left upon entering the lobby and they were fitted with every modern convenience. A pianist was hired by the name of Lucy Bolton and she was assisted by the Mount Royal Orchestra. Since the showing of films was still banned on Sunday nights there were concerts held instead.

It was shaping up to be a good summer and with the theatre reopened, the King Edward Block under construction and the tourists in the thousands visiting the small town, life was looking up for Norman. His mother had come up for the summer to visit her three sons and her granddaughter Eleanor. It was nice to have so many of the family together. Norman even managed to find the $20 needed to renew his Banff Springs Golf Club membership. Golf was a pastime that he and Georgie enjoyed together.

On August 4, 1914, the Duke of Connaught was visiting Banff with his daughter Princess Patricia. They had decided to take a leisurely canoe trip down the Bow River from Lake Louise to Banff. That morning the Duke took his position in the first canoe and sat directly behind Jim Brewster. It was a beautiful day but the spectacular trip would soon come to an end. Just ahead was the final bend in the river just before you reach Banff. As the first canoe rounded the bend the Duke gasped, "Oh my God!" There on the banks of the Bow River he saw them—a group of RCMP officers in full uniform. The Duke and Jim quickly paddled to the wharf where the official documents were handed to the Duke. Great Britain had declared war on Germany at 4:00 pm, Mountain Standard time. By 7:00 pm a train had arrived from Calgary to take the Duke and his daughter back to Ottawa.

With the outbreak of war, George decided to move back to Minneapolis and along with his mother and his wife Ada they made plans to leave as soon as they could. Sarah had been up visiting her boys in Banff over the summer.

Life in Banff would never be the same. Canadians still had such close ties to Britain that Canadian soldiers were eager to enlist. The first recruits from Banff had already signed up before the end of August, less than a month after war was declared.

Norman held the first Patriotic Fund concert on August 30, at the Lux Theatre. He had signed on as president of the Banff Patriotic Fund. All proceeds raised from the concert would go to the fund whose mission was to provide money to the wives and children of Banff soldiers who had enlisted to fight in the First World War. Norman was unable to volunteer for active duty due to back injuries he had suffered in a riding accident years before. He would do his best to contribute financially and he took his role very seriously. The first concert at the Lux Theatre raised $43, it was a start.

Before the end of September the government announced that all aliens who were from countries at war with Great Britain could no longer have arms or explosives and must surrender them within 10 days. If any alien was caught after this 10-day period he would be fined $20.

To raise money Norman announced that henceforth 20% of all proceeds from the Lux Theatre would go to the Patriotic Fund. The troop trains from the west coast were already going through Banff on their way to Calgary. While on leave from training camp the boys would come up from Calgary to see Banff and say perhaps a final goodbye to the mountains before being shipped overseas. For Canadian boys the pay offered to a soldier was $401.50 per year for an unmarried private and $565.75 for a married one. Canada ranked highest in the world for army pay, with the average British soldier receiving only $85.16 per year, French soldiers $20.40, and an Austrian soldier only $8.12 a year. The first Canadian boys landed at Plymouth, England on October 14, 1914. The boys from Banff had promised to write Norman in care of the *Crag and Canyon* so that local friends and family could be kept updated. Letters soon began to arrive and many were printed on the *Crag and Canyon's* front page.

Georgie had gone to Morley in the fall with little Eleanor. While visiting the family, Georgie's father David was suddenly taken ill. Annie and David immediately left for Calgary where they consulted a doctor. The doctor advised David to stay quiet and not exert himself in any way for awhile. He was told to eat only light food for the time being. Georgie was worried and wrote Norman that she hoped her father would stay in

Calgary for a while as it certainly was more comfortable than the home in Morley. Meanwhile Georgie would stay and manage the house while her parents were away. Everyday she would drive the team of horses across the river to get the mail. She looked forward to Norman's letters; they were always so enjoyable to read and always interesting. Eleanor enjoyed her holiday away from Banff but Georgie had been suffering from a cold although it was getting better with just a cough lingering on.

No one was too concerned about the war, as most people believed it would end by Christmas, and so life continued as usual. What to them was more likely to cause an impact was that by the following summer, automobiles would be allowed to run in Banff. That was sure to bring a lot more tourists and would ease the current financial situation. Norman's bills had piled up since the hotel fire and many remained unpaid by November. Among those bills were the wages owed to Mr. Thomas Leslie Stonnill who served as engineer on the *Aylmer*, Norman's passenger launch on Lake Minnewanka. Thomas was still awaiting payment of $190 from the previous May and had now hired a lawyer to collect. The lawyer advised Norman that unless the money was paid by 5:30 pm that very day a summons would be issued the following morning. Thomas got his money.

With all the financial worries it was a difficult time but Christmas was just around the corner. A holiday feast was planned at the King Edward Hotel and this year's menu was surely fit for royalty:

King Edward Hotel Christmas Dinner Menu (1914)

Soup   *Fish*
Cream of Oysters or Consommé   *Columbia River Salmon with Egg Sauce*

Entrées
Wild Mallard Duck with black currant jelly
Prairie Chicken with sage dressing
Rocky Mountain Sheep with bacon, apple fritters and orange sauce

Roasts
Haunch of Venison with red currant jelly
Alberta Moose with joulouse sauce
Young Turkey with oyster dressing and cranberry sauce

Salads

Lobster mayonnaise   *Olives*   *Crisp celery*
Vegetables
Baked B.C. potatoes   *Baked sweet potatoes*
Mashed potatoes
Asparagus with butter sauce   *Corn on the cob*

Dessert
English plum pudding with brandy sauce
Deep apple pie   *Hot mince pie*
Washington cream pie   *Raspberry jelly with whipped cream*
Strawberry ice cream   *Christmas Cake*

Fruit
Japanese oranges   *Grapes*   *Apples*
Raisins   *Cheese*   *Assorted nuts*

Tea, Coffee and Milk

Perhaps the meal had seemed indulgent but it was a time for family and friends to appreciate what they did have.

Norman received a Christmas letter from his brother-in-law, Ed Hoskings, who said that Malloch (still living in Banff), had written complaining that no family had written to him for over 4 months. He was worried that something had happened to the folks in Minneapolis. Ed assured Norman that everyone in St. Paul was well and hoped that Norman would soon see an end to his business woes. George and Ada had been to visit only the day before and were doing fine.

Other Banff organizations raised money for the war effort and the annual bonspiel even found Norman on one of its curling teams. The Banff Winter Sports Club had plans for a Patriotic Fund Carnival to be held on Wednesday, January 13, 1915. All the proceeds would go to the Red Cross. Many of the local boys continued to sign up for duty. Minimum requirements were a height of 5'2", written consent from the spouse if they were married, and they must be no younger than 18 and no older than 45 years old. Many of the boys lied and were well under the minimum age. The youngest of these boys from Banff was Carl Olsen who was only 15. Carl promised to write to the *Crag* and keep them informed as to what was happening. He went off to Revelstoke to enlist.

On Monday, February 7, a recruiting officer by the name of Major Parry, officer of the 50th Battalion, arrived. He was looking for new recruits and by the time he left, 20 men from Banff, 12 from Bankhead, and 2 from Exshaw had been accepted. There was little time for them to say goodbye as that same day all the men boarded the train and headed for Calgary. Total recruits from the Banff area now numbered 102 men. Keeping in mind that the winter population of the entire Banff area was only just over 1,000 this meant that enlistment was 10% of the total population. More men per capita signed up from the Banff area than any other town or city in Canada.

The latest Red Cross campaign was to get each town to buy beds for the Canadian Red Cross Hospital at Cliveden, Buckinghamshire, England. Each bed purchased would bear the name of its town. If possible, an injured soldier would be placed in the bed from his hometown. The beds cost $50 apiece and the little town of Cochrane had already bought 16 beds; Lethbridge, although much larger, had only purchased 10.

The King Edward Block had been renamed the Lux Block and now housed the King Edward Hotel, King Edward Bar, the Silver Grill Café (open 24 hours), the Gents Furnishing Store, the Lux Theatre and the Banff General Agencies law offices.

A little good news came with the arrival of a new niece born on April 7, 1915. She was the daughter of David McDougall Jr. The following month Norman's mother arrived along with George and Ada. They were planning to spend the entire summer in Banff and it was wonderful to have the family together again.

The war carried on and Norman continued to raise funds for the Patriotic Fund. The local ladies' branch of the Overseas Club was asking that every Banff citizen donate two pairs of socks. They put on a play and admission was two pairs of socks. The socks had to be woolen as no others were used by soldiers fighting at the front. Even though the war seemed a long way from Banff there was potential danger on Canadian soil as well.

The Canadian government felt that Germans and Austrians living in Canada, but not yet citizens, could prove a threat to national security. These were men who were unemployed or were planning to return to their respective countries in the near future. The government decided an internment camp should be opened at nearby Castle Mountain. The camp would start with 260 internees and 40 guards. The majority of the internees at this camp were Austrian.

July brought the Indian Days to Banff and this year they were held on July 19 and 20. There were 600 Indians taking part this year and 65 teepees were erected. The internment camp and the Indian camp were almost the same size now. Over at the Castle Mountain camp another 500 Germans and Austrians had arrived. The internment camp was scrupulously clean that not even a fly could be found there. This was thanks to the sanitary arrangements made by none other than Dr. Brett himself. An incinerator disposed of all refuse from the cook tents. Bunks, cots, and beds were regulation height from the floor so no dust or dirt could accumulate underneath. Food was abundant although it did lack in variety. With the war now so close to home more local boys were very keen to sign up for duty. By the end of the first week of August one out of every five Banff residents had signed up for active service. Many were already serving overseas. Even Reverend Harrison, who had tried to enlist for over a year, was finally accepted as chaplain. Another local boy, Phil Moore, had been promoted to Brigadier Major, which meant he was now in charge of 140,000 men. Not only had Banff sent the most soldiers to war but the Province of Alberta now ranked number one in the rate of enlistments.

That first week of August 1915, saw another young Banff resident sign up. His name was Malloch Luxton, Norman's baby brother. He was 32 years old and he had spent the last several years living in Banff. He was a very popular man with an outgoing personality and strong athletic skills. Malloch left for Calgary and signed on with the 63rd infantry.

With the war raging in Europe the American tourists headed up to Canada to spend the summer. The summer of 1915 found such celebrated visitors as Theodore Roosevelt, the former President, Mrs. John Rockefeller, and Mrs. Spaulding. Spaulding was the former Catherine Barker who was the famous $30 million orphan heiress from Chicago. The rich and famous flocked to Banff as they felt it was a good place to hide from reporters and photographers who hounded them in the States.

Norman was busy promoting Banff and published a local travel guide titled, "*Fifty Switzerlands in One.*" It was 84 pages long and compiled by Mr. H.C. Stovel of Winnipeg. Norman printed up between 3,000-4,000 copies just for Banff as souvenirs. Another 20,000 were printed to promote the little town in the Rockies to people from around the world. It was the largest job Norman had ever undertaken and over 2½ tons of paper were used in the printing. At only 10¢ a copy the book was for promotion purposes and never designed to make a profit.

One summer's evening, visitors were witness to a large meteor shower that streaked across the sky in the direction of Cascade Mountain. It seemed certain it would strike the mountain. The meteor appeared as a thousand blue-and-red coloured lights that formed an arch, and put an otherworldly glow over the town. The sky lit up so bright one could read a book by it. Residents were equally amazed that they could hear it "sizzle" as it flew by. It was a spectacular sight to behold.

Malloch completed his training at the Sarcee Training Camp in Calgary by the end of August. He just had time for a quick trip to Banff for one last visit with his brothers. Luckily his mother was still in town so he was able say goodbye to her also. Malloch arrived in Banff with a few of his training camp buddies and they all received a royal welcome. On Wednesday, September 1, 1915, Malloch and his friends left Banff and returned to the Sarcee camp to join a special "draft" for the firing line in France.

Fall came and with it many letters from soldiers writing home. A former clerk, Jim Smith, of the King Edward Hotel was now a member of the 4th Field Ambulance and stationed in France. Soldiers' letters still appeared regularly in the *Crag and Canyon*. Banff had not yet suffered any loss of life in the war and spirits were good. Dr. Brett had been given the office of Lieutenant Governor of Alberta and the locals were very proud of him. The Lux Theatre continued its patriotic movie night where all the services of the employees and the theatre were supplied free of charge. All the money raised would go directly to the fund. Canada was expected to raise over $7 million for the fund and of that Banff was designated to raise at least $3,000. Single working men were expected to pay 2 days' salary per month toward the Patriotic Fund and married men were to pay 1 days' salary.

The government had decided that Castle Mountain was not suitable for a camp during the long winter months and so it was decided another camp would be built up at the Cave and Basin. Construction began right next to the pool and the plan was that the relocated internees would build a few much-needed roads for the tourists. To make the locals feel safe the *Crag and Canyon* printed the number of prisoners along with the number of guards that would be held up at the Cave and Basin camp. The prisoners were soon put to work cutting trees, clearing bush and ground for the new carriage road that would run 5 miles up the Spray River on the north bank.

Patriotic nights at the Lux Theatre were held every Wednesday and usually raised between $40 and $50 each week. Banff's promise of $3,000 had already exceeded $4,225 by mid November. Even so, Norman would confront people on the street, making sure they had given their money to the fund. If anyone refused to contribute they would have to withstand Norman's fury in full view of anyone nearby. One such man had refused to give even 5¢ and Norman decided to do a little research on the man. What he found was this man's entire contribution to the war effort was exactly $2, this being given to the Red Cross. Norman decided to humiliate the man by writing an article in the *Crag and Canyon*. Norman's article said that there were not enough suitable words with which to express his contempt of this man. He then offered a year's free subscription to anyone who could come up with a suitable name for this pathetic excuse for a human being.

Early December another curling bonspiel was held to raise money for the Red Cross. Norman was out curling with his team doing what he could. They managed to raise another $70. Norman also made sure a copy of the *Crag and Canyon* was sent to several Banff boys overseas so they could keep track of what was going on at home. Those boys would pass them around so all the boys from the Banff could read up on the latest news from Banff, Canmore, Exshaw, and Cochrane. Many boys had leave coming up at Christmas and were planning visits with extended family members still living in England. Most of the Canadian boys were at Bramshott Camp in Hampshire, England. They took pity on those returning from the front, so many were sick and wounded. The English treated the Canadian boys like royalty, which came as quite a surprise to them. Once stationed at the front the routine was so many days in the trenches followed by so many days of rest. The boys often found it colder in France than in Canada as they were always soaked with mud and water. The water in the trenches was always up to their knees.

Christmas meant it was time again for the Banff Rifle Club to hold their Christmas turkey shoot. Norman was in good form and managed to bag two. Banff had quite a rush of tourists as many soldiers from Calgary were on leave and visiting the mountains over the holidays.

The telegram arrived from Ottawa on January 4, 1916. Malloch Luxton was dead.

"Deeply regret to inform you No. 467056, Private Harold Malloch Luxton, 31st, formerly 63rd battalion reported killed in action on 18th December."
(Adjutant General)

Malloch was the first Banff boy to be killed in action; he had made the ultimate sacrifice. He hadn't even lived to see Christmas. More news followed on Thursday when the chaplain of the 31st Battalion sent a letter to the family. Malloch had been passing among the trenches at Ypres with a comrade to fetch his dinner. There was a spot where a portion of the parapet had been destroyed and it had been impossible to stoop low enough to completely conceal one's body. While making the dash for dinner, a sniper's bullet had killed both boys. Malloch had been very popular and was one of the battalion's favourites. He had always done his duty without complaint and always tried to be cheerful. He believed that giving his life for his King and country was the proper thing to do. A person must fight for justice and what is right. He would be buried at Kemmel Cemetery in Belgium along with many of his comrades. Eventually a cross would be built to mark the grave and a metal plate bearing his name and regiment would be erected.

Malloch had always been described as having a jovial personality and happy disposition. He easily made friends wherever he went. While still living in Winnipeg the young Malloch had taken a course as a civil engineer and graduated with honours. This profession didn't suit him and he followed his family to St. Paul and got work as a photographer for the *Journal*. He eventually moved to Banff to help Norman and Lou at the curio shop. Later Malloch got on with the Eau Claire Lumber Company and worked his way up from the bottom to become a manager. His employees loved him. He was an expert with a rifle just like his brother Norman. Banff had been the perfect home for Malloch as he loved the outdoors and sports of all kinds. After arriving in England he had almost immediately been sent to the front. Malloch had been in excellent shape and was considered to be very athletic. Just prior to his death, Malloch had managed to send one final letter home to his sister in Winnipeg. She received that letter on December 14, just 4 days before his death.

That January in Banff was a depressing time for the Luxtons. Malloch had died and the end of the month brought the worst snowstorm in Banff's recorded history. The temperature plummeted to -46.5°F and 26 inches of snow fell. All the trains coming from the west were cancelled. Norman had managed to get away a week earlier to attend a curling bonspiel in Calgary. He had gone with Jim Brewster and Dave White. The only good news was that the socks sent to the front from the ladies of Banff had arrived. The socks often contained slips of paper bearing the name of the donor and her address. A letter arrived saying that all the socks had reached Flanders.

Norman was the "skip" for his curling team at the Banff bonspiel in February and curled alongside his teammates O. McMahan, J.T. Child and J. Campbell. There was also iceboating up at Lake Minnewanka and cars were now allowed to drive up there.

Letters continued arriving from the front and local boy Sidney Unwin was now an artillery sergeant. He often wrote his letters in the trench while bullets flew over his head. Sergeant Major H. Lecock of Banff had written of his recent promotion to Battery Sergeant Major. That meant he now had control of 4 guns, 164 horses, 8 ammunition wagons, and 140 men. Mail slowed down dramatically due to an outbreak of measles in England. All mail was now required to be disinfected before leaving the country.

Norman had a little fire at the curio shop that destroyed his workroom so he was busy rebuilding it and would resume business shortly. It didn't seem of much importance compared to news of the possibility of soldiers arriving from the trenches to recuperate in Banff after being gassed. The old Brett Sanatorium, now called the Grand View Villa, was being considered as a prospective home for invalid and convalescent soldiers.

Up at the Cave and Basin internment camp there had been 4 internees escape but they were soon found in Canmore, harboured by 4 fellow Austrians. Although 4 prisoners escaped from camp it was 8 that returned!

In April, the second boy from Banff was killed in action. His name was Fred Woodworth and he died April 16. He was only 21 years old and was the first native-born Banff resident to die in the war. Two more deaths followed in June and Banff mourned the loss of G.J. McDonald and Cecil Dude. McDonald was only 18 years old.

On June 10, 1916, the government decided to impose a moving picture theatre tax. If the performance was a motion picture the tax was 1¢, if it was an opera, drama or vaudeville the tax was 2.5¢. If the total admission was $1.00 the tax increased to .5¢. Even guests of management were required to pay the tax portion.

Norman was busy planning Banff Indian Days once again and in early July he travelled to Morley to hold a conference with the chiefs. This year the Duke of Connaught would be attending the celebration. The chiefs agreed that this might be a good opportunity to make the Duke an honorary chief. Before they could begin making preparations they had to obtain permission from Ottawa. Their request was approved and plans for the ceremony were soon underway. While Norman kept busy organizing the event, his brother Lou was busy training a little bear cub to turn somersaults up at curio shop. A wealthy American collector was so enamoured with the talented little cub that he offered a good price for the little acrobat. Again another bear would leave his friends behind at Luxton's store. Lou was okay with losing the bear as he had another little someone at home to care for. His wife had given birth to a baby girl at their home on the previous Tuesday, June 27.

At the end of June, little Eleanor Luxton had graduated from grade one. The Duke and Duchess arrived on schedule along with their daughter Princess Patricia. They were staying up at the Banff Springs Hotel. They had planned a nice 2-week holiday in one of their favourite places. The ceremony to bestow the title of Honorary Chief was held during the Indian Days festivities. Two teepees were erected and the ceremony took place with Reverend John McDougall interpreting. The welcoming address was in Cree and John acted as interpreter. The Duke was given his new Indian name "Teenchaka Eeyake Oonka" meaning Great Mountain Chief. Norman was happy to learn that a picture of himself and the Duke was later published in the *London Daily Mail*, one of England's most popular newspapers.

One of the local boys returned from the war that August. Don Bannerman had been badly injured and would be arriving by train on the Monday night. A huge crowd gathered at the station to welcome the young man home. Don had been wounded way back in January while rushing to the aid of a wounded comrade. Initially Don had been reported dead but it soon became apparent that he was in fact alive and had spent the last 7 months in hospital.

Norman got a letter from another local boy named Carl Friesen. Carl was in Belgium near Flanders and had recently made a cross for the grave of Malloch Luxton. He wanted Norman to know that Malloch now had a marker for his grave.

That August the King Edward Hotel overflowed with guests. They were put on cots in the parlor, corridors, and sometimes even the bathrooms. They seemed content enough as long as there was room for them all in the dining room. That fall even Henry Ford paid a visit to Banff in his private car. The tourist season was drawing to a close and it was decided that the winter population of Banff could not support both the Lux and Harmony theatres. The Harmony theatre remained open and the Lux closed down for the season.

Norman played in the local golf tournament in October followed by his annual hunting trip. It was a quiet winter and the names of the latest war casualties continued to appear in the *Crag and Canyon*. Captain Johnson had died; he had been the sergeant in charge of the Banff detachment of the RNWMP after purchasing his discharge from the Mounties so he could enlist. Fred J. Grant was dead and Jack McLennan, a porter from the King Edward Hotel, also had been killed. Pat Brewster had recently enlisted and was now with the Canadian Flying Corps although he was back in Banff after a little accident he had suffered during training. Norman decided to step down as president of the Patriotic Fund. He was just too busy now that he was the new owner of the Stoney Trading Post in Morley.

By the summer of 1917 there were 14 Banff boys that had given their lives for their country. Another 31 had been wounded. Down at the Hub Cigar Store hung 71 photos of local boys who had gone overseas. Norman continued expanding his business activities and had recently opened a garage on Banff Avenue for cars. People could have repairs done on them or even store them on site over the winter. The previous winter the town held a small winter carnival with little fanfare. Still it had been quite enjoyable and so it was decided that the carnival should become an annual event. They looked for donations and managed to raise $400 and the second annual Banff Winter Carnival was scheduled for February, 1918. Norman didn't want anything too elaborate, funds should be going to the war effort. Still everyone needed something to lift their spirits. Lou Luxton was made the official Chaplain of the Carnival. Committee members also included Lorne Orr, T.A Dunsmore, G. Standish, D. McGowan, and William Mather. Events were decided upon and would include curling, art skating, skating races, swimming races, ski jumping, swimming races in the hot springs, an illuminated ice palace, tobogganing, dancing, fireworks, trap shooting, and sleigh rides. The *Crag and Canyon* really pushed the event. The entire front page of the January 26, 1918, issue was dedicated to the upcoming carnival. The internees from the Cave and Basin Camp were commandeered to build the ice palace on the vacant lot on the corner, directly in front of the *Crag and Canyon* office. This would be the internees' last winter in Banff as it had been decided that the internment camp was to be torn down. Some of the buildings would be relocated around Banff for those in need of them.

The approaching winter carnival brought with it a shortage of available rooms. Locals were being asked to make rooms available in their homes and the Mount Royal Hotel agreed to reopen for 10 days. The carnival would begin on Friday, February 8, with the official opening to be held the following Monday.

Norman had his own guest coming to stay and he was very excited. His old friend Ollie Ormond from Victoria was coming for a visit. Ollie had remained a close friend through many letters and it was wonderful to see him again. It was hard to believe that almost 17 years had passed since that crazy evening prior to the *Tilikum's* departure. There was so much news to catch up on. Ollie's little bookshop, where George Luxton had worked, continued to operate for a few years. Eventually Ollie gave up his shop and got himself a job as bookkeeper for the Poppham Brothers Biscuit Company. The factory was located at 242 Mary Street and supplied Vancouver Island with biscuits, cookies, and crackers.

The Ormond family had originally come from Peterborough, Ontario where the father had worked in the jewellery business. Ollie had been born in 1871 and by 1887 the young man had decided to head west and settle in Victoria. He loved the city so much he sent a letter to his brother, A.E. Ormond, and convinced him to move out to the west coast. A.E. bought a farm which he later sold and with the money he purchased the Poppham Brothers Biscuit Factory. The name remained until one of the Poppham brothers began to get into such trouble that the Poppham name became a bit of an embarrassment and thus it was changed to Ormonds Biscuit Factory. A.E. hired his brother Ollie who began as a bookkeeper but soon was selling biscuits and cookies all over the Island and in Vancouver. The large red brick warehouse where the cookies and chocolates were manufactured was an imposing building and out back was a large livery. Usually Ollie would travel by horse and cart to sell his confections but sometimes he took the train. Ollie had married a girl named Mary but in her early twenties she developed rheumatoid arthritis and for much of her life she would be confined to a wheelchair. The couple was unable to have children but she was a lovely woman and Ollie adored her.

The Ormond factory supplied Vancouver Island with crackers, graham wafers, Arrowroot cookies, coconut cookies and a luscious chocolate mint cookie dipped in chocolate. The chocolate mint cookies were so much in demand that it was almost impossible to keep them in stock.

Norman and Ollie had a wonderful visit and promised to keep in touch. The carnival had been a great success and Eleanor Luxton took first prize in the ladies' swimming race. The winners were all listed in the *Crag and Canyon* and even the little paper had won its own race. During the war, the newspaper industry had been hit very hard and over 800 newspapers in the United States and 84 papers in Canada had gone out of business. The *Crag and Canyon* defied the odds and carried on.

In the spring, a new employee was hired at Norman's garage. Mr. R. Duncan was a retired veteran and had served overseas driving transport cars and motor lorries. The war continued and by the fall, the *Crag and Canyon* had begun publishing draft notices. Even though the paper had survived there wasn't enough revenue to keep it operational during the winter of 1918. Publishing was suspended on September 21, 1918. The editor, P.W. Stone, had left the paper the previous week. Norman was sad to be forced to discontinue the paper over the winter but he had no other choice. There was one final paper printed that year. A special issue was requested by the government to raise money for the Victory Loan Campaign. They thanked Norman for his patriotic stand when he agreed to publish the special issue. The paper made mention that Jim Brewster had joined the Siberian force and had already left for England. Also in that issue there appeared a little poem written by a Lieutenant Colonel Dr. John McCrae of Montreal. The Canadian doctor had been killed in the second battle of Ypres. The name of the poem was "In Flanders Fields."

The war would soon be over but along with the returning soldiers came something so insidious that over 50,000 Canadians would lose their lives.

TEN

The Stoneys

Nina Edith Potts, a young girl of 23, had died. A resident of Banff, she had been suffering from the flu when suddenly it turned into an acute form of pneumonia and just a few days later she was dead. It started just like any other flu, with chills, aches and a fever but this wasn't just any flu. This was the Spanish Influenza. Although the name indicated that the flu began in Spain it actually began in Kansas. Soldiers from the American state had carried the flu to the French front where it rapidly spread. The flu originally was known as the American flu but was conveniently renamed so as not to lay blame on the Americans. This deadly strain of flu was a mix of a human flu virus and a pig virus. Twenty-one million people died worldwide including 450,000 Russians, 375,000 Italians, 228,000 British, and the worst toll, India, with over 5 million dead. Alberta was not immune and the deadly virus took over 3,000 lives in the province. Canadian soldiers had brought the airborne virus home with them. As the deadly virus spread, the public were soon donning masks and all public gatherings were cancelled.

One day in the early winter of 1918, Norman went out to Morley to check on his trading post, the Morley Trading Company. He had purchased the store in 1915 from Leeson and Scott. Norman arrived early that frosty winter's morning and found the store deserted. A few hours passed with still no sign of a customer. Norman knew something had to be terribly wrong. At 11:00 am, a small boy about the age of 8 entered the store looking for chewing gum. Norman asked him where everybody was.

"They're dead!" he replied. With that the boy grabbed his gum and ran out.

Norman followed him out the door then turned and jumped into his small Ford truck and sped off to Chinequay Village. It was only a couple of miles from the store. As Norman drove along he simply couldn't believe that everyone had died. Norman stopped at several houses knocking on each door but there was no answer. Every home appeared to have been abandoned. At last Norman found someone at home' in fact, the house was crowded. Inside there were 30 Indians, all plainly in grief. They told Norman that as of the previous day there were at least a dozen houses with one person dead in each. If that were true, Norman wondered where on earth the Indian agent was and why wasn't he doing anything? The Indians told him the agent was at home but refused to come out. That was all Norman needed to hear. He jumped back into the truck.

Upon arriving at the agent's house Norman proceeded to pound on the door. The agent answered and told Norman to go to the window. The story he gave Norman was that he too was sick with the flu but that Norman could have the key to the ration house. He passed the key to Norman and told him to take what he needed. He then disappeared back into the house. Norman drove to the ration house and unlocked the door but the shelves were virtually bare. All that remained was a few sow-bellies and some tea.

Norman knew he had to act fast so he immediately sent a wire to the Indian Department in Regina. He wanted a doctor and a nurse sent to Morley immediately. The next call he made was to his own doctor in Banff, asking him for advice on what best to do. He was told that the virus was still too new and most doctors had no clue how to treat it. The best advice his doctor could give him was to treat the Indians with whiskey and aspirin. There was no other medicine available.

As evening approached, Norman gathered all the healthy men together and organized them into teams. The dead would have to be buried and the sick would need to be quarantined if there was to be any hope for survival. It was December 10, 1918. The elders told the younger Indians how to bury the dead while Norman began the difficult task of visiting every home and assessing the situation. In his pocket he kept scraps of paper and on each would be noted the conditions in each home.

"Double-Old-Man - girls sick, been sick 3 days-not very bad

"Enoch Baptise - 7 in house, including Amos Amos. Enoch's wife pretty sick, temperatures 101, send aspirin. Enoch temp 99. Amos baby sick, no milk"

"Peter Bearspaw - 6 in house, all sick"

"John Powderface - boy 7 years, temp 104, John sick, temp 99"

"Issac Rollingmud - 4 small children, all with colds and some temperatures"

The list went on and on and Norman noted what things he could bring from home like aspirin, food, blankets, cod liver oil, and whiskey. There were no other medicines available but he would share what he had. Prohibition was on but Norman had several dozen cases of scotch, rye and other hard liquor stored away at the King Edward Hotel. He would give all he had if it meant saving the Stoney tribe. The liquor would help keep them warm on the inside and help ease the pain. Georgie was put to work to locate other supplies including as many thermometers as she could find. She managed to gather up a dozen and by the following morning the supplies were ready to be taken out to Morley. Before leaving Banff another wire was dispatched to the Superintendent-General of Indian Affairs in Ottawa advising them of the desperate situation on the reserve.

Now back in Morley, the first order of the day was to fill the shelves of the Trading Post and open the doors. Money was not an issue; whatever the Indians needed, they could take. The second issue was that of the conditions on the reserve. Most of the houses were unfit to live in and bitterly cold during the winter. Norman decided to visit every house, determine which people were the sickest and then quarantine them. The sickest were moved to the warmest houses, giving them a better chance at survival. Several groups of Indians were assigned the job to relocate the people based on their needs. The thermometers were handed out and temperatures were to be taken every 6 hours. Any person with a temperature was isolated and given what medicine was available.

Daily Norman continued his rounds updating his lists. He had received a brief telegram in answer to his wires offering little in the way of help. Norman decided a more detailed letter might better explain the dire circumstances, so on January 3, 1919, he wrote to William Graham of the Department of Indian Affairs Canada, Regina, Saskatchewan.

"Mr. Wm. Graham,

I am anxious to call your attention to the conditions existing on the Stoney Reservation regarding the flu and in so doing that proper action will be taken to check this terrible plague. The first of these cases came to my attention some time before Christmas. The flu is in almost every house on the reservation and no attempt at any quarantine or sanitary arrangements have been made. The well now eat, sleep, and live in the same house with the sick, and the dead have lain for days without being put away. I have personally attended to cases where actual want was in force for food, wood and water. Not only are the Indians a danger to themselves but also to the entire country. In the last few days the following have died at Morley:

Amos Amos wife, his mother and sister, Stoney Joe and his wife, John Steven Simmeons' two sons, William Powderface......(the list continued)

Might I suggest something in Bearspaw and Chinequa Village. There are two large halls, these places could be fitted up as hospitals. One of the doctors could be called in for constant attendance. I have in mind Doctor Atkin who has large experience of the flu both in France and here. So far to my knowledge there has been one medical call in the last two weeks (a doctor was sent out once after Norman's initial telegram). Possibly it is hard to get medical aid.

I could go into gorier details but is it necessary? Conditions could not be worse and those responsible should receive such attention as the law allows.

If in any way I can be of assistance command me, I feel sure you will act at once."

Norman was aware that spending time surrounded by the sick and dying meant that he too would likely contract the virus. With a family of his own to worry about it was time to think about writing his will. If anything should happen to Norman the estate was to be left in its entirety to his daughter Eleanor. So far Norman had been lucky and remained free of the virus and he continued his work at the reservation. All the supplies taken from Norman's store were at his own expense. Hundreds of miles were covered going house to house attending to the sick and waiting on word from the government office in Regina. The letter came just over two weeks later but its contents shocked Norman. There would be no help, financial or otherwise. They acknowledged receipt of Norman's request for help but explained that the epidemic had made its way on to a large number of reservations in the three prairie-provinces, and in most cases the mortality rate had been high. The letter continued:

"It is a circumstance very much to be regretted, but generally speaking the problem has been well met by those called upon to handle a very difficult situation. I shall be glad of the opportunity of meeting you when I have occasion to visit the west."

That was it— no help, no offer of assistance, nothing. That wasn't satisfactory as far as Norman was concerned and he started a letter-writing campaign until he got some sort of assistance. Finally a message arrived from Ottawa. After another 2 weeks had passed, they agreed to send a doctor and two nurses. Norman met them at the train and updated them with the current conditions. With so many Indians dying it was difficult to remain upbeat but Norman tried to be cheerful and smiled even though his heart was breaking. Often the sick ones would ask Norman if they were going to die. He always gave them the same answer.

"Do you owe my Trading Post money?" The answer was always in the affirmative. Norman would then reply,

"Well God won't let you die owing my Trading Post money."

That would be followed up with a little pep talk to keep their spirits up. He made up stories about dreams he had about God and found that the stories seemed to give them courage and trust in the white man's God.

Norman stayed on to help the doctor and nurses until they had everything under control. He had stayed at great personal expense and risk to his own life. The Stoney Indians did survive although they lost 25% of the tribe. Not long after the doctor's arrival Norman was stricken with the flu and returned to Banff. Georgie came down soon after with the virus but they both managed to beat the illness within 2 weeks. Norman returned to the reserve and found that the flu had now passed through and no further cases were reported. The members of the tribe now held Norman in the highest esteem and someday they would find a way to thank him properly. As for the Indian agent he never did have the flu and did not pay Norman for any of the food and supplies that were taken from Norman's store. No money at all was paid to Norman in compensation but it didn't matter. To have saved the Stoney Indians from extinction was payment enough.

Norman's reputation of having a wonderful collection of Indian artifacts had reached all the way to Washington, D.C. The bureau chief on aboriginal research, J. Alter Fewkes, from the Smithsonian had written a letter to Norman. The museum was interested in Norman's collection and were looking for more information. The Smithsonian had only limited knowledge of the Banff area. They knew only that the Peigans were a division of the Blackfoot who were in the area and that some time before that Kutenais had originally been on the east side of the Rocky Mountains. Norman was always eager to share his information and told them what he could.

During 1919, soldiers continued to trickle back across the sea. Norman was busy adding an extension onto the rear of the King Edward Hotel, a new garage that could hold a large number of cars. He had his top-notch mechanic and he wanted to be able to sell gasoline for the many vehicles now coming to the town. Norman approached M.D. Greene who was the Alberta representative for Imperial Oil. He managed to convince Mr. Greene to come to Banff and install a new 35,000-gallon oil tank at the new garage. The price was set at 50¢ per gallon and Norman served as the local agent for Imperial Oil. The previous year it was estimated that the King Edward Garage had sold approximately 50,000 gallons of gasoline. With the increase in tourism after the war it was obvious that sales would increase, especially with the planned completion of the road to Lake Louise. Imperial Oil had sent all the supplies for a new warehouse, to be built at the gas station by early April. They were sending a crew to construct the warehouse that were to arrive by the third week of May. The new storage tank would then be affixed and a tanker car of gasoline would be shipped.

The King Edward Hotel still had its livery but now added a new tally-ho motorcar to its collection. One Sunday in May the new motorcar was to be tested and a number of invalid soldiers from up at the Brett Hospital got a joy ride around town. There was also joy in Minneapolis with the announcement that George Luxton and his wife Ada, had a new baby daughter, Patricia, born May 17, 1919.

Summer saw another successful Indian Days at Banff. Norman, Jim Brewster and Tom Wilson served on the committee. The *Crag and Canyon* was up and running again after the winter break with an increased subscription price. The cost had been raised from $1 to $1.50 per year. Little Eleanor Luxton had graduated from grade 6 and she had a new cousin, born on July 1, the newest daughter of David McDougall Jr.

Along with the usual business problems there were now automobile issues to contend with. A man by the name of James Newhouse was trying to sue Norman for damages he incurred by way of one of Norman's tour cars. The accident had happened on the road from Banff to Castle Mountain, about 4 or 5 miles outside of Banff. James said he was driving his rig when one of the tour cars belonging to the King Edward Livery, came up behind him. James signaled the car to go "steady" as his horses were becoming uneasy. According to James the car decided to pass, on the wrong side of the road, and ran over his dog. James swore that the dog was very valuable and now it was dead. He also claimed his outfit was damaged and that the car had not even stopped to inspect the damage. James was looking for a settlement of $100.

The other problem in Banff that summer was the complete lack of coal due to the recent miner's strike. Norman decided that if it didn't end soon that perhaps he should see about buying and operating his own coal mine at Anthracite. He made inquiries. The government was willing to grant a permit to anyone they deemed competent to take charge of a mine, provided they not employ more than 30 men underground at any one time. They did caution Norman that mining an anthracite field was probably the most dangerous mining in the province and he should reconsider. They also advised him they believed the strike would soon be over. Norman agreed and his possible career in mining came to an abrupt end.

George and his family had decided to stay in St. Paul and had purchased a house there some years before. The problem was he wasn't making enough money to keep his family and pay the mortgage. George still had some shares in the King Edward and knowing that the summer was Norman's best time financially he sent Norman a letter. He came to the point quickly and came right out and asked Norman for money. He said that with the new baby, combined with the interest on various mortgages, he simply had no money to pay off most of his debts. If he couldn't pay the debts that could mean losing his home, leaving nowhere for his wife and baby to live. George hated to ask Norman for money and had put off writing the letter for some time. He had hoped to pick up some extra work for the local newspapers on Sundays or evenings, over and above his regular salary, but it still wasn't enough. He mentioned that he wished that the new baby had been a boy but was happy with his lovely little daughter. Norman had often told his brother that a man does not begin to live he agreed with him.

By September everyone agreed that the summer of 1919 was among the busiest yet. The problem now was the lack of rooms for the many tourists. Everyone felt that enough hotels existed and so people were encouraged to build cottages, perhaps in the style of the new California bungalows which contained 3 or 4 rooms. There were always a few tourists that complained of the bad road between Calgary and Banff but it still was an easy trip one could manage in just over 3 hours. Whatever the road conditions that summer, it hadn't stopped Cornelius Vanderbilt from arriving with his friends to do some motion picture filming. Along with Mr. Vanderbilt came many motion picture men and writers who wanted to make movies in the mountains.

That winter Norman was appointed Director of Events for the annual Banff Winter Carnival. Arthur Wheeler from the Alpine Club suggested that perhaps Norman might try to include the visiting public in the events. He also suggested they incorporate a torch light procession with all the locals dressed in their sports equipment. After the parade, there could be a big bonfire with singing. The carnival was a huge success that year, with hotels filled to capacity; locals who could offer board and lodging were encouraged to make rooms available.

The highlight of 1920 was an official invitation from the Director of Exhibits for the Canadian National Exhibition in Toronto asking Norman to help with the exhibition. This was indeed an honour and an Indian exhibit was soon organized. The Canadian National Exhibition was world famous and had begun officially in 1879. It made history in 1882 when its exhibition grounds were the first in the world to be lit by electric light. Thomas Edison had also made a sound recording of a talk given by Lord Stanley. This recorded speech remains today as the oldest existing sound recording. The Exhibition insisted on covering all expenses and handled all Norman's transportation arrangements. Norman decided this was a great chance for a family holiday so along with Georgie and Eleanor, the family went east in August to take part in the Exhibition. The booth was manned by the Luxton family, complete in their Stoney Indian costumes. Even 10-year-old Eleanor looked splendid in her Indian dress with her long dark hair done up in braids.

Norman had started up another little venture that summer and now had a tour bus and jitney service. Little did he know that at that same time, somewhere in California, a certain Captain Voss was also running a jitney service. Norman published a brochure promoting the new tour service:

"Why be held up when you see the park? We can save you 25% of your expenses while you stay in Banff. CPR monopolies no longer exist. We book for any drive, river or lake trip in the mountains, with the best livery turnouts in Banff. Seven years in the livery business, and we have never had runaway accidents, upsets or lawsuits yet [well maybe just that one with the nasty run over the dog business]. All our drivers are Government inspected and licensed. We tell you where to go, then take you there."

Norman's company offered three different trips. The first was a general drive which took in the Bow Falls, Tunnel Mountain, the Buffalo paddocks and animal corrals. It covered 20 miles and cost just $1. The second trip was the "Lake Trip" which took in the Buffalo corral, Bankhead Village, Devil's Creek Canyon and the *Aylmer* Launch Excursion on Lake Minnewanka. The distance covered was 42 miles and cost only $2. The final offering was the "Combination Trip" that covered the general drive and the lake trip, covering 62 miles, for $3. This trip left Banff at 9:30 in the morning and didn't return until 6:00 pm. Tickets could be purchased for all trips at Luxton's Free Museum (the curio shop) and at the King Edward Livery.

Over the next few years Banff continued to grow and Norman kept busy with the hotel, curio shop, and various other businesses. Norman had managed a trip to Victoria in the summer of 1921 and was able to visit his long-time friend Ollie. Over at the Lux Theatre, there was much excitement when the theatre held its first world première. The film was "The Valley of the Silent Man" and it had been made in Banff. The story featured Sergeant Kent of the Royal Mounties and his adventures with a woman, dog trains, and fur trappers. It debuted in the fall of 1922. By the summer of 1923, the revised and updated edition of "*Fifty Switzerlands in One,*" with Norman acting again as publisher, was printed. Norman had decided start a special feature in the *Crag and Canyon*. The feature would contain stories and pictures of all the newspaper editors of the West. Of course Norman was featured in one of those stories. The other changes to the *Crag and Canyon* included its new release date. The paper would now come out on Fridays. Local businessmen persuaded Norman that by releasing the paper a day early they could run ads for their Saturday sales. Many merchants wanted to run weekend specials and so Norman happily complied. He was all for promoting local business and was a strong standing member in the Banff Citizens' Association. The *Crag and Canyon* also looked for other publishing business and offered their services for printing letterheads, envelopes, noteheads, billheads, statements, shipping tags, and ruled office forms. Norman's motto was, "If it is printed we can do it. Phone us at 143".

Always looking for ways to make more money, Norman now was selling coal serving as the local agent for Galt and Saunders. He was happy to have the support of the Alberta government who supplied him with brochures to mail out to his customers on how best to use their coal. Norman mailed out 100 of these money-saving brochures titled, "Coal Truths of Alberta Domestic Coal." The booklet advised that 50% of all soft coal is made of gas and that it was not necessary to let this useful gas go up your chimney. It had tips to the customer on how to use this gas and how better to burn their coal. For just $11 you could purchase 1 ton of Super X Coal.

Prohibition was still in full swing and many a liquor referendum ballot would appear in the *Crag and Canyon*. It boiled down to whether a total ban was required except for medical use or whether hotels could sell it. Better still, the government thought they should control the liquor by selling it themselves.

Norman was busy organizing the Banff Winter Carnival but when he went looking for support in late 1923, only 20 businessmen responded.

There had been 78 invitations for support sent out. The lack of support was disappointing but the 1924 Winter Carnival went ahead as planned. This year Norman introduced an amateur boxing tournament that would be held at the 500-seat Lux Theatre. A good snowfall meant everything would run smoothly. An illuminated ice palace was built at the north end of the Bow Bridge. Alongside the palace would be Indian teepees. Dog teams would take visitors along mountain trails on toboggans and sleds.

Along with the usual activities during the summer of 1924, it was decided that the time had come for Norman to add on to the King Edward Hotel. By the end of September the building of a 24-room extension commenced. The new rooms were built over top the existing businesses in the Lux Block and contained tiled bathrooms, hardwood floors, plus hot and cold running water. By the end of construction, the Lux Block was now two storeys high. The hotel's manager, Lorne Orr, was sent east to purchase furnishings for the new extension.

With the approaching holiday season, the local veterans had decided that no child in Banff should be without a Christmas gift. Tickets were printed and distributed to all the children in the town. Any child under the age of 12 could exchange the ticket for a present from under the giant tree. Local businesses, organizations and private individuals donated to the cause. Among the generous contributors were the Banff Rotary Club, the Masonic Lodge, Dave White & Co., Brewster Transport, Pat Burns & Co, the King Edward Hotel and, of course, Norman. The total raised was $167 and the event was a huge success. Some 400 children had tickets and each was given a present. The local mothers were treated to tea and cake in the afternoon and Santa was present to hand out the gifts.

Enthusiasm for the 1925 Winter Carnival increased when Norman was approached one day by a young lad by the name of Reg Harris. The young man had arrived in Banff in 1923 and was working as a fire lookout on top of Tunnel Mountain. His idea was to get together a team of dogs and a sled and travel to Calgary to promote the Banff Winter Carnival. The trains were running in the winter now and perhaps a little promotion might bring out a few Calgarians to the carnival. Norman agreed and Reg began preparations for the trip. Reg had convinced two of his friends, Harry Knight and George Child, to accompany him. The boys gathered up a rather sad collection of 12 of the most mismatched and scruffy dogs available. Everything from Airedales to Bulldogs were part of the team. The dogs were hooked up to two sleighs but the dogs were not strong enough to pull the sleighs with the boys riding on them. Reg, Harry, and George would have to walk alongside. It was January 7,

1925, when the boys and their dog teams left Banff. By the time the group arrived at Exshaw they had been adopted by another stray dog, a Collie. The first night they made it to the Morley railway station, where they spent the night. The second day they arrived in Cochrane where friends had arranged a big party and dance. It was a great night but they still had another 20 miles to go until they reached Calgary. The following day they made it into Calgary and stopped outside Perry's Drugstore, 328a 8 Avenue. The owner gave the boys $25 which came in handy and they happily posed for pictures outside his shop. They continued on to the Capital Theatre on Stephen Avenue where a reception was held. A big crowd gathered while Reg extolled the benefits of the Banff Winter Carnival to the onlookers. The theatre's organist supplied the music while the dogs howled along in accompaniment. That evening, a local hotel manager put the group up for free. While in Calgary, Reg had managed to spend time with his sister Nan and convinced her to come back with him to Banff. He paid her fare on the train but thanks to Norman's generosity the rest of the group travelled home on the train at Norman's expense.

The trip had been a success and Norman was pleased. Reg and Norman would remain friends from that day onwards. Reg would later become an electrician for Parks Canada and usually did Norman's electrical work free of charge. Reg later married Elsie Williams who had been a schoolmate of Eleanor Luxton. Norman was most impressed by Reg's artistic talents as a wood carver and collected several of Reg's copper engravings, including a copper plate done in Norman's likeness. Reg's totem poles can still be seen in front of the Whyte Museum, and next to his house, on the left, on the drive up to the Banff Springs Hotel.

In 1925, it was decided that in order to encourage tourism between Calgary and Banff that a "Booster Club" should be formed. The new club would "boost" tourism by promoting each other's attractions and activities. There would be 12 men in the club, 6 of whom would be from Banff and 6 from Calgary. An election was held and the representatives from Banff included S.M. Armstrong, Byron Harmon, R.S. Stronach, Lorne Orr, Jim Brewster and, of course, Norman Luxton. The Calgarians elected were J.W. Davidson, John H. Hanna, Reg Smith, R.W. Ward, A.B. MacKay, D.E. Black and Mayor G.W. Webster. They called themselves the Banff-Calgary Development Association.

Later that year, Norman could be found on the council for the Trail Riders of the Canadian Rockies, along with most of the Brewster family, Byron Harmon, Bill Potts, James Simpson, Mary Schaeffer, Tom Wilson and many others. Norman had also been enlisted by the Calgary

Stampede to serve as an Associate Director, a position he would retain for the next 36 years. That year the Calgary Stampede Board had submitted a list of planned floats for Norman to evaluate. This year's theme was to be the history of Alberta and all floats were to represent a certain piece of that history. Along with the proposed list, Norman suggested that a float should be added to represent the McDougall family since they built the first protestant church in Alberta and established the mission at Morley.

In Morley, where the mission was located, there seemed to be some confusion over who exactly owned the mineral rights. Norman was always looking for a good investment and had hired a geologist to check things out. After being told that oil could possibly be found in the area, Norman gathered a few possible business associates together and then sent a letter to the government expressing interest in the mineral rights. He knew the actual Indian reserve was off limits but the mission property had just recently been transferred to the Indian department and that possibly the mineral rights could be obtained. David McDougall and Fred Green joined with Norman to secure the rights even though others had earlier been refused. Norman knew the Methodists had owned the property in the 1870's and therefore had settlers' rights so the Indians could not lease the land. Inquiries were made into who exactly owned the land now. Word came that the government actually had no clue who owned the rights. The Indian Department did indeed own the land now but mineral rights were never established. Even so the final transfer papers hadn't even gone through yet so no leases could be granted. Norman asked if his name could go to the top of the list but he was refused. Later the government determined the mineral rights were not part of the transfer and therefore they could not sell the rights to anyone.

In June the Calgary Exhibition and Stampede approached Norman and advised him he had been selected, along with Frank Sibbald and Jack Marshal, to select and distribute the awards in connection with all the Indian competitions during the Stampede. Prizes were to be awarded for best painted teepee and best equipped teepee. Judging was to take place on the grounds and prizes would be awarded on the platform at the grandstand. It was an honour to be picked to do the judging and award presentation. Attendance at the 1925 Calgary Stampede broke all previous records and Norman was thanked for all his cooperation over the years in making it such a continued success.

In the fall the Luxtons sadly said their farewells to Eleanor who had been accepted at the University of Alberta. Eleanor was packed and on her way to Edmonton. The school had an excellent reputation and seemed to care very much about their students. The university had sent Norman a letter asking him to write a brief biography on his daughter. The biography was to contain information on her individual qualities and needs so they could better understand her and help her in achieving the best education possible.

With Eleanor off at school, it was time for Norman's annual hunting trip. The previous year Norman had gone with his good friend, Eugene LaPorte of Baltimore. Eugene had written to say that he wished he could be along for the trip but instead had to be content to stay home in front of the fire. Eugene's only child, "Bill," was away at school now and Eugene felt he should stay home and keep his wife company.

The hunting trip was a pleasure as always but the grouse had been very scarce that year. These annual-hunting trips often lasted more than a month, but it was Norman's way of treating himself for his hard work throughout the summer months. This year Norman managed to spread the trip out to 37 days. Some of the grouse Norman killed he sent off to his friend Ollie in Victoria. Much to Ollie's surprise they arrived in wonderful condition and were excellent eating. In Victoria they didn't call them grouse but referred to them as mountain quail. He hadn't tasted grouse for 12 years so he was pleased that Norman had sent him a few. Ollie always sent Norman a long letter at Christmas but this year he felt bad for not getting a letter out until January. He had been writing Norman for over 24 years. His excuse for the letter's delay was that on New Year's Day his mother-in-law had died. Ollie had thought her an exceptional woman and was as devastated as his wife at the news. The bright spot was that Norman said he was planning a trip to Victoria and Ollie was looking forward to seeing him again. Norman wrote to Ollie complaining about his various aches and pains. Since Ollie was older, he was someone to commiserate with now that they were both "so old." Ollie would have none of it. He told Norman that he was the elder of the two of them and in his mind, he was still a kid. Ollie's answer to getting old was that whenever he woke up feeling achy he would just do his push-ups harder than ever. He did admit that his eyesight was going and now he had to wear spectacles for reading; he referred to them as his "windshields."

In the spring of 1926, a letter arrived from Eugene who decided that he wanted to come on a 2-week trip to Banff for some fishing and hunting. He wanted to spend time with his son, who was attending Princeton, and would bring along a couple of his son's schoolmates.

Eugene wanted the boys to know what living out West was really like and expose them to the wilds of Alberta and the Rockies. He desperately hoped Norman would join them and so in order to convince his friend, Eugene began an intense letter-writing campaign.

For the next 3 months it hardly seemed a day went by that Norman did not receive a letter from Eugene. This was going to be the best trip ever and Eugene wanted Norman to arrange everything in order to impress those "Princeton" boys. The plan was that as soon as finals were over, Eugene and the boys would travel to Montreal. From Montreal they would continue west by train, departing on June 16. Always the letters were always full of questions. Did they need to bring their own rifles? What about flies and mosquitoes? Should they bring rods and reels for fishing? What about beer? Could Norman arrange for some Canadian ale and beer? Of course other liquor would be equally welcome, for all those stomach cramps and snake bites. Eugene knew that Norman would have difficulty putting all of them up in his home and they were more than happy to stay at the King Edward Hotel. Norman had assured his friend that he would join them on the trip and Eugene was thrilled. There was nothing better than a trip with Norman. That summer Norman decided to buy himself a brand-new 1927 Dodge Sedan. After laying down $1,680 the car was his.

The final letter from Eugene arrived confirming that the men would all leave New York on June 15, as planned. They would be in Banff by the June 19, and they were all looking very much forward to having a "bully" time. Good friends, good things to eat, smoke and drink, shooting, and of course, plenty of fishing. There was no reason at all that they shouldn't have the best time ever. The final words told Norman to look out for them when the "blooming train" pulls into the station.

There was no better guide than Norman and the trip was sure to be a spectacular success. Norman finally met Eugene's son Bill along with the other boys Morgan A. Reynolds and Donald Q. Coster. Eugene could hardly believe all the work Norman had gone to on their behalf. There was a cook named Wally Pots who would serve up the wonderful meals and Max Brooks was to be their guide and packer. Bill Potts came along as an additional guide and counselor. There were 16 horses in total, some serving as packhorses and the rest for riding. The packhorses were loaded down with camping equipment, provisions, and suitable clothing.

That first morning the party had set out from Banff before sunrise and soon civilization was left far behind. By nightfall they reached Porcupine River where they set up camp for the night. Early the next morning the party awoke to a most glorious sight of the early morning sun glinting off the fresh snow-capped peaks. Eugene stared in awe and said that in all his years travelling through Alaska, the Swiss Alps, and the Pryenees of Europe, that only the Rockies of Alberta provided such grandeur. The mountain streams overflowed with Cuthroat and Dolly Varden trout, weighing in between 2 and 6 pounds each. The deer were in such abundance that it was an embarrassment to call it hunting.

The next stop was Pocoterra where the group saw their first bighorn mountain sheep; it seeming completely indifferent to their presence. It was not hunting season for big game so it was a time for them to simply enjoy the beauty of the park's animals. From Pocoterra Creek the party headed to the Kananaskis Range where they found the rivers so deep that the horses had to swim across. Luckily the horses were strong and landed on the opposite bank even with the swift currents. That evening they camped at Spray Lakes where they were met by the local game warden, Johnny Kerns. He kept them up most of the night telling them stories about the area and of his adventures as a trapper before becoming the warden. He showed them where beavers built their dams and houses. The area was full of deer, bear, coyotes, elk, moose, mountain goats, porcupines, and squirrels. At one point they heard the coyotes begin to howl and Norman knew that meant something was up. Three of the party crept through the bush, following the noise, when suddenly they saw what all the commotion was about. There in a clearing in front of them was a mountain lion, feeding on a deer.

Eugene again remarked that the Spray area was one of the most beautiful spots he had ever been. The upper and lower Spray Lakes were breathtaking and the party took an excursion to Watterich Lake.

From Spray Lakes, the group continued on and made their way to the Morley reserve where Norman introduced them to many of the native Indians. The American boys were told that the Stoneys were descendants of the Sioux. Eugene was thrilled to meet many of the chiefs including David Bearspaw, Simeon Bigwoman, Enos Hunter, and Jonas Rider. As a special treat the party rode to Kananaskis Lake where they were taken to a large spruce tree. The tree had been carved into a life-size sculpture of an Indian squaw. The mystery was how the tree had survived the carving as it was still very much alive. No one knew quite how old the sculpture was or who had carved it, but it was most impressive.

Since it was still June and very cold the group sometimes had to break the ice covering the river so they could take a quick dip. When the weather got really bad they got a chance to sleep in a teepee. An authentic Indian teepee was much warmer than any house and very comfortable. Norman was such a pleasure to have along as with all his newspaper experience, the boys found him both instructive and entertaining. The exhausted but happy group returned to Banff and the boys promised to write the story of their Wild West adventure in the Princeton paper.

ELEVEN

Family

Ed Hoskings had become a wonderful brother-in-law and always kept in touch with Norman, writing often from his home in St. Paul. It was back in 1901, while Norman was on the *Tilikum*, that Ed had proposed to Olive "Ollie" Luxton, much to the dismay of the family. Perhaps it had been true love; what was certain was that Ed had become a strong member of the Luxton family. Ed and Ollie had two daughters, Dorothy and Mary, plus two sons Louis and Bill. Both boys had grown to be fine young men. Louis was now off in Michigan selling woolens and Bill was selling cars for the Ford Motor Company. Ollie and Ed had really hoped that Eleanor would attend university in Minnesota as they felt it was very valuable to visit other countries and meet people whose cultures were perhaps a little different than her own. Besides, she had two attractive cousins, both over 6 feet tall, ready to escort her around town. They wondered if she might reconsider going back to the University of Alberta and finish her 2 years of schooling in Minnesota. She would be surrounded by the Hoskings family and her Uncle George, Aunt Ada, and her grandmother Sarah.

It had been a difficult 20 years for the Hoskings, after William F. Luxton had died. They had taken Sarah in and cared for her. They all agreed she was a wonderful woman but the demands—physically, emotionally, and mentally— were tough on the family. They were most grateful to Norman as it was only he that contributed financially and always paid all of his mother's bills. Often Ollie would complain about the difficulties in caring for her mother but it was never intended to make Norman feel bad. Sometimes they worried that he felt they were not thankful for his generous financial support but it wasn't that. They just wished they had more privacy and their small house made it difficult for young Dorothy to entertain friends.

George and Ada had repeatedly offered to have Sarah stay in their home but she always backed out at the last minute. She didn't want to move all her things and start again in a new home. At last they convinced her to move to George's and she had seemed to settle in well. Pat would often walk with her grandmother in the garden and they would talk about old times. One night Sarah and Ada sat down in front of the fire and talked about the days in Winnipeg when the children were young. Sarah's mind was sharp but her health was starting to fail rapidly. The doctor often came but there wasn't anything he could do for her and no medicine would help her. The simple fact was that Sarah was 81 years old. Sarah had recently become a Christian Scientist and took great solace in her new religion. She had only been with George and Ada a few months when she came down with a nasty cold. Combined with her age and weak condition she had no strength with which to fight it. She passed away in her sleep, early October of 1927.

George had been in the room with her, along with Ada and his sister Ollie, when the phone rang. It was Ed calling to ask how Sarah was doing. By the time George finished the call and got back to the room, Sara had already passed on.

Norman wrote his sister Nellie in Winnipeg and another letter to Ed, upset because he felt that Ollie somehow blamed him for not helping with their mother more, even though he paid all the expenses. Ed asked Norman to write to his sister and try to patch things up. He knew his mother-in-law would be unhappy if she thought they didn't get along because of her. Ed had helped Sarah prepare her will sometime before and asked if Lou or Norman wanted any of her personal effects. There wasn't much really, apart from a desk pen, paper cutter, paper weights, a small vase, and some books. There was one thing that Sarah had stipulated in her will especially for Norman. During her time at their beautiful home in Winnipeg she had taken to writing poetry and verses. Sarah continued her writings after she moved to St. Paul and the family thought they were very good. Ed had hoped someday that they could even publish them in a book. It was these writings Sarah left to Norman.

Norman's sister Nellie and her husband Fred still lived in Winnipeg and they had offered to pay half the funeral expenses. Norman appreciated the offer but insisted on covering everything himself. The funeral would be held at Lakewood Chapel in Minneapolis on October 4, 1927, and Sarah's body would then be sent to Winnipeg to lay beside her husband William. There would be a separate service at St. John's in Winnipeg. The undertaker in Winnipeg had so admired the Luxton family that when it came time to pay him he refused. He had often gone hunting with Norman, Harry and their father William. This would be his way of expressing his appreciation for the family, his way of saying thank you.

Ed travelled to Winnipeg with Sarah's body and the ashes of his brother-in-law Harry Luxton. After the service Ed, Nellie, and Fred all went to Elmwood Cemetery and scattered Harry's ashes on the ground, under a big tree, just as he had wanted. They then placed flowers under the tree and said their final goodbyes.

All that remained of the Luxton family now was Norman, Lou, George and the two sisters, Nellie and Ollie. The family remained strong and cared deeply for each other. The oldest son William had disappeared as a teenager and the family believed he had likely been shot after he had landed in Montana. He had been the black sheep of the family and had left Winnipeg while still a teenager.

Lou had been on holiday in Victoria, B.C. when his mother died. Neither Norman nor Lou were able to attend their mothers funeral. Eleanor had already returned to Edmonton to complete her university and had acquired a small black cat to keep her company. A letter had arrived from Eugene who had become quite ill and had been confined to his home for 2 weeks but he was on the mend. Poor George was still having a tough time financially as the theatre he worked for was now on strike and he hadn't been paid for 6 weeks. Again he had to ask for Norman's help and felt horrible because there had been the large funeral expense just the month before. He had so wanted to help Norman pay for things and insisted that half the expense should be put down as part of what he owed Norman.

Sarah hadn't been the only parent to pass away that year. Georgie's father, David McDougall, had also passed away.

In January a parcel arrived for Norman. It contained a black Japanese writing box that had belonged to his mother. Norman remembered the box from his childhood in Winnipeg when they lived in the house at Assiniboine Pointe. He remembered that the box had sat on his mother's dresser and held her letters and poetry. George sent a letter along with the box which expressed how he felt that his mother's beautiful soul came through in her writings. He knew she was the best mother any boy could have had. Sarah had saved a few dollars and these were returned to Norman as he had been the one to support her. George wrote about going to Winnipeg for the funeral and while there he had decided to wander down by the river near their old house on Assiniboine Avenue. As he walked along the river's edge he was spotted by Mrs. Col Rattan who now owned the old Luxton home. She called out to him and invited him inside for a look around the old place. It brought back many wonderful memories and he wished he'd had the money to buy the place and fix it up. Mrs. Rattan now lived alone except for her maid, and the house was slowly falling apart with no one to maintain it.

Lou had remained in Victoria for the winter but in early February he sent Norman a letter overflowing with excitement. While in Victoria, Lou had met a Mr. Harry Barns who had been a close friend of Captain Voss in earlier years. After his death, Voss had left the original log book of the *Tilikum*, along with the original manuscript of a book he had published in 1913, to Mr. Barns. Harry also had a copy of the published book and upon discovering that Lou was Norman's brother he offered to loan the book to Norman to read. Norman wrote back saying he was very interested in the book and it was quickly sent off to Banff.

In book titled, *The Venturesome Voyages of Captain Voss,* arrived in March and Norman began reading it immediately. It brought back many memories and Norman got quite a kick out of it. He was a little upset that Voss had written it since they had agreed that the rights to the story belonged to Norman. Still he hadn't had the time to write of his adventure and the information contained in the book certainly would have saved countless lives. Perhaps one day he would write his own account, with the help of the diary he kept daily while on the *Tilikum*. Harry told Norman that the original manuscript far surpassed the book. It was clearly written in Voss's own words. You could almost imagine you could hear him speaking. Still the book was quite good and captured some of the voyages that Voss had been on.

Norman decided to type out the entire book word for word, making two copies, both of which he had bound. One copy he kept and the other he sent off to Harry with his thanks. Harry was a bit of a sailor too and told Norman that he would be more than happy to take him sailing should he ever make it out to Victoria again. Harry's boat was the *Minena*. He planned to put the bound copy of Voss's book in the little bookcase onboard.

Spring of 1928 had arrived and Norman was thinking that if he erected a few teepees next to his curio shop they might bring in some additional tourists. Since it was just for advertising purposes and no one would actually live in the teepees, there should be no problem. He also thought about expanding Indian Days, perhaps inviting the Kootenay Indians from the Windermere area. He approached the CPR about bringing the Kootenay Indians east but the CPR thought it best that the Kootenays stay away from the Blood Indians.

With tourist season still a couple of months away Norman decided to head out to Victoria. Unfortunately it rained the entire time and Norman came down with a nasty cold. What surprised him was that he noticed that drinking whiskey in Banff had twice the kick that it did at sea level.

While on holiday Norman decided to look up a few old girlfriends but he soon found that many of them had already passed away; one had even committed suicide. He was just glad it was through no fault of his. He realized that he was no longer the young lad that had sailed on the *Tilikum* those many years ago. He didn't walk like he used to and he had the aches and pains that come with age. He needed some cheering up so he wrote a long letter to his buddy Eugene in Baltimore. He told Eugene about how some days he just felt rotten and he'd always been so wonderfully healthy until now. He talked about how he would cry like a baby now if he got so much as a wart on his toe. He wasn't one for doctors and still firmly believed the best cure was a drink of scotch and good company. He had recently read about the possibility that aluminum cooking pots caused cancer. The article was very convincing and as soon as Norman got back home to Banff he immediately threw away all of his aluminum pots and wrote letters to his family encouraging them to do the same.

Eleanor was coming home from university at the end of the month, having just completed her final exams. She had never been a strong girl and had missed much of her early schooling due to illness. Even though she was older now she had been very unwell of late and Norman was glad that she would soon be home. He hoped to send Eleanor and Georgie out to the coast for part of the summer.

The debate continued about bringing the Kootenay and the Blood Indians to Banff for Indian Days. The town of Standoff agreed to pay all the expenses for the Bloods to attend. Norman was okay with that but said that no special favours would be granted and that they must arrive and depart the same day as the Stoneys. He was adamant that every tribe would be treated equally.

Back in Banff the curio shop was looking better than ever. The grizzly and polar bear heads were the best he'd had in years. As Norman looked over his little shop he knew he loved this little business the best of all. The summer was always so busy but Norman loved when the tourists came. There was never much free time and things like letter writing took a backseat until the tourists had gone home. Though Norman didn't have time to write he could always count on lots of letters from Eugene in Baltimore. Mostly Eugene bugged him about when Norman was going to sit down and write his book on the trip to Australia in the canoe. Norman thought he could maybe manage some sort of serial-story for the *Crag and Canyon*. That might make better use of his time. Perhaps this winter when things had slowed down a bit he might just do it.

In addition to all his other business, Norman signed on as president of the Banff chapter of the Alberta Game and Fish Protection Association. That meant his usual posse of friends would serve along with him. Bill Potts became vice president and Jim Brewster, Lorne Orr, William Brewster, and N.J.T. Frost signed up.

The idea to expand Indian Days was finally shelved for the current year as there wasn't time to get it organized. They had thought about adding 2 additional days on but Norman decided the time wasn't right. There would be one new feature of Indian Days and that was to be a special prize for best-dressed pinto horse. Norman wrote to Jonas Benjamin at Morley and told him to be sure to bring every pinto they had. Next came the food rations since Banff paid for all the food that the Indians ate during their stay. The government always paid for the meat and that year sent three buffalo. With the buffalo now almost extinct, buffalo meat was a real treat. The Stoney Indians had eaten buffalo for so many years that they actually craved it. Although it was never said out loud, the buffalo meat was one of the main factors which drew the Indians to Banff. The buffalo were sent out from the east and the Indians were allowed to slaughter it and use the animal as they had in earlier days. The available buffalo weren't like those of the past, now you were lucky to get a bull weighing 800-900 pounds. In the old days a buffalo could easily be double that weight. All other food had to be purchased by Norman including 1300 loaves of bread, 1000 pounds of potatoes, 15 pails of jam, 25 plugs of smoking tobacco, 100 pounds of tea, 20 pounds of baking powder, 720 pounds of flour, and 10 pounds of sugar. The merchants of Banff covered all these expenses plus the prize money. Indian Days were Norman's way of giving something back to the Indians who he felt had been unjustly treated. The amount of food supplied in Banff exceeded that of the Calgary Stampede which also supplied food to the Indian encampment at the fairgrounds. The total cost for food and prizes that year for Indian Days came in at $2400.

N.J.T. Frost was the editor of the *Crag and Canyon* and felt badly when he was forced to resign due to health and family matters. He assured Norman that everything was in good shape for a new editor. Still it was more worry for Norman.

September came and Eleanor was again on her way to Edmonton to continue her classes. Her health had improved a great deal over the summer; her expanded waistline could attest to that. Still Norman didn't care how big she got as long as she was healthy. She worried about her weight but Norman didn't at all. She was already larger than either of her parents but still resembled her mother the most.

George had written from Minneapolis with word of his new job as a modern motion picture operator, or 'projectionist' as they were now called. It was quite different running the new equipment from his days at the Lux Theatre, and he had to complete all new training. The local union had accepted him as an extra man and he had passed the exam and already worked 3 weeks. Two of those weeks George was left on his own, he was proud that he had not yet had any mishap. It was difficult though because he still worked his regular job at the paper. With this new part-time job he was working 16 hours a day, 7 days a week, including Sundays. Unfortunately, working so hard caused him such physical exhaustion that after just a few weeks he was forced to take a week off without pay in order to recover. Still the union had lots of potential work now. The new talking pictures were very popular and there was talk about the latest invention, something new called television. George had hopes that his latest training would turn into a very lucrative profession and that life would become easier.

The tourists were gone and Norman had enjoyed another month-long hunting trip in October. He had decided that the time had come to write of his *Tilikum* voyage, the *Crag and Canyon* would run the story over several weeks. He thought it best to start the serial story in late December. It would give the locals something to read over the winter. He also intended to send copies of the papers to his friends and family down in the United States so they could, at last, hear the details of his journey.

The Stoneys had always held Norman in high regard and often he received letters from the chiefs with the latest news and sometimes requests for help. In January of 1929, a rather lengthy letter arrived from Jonas Two-Young-Men. Chief Bearspaw had died and Jonas was now chief. He just wanted Norman to know that he was welcome to come to Jonas anytime he needed anything from the Indians. Jonas greatly respected Norman. Enos Hunter also wrote Norman about the great fun he'd had in Banff recently at the ice palace. It seems there had been much singing and Enos thoroughly enjoyed himself. He said the music was like the sound of wind against the trees or like waterfalls. He hoped that singing would become a part of future festivities in Banff.

Not only did the Indians think highly of Norman but he was regarded by many people as the ultimate authority on Indian customs and traditions. A writer from California, J. Roy Lee of Los Angeles, was writing a book about the West and asked Norman for assistance in describing the Sun Dance. Norman was more than happy to help.

Just when some men reach a certain age and think about slowing down, such thoughts never entered Norman's mind. Eugene wrote teasingly that Norman's eyesight must certainly be failing as he sent the last letter to the wrong address. He also complained that Norman's letters were too short because he was likely too busy with some Indian celebration, rodeo or carnival to write a decent letter. Didn't Norman know that he is too darn old to keep the pace up and that one day old Norman would just drop stone dead?

It was winter carnival time again and much to Norman's delight the *Calgary Herald* had provided huge coverage for the event. Stories ran up to 10 days in advance, bringing large crowds up from Calgary. The weather had been bad in Banff during the carnival and a lot of people were sick so had it not been for the Calgarians, it would not have been the success it was. Special excursion trains ran from Calgary but the trains west of Banff were blocked due to a bridge being out. Still a few travellers managed to make it from the coast. The trip from Vancouver which normally took 24 hours, lasted 72 hours when passengers had to reroute through Edmonton and Kettle Valley. Some competitors for the carnival came up from the United States and a young Montana boy had won this year's speed skating prize. Norman was extremely grateful to the *Calgary Herald* for all their publicity and sent a long letter of thanks to Charles Hayden, editor of the paper.

Norman had kept his promise and wrote the *Tilikum* series for the *Crag and Canyon*. Letters began to pour in, thanking him for writing about his adventure. Eugene received his copy and was so impressed he thought surely if Norman had sailed a boat to Australia then he was as much a sea captain as Voss. From this point on his letters to Norman always started with "Dear Captain." A letter from Eugene, now nicknamed "Pop," always made Norman laugh. The latest joke of the day was always included and this latest letter was no exception.

"I asked a friend how he was feeling and he said not very well."

"What's the trouble?"

"I have matrimonial indigestion. My wife doesn't agree with me."

Eugene was planning on coming out again in late May and was looking forward to the trip. This time he planned to bring a friend. Norman assured him that he would happily take them wherever an automobile would go. Lorne Orr, over at the hotel, would make sure a room was ready with two beds and a bath. Norman told Eugene that any friend regardless of creed, colour, or sex, was more than welcome at his hotel.

Poor George always seemed to be having a tough time down in Minnesota. No doubt he was working too hard but now he was also having some heart trouble. In early March, Ada had found him unconscious on the bedroom floor in the middle of the night. George had known for some years that his "pump" wasn't quite right. He took comfort in that a man he knew, who had suffered from the same problem for over 20 years, was still going strong at 70. In fact the guy had recently remarried. Perhaps there was no cause for alarm but George would feel better knowing that his business interests in Banff were safe. He already had a small life insurance policy for Ada and Pat but they would need the money from his Banff investments as well. Over the years he'd asked Norman for something in writing regarding his various Banff holdings. It wasn't that he doubted Norman's word; he just wanted to be sure that the money was there should he pass on. He decided to ask Norman for written details of his investments. Often George had been asked to remortgage his house in order to provide money for the Lux Block. Reflecting back on his life, George felt the best two things life ever game him was Ada and his daughter Pat. He felt very lucky that Ada was still his sweetheart even now that they had been married over 20 years. He didn't have to explain to Norman the joy of having Pat knowing that Norman had his own wonderful daughter Eleanor.

George was happy that Norman had written the story of his ocean voyage with Voss. Every week he looked forward to the next edition of the *Crag and Canyon*. Norman had mentioned again about the mysterious visit from George Grieves on board the *Tilikum*. It didn't surprise George that Norman had received the ghostly visit as it seemed that George, along with Norman and their mother, often had communication with these "outside" forces. Along with the serial in the paper, Norman had typed up his story in book form and along with Voss's account, had sent it to the head librarian and archivist at the provincial archives in Victoria. They hoped the gift would be a permanent gift for the archives.

A few weeks passed when at last George received his package from Banff. George was thrilled as now he had full details of all his holdings in Banff. Norman had set to work immediately to put his brother at ease and George now had the paperwork should Ada or Patty ever need it. George continued to have "spells" with his heart but for the most part he hid them from Ada so as not to worry her.

At the end of May, 1929, Eugene had arrived in Banff along with his brother Robert for a much- anticipated visit with Norman. He had shipped a large trunk and suitcase earlier that he asked Norman to pick up. It was during this visit he became friends with Lorne Orr (Lorry) at the King Edward Hotel. He liked to joke that he would eat with Lorry when he could find the time but would drink with him anytime. They all had a good visit but Norman decided to kidnap Eugene and his brother and take them to Calgary. Although the kidnapping was all in good fun, Eugene felt bad that he didn't get the chance to say goodbye and thank his friends in Banff. He gave Norman a bit of a hard time over that.

Always up to something, Norman had recently purchased 100 shares in Outwest Petroleum stock of Calgary. It was, in some ways, like the old gold rush where one hoped that their company would stike oil. Not that it mattered as financially Norman was in the best shape he had ever been. He bought a new car and was thinking about either buying an existing cabin up at Lake Minnewanka or building a new cabin on the 2-acre lot he had there.

That summer some men came around Banff, scouting out a possible site for a Banff airport. The bad news was that the most suitable place for an aerodrome was on the rodeo grounds where the Banff Indian Days were held. Norman agreed that Banff would likely need some sort of airfield in the future but was only willing to give up the rodeo grounds should a suitable alternate location be found. The Indian Days committee drafted a letter indicating their concerns. The letter was then signed by Jim Brewster, S.M. Armstrong, and Norman who sent it off to the appropriate government department.

As usual, letter writing took a backseat during the summer and Norman's friends usually started their whining by early November. Eugene had worked himself into quite a state believing that one of his insulting letters to Norman may have been taken the wrong way. He meant the insults in a funny way, hoping for a laugh. Since he had heard nothing from Norman since his last trip he was really starting to worry. At first he tried to humour Norman into writing him but then he thought that perhaps his insults had become too serious. He was certain now that he'd overdone it and that Norman no longer wished to correspond with him. He wasn't sure which letter had offended Norman but he was devastated. The friendship with Norman was not something he was willing to give up. Eugene had written at least twice a month and now he worried that the friendship had ended because of something he had said that Norman must have misinterpreted. The letters to Norman became more desperate, at first asking if he had offended him but then in the same letter he would accuse Norman of just getting old and crabby. Perhaps Norman walked around Banff like an old grouch now, cussing his friends. He didn't really mean the insults but now he was hoping for any kind of response. Another letter was sent asking Norman what the big idea was. If he had offended Norman he wanted to know in what manner so he could at least defend himself. He told Norman that he considered him to be one of his very best friends and appreciated their friendship above all. The only thing he was guilty of was bragging to his eastern friends about his wonderful friend in Banff. His latest letter included photographs of their trip the previous June and some films that Norman had loaned him.

At last a letter arrived from Banff; the friendship was back on track.

William Fisher Luxton (c1900)

George E. Luxton, Harold Malloch Luxton, Lou Luxton, William
Fisher Luxton - Winnipeg, Manitoba (c1906)

Voss, Captain John (c1890)

Norman Luxton, George Luxton and Malloch Luxton (c1913)

Georgiana Luxton (McDougall) - Banff, Alberta (c1904)

Eleanor Luxton (c1913)

King Edward Hotel Fire - Banff Avenue (c1914)

Norman and "Larry" with the Tilikum model (c1923)

Eugene LaPorte (c1923)

Earl Massecar (c1940)

Eleanor and Norman Luxton (c1950)

Guy Weadick (c1910)

TWELVE

A Busy Man Never Retires

At an age when other men think of retiring, Norman was at last a successful businessman and continued to work hard with the comfort that his financial affairs were no longer a worry. Even with the crash of Wall Street in 1929 the beginnings of the Great Depression did not yet affect him. In fact had he not read about the crash, he would hardly have known it had happened at all.

Eugene continued to write several times a month and was usually off visiting New York or Atlantic City, two of his favourite spots. Every year Eugene made his way to Banff to visit Norman, a man he admired and counted as one of his closest friends. Eugene had been sick with a cold that he couldn't seem to shake but his letters were never anything but upbeat. They were always full of news of his latest trip and always contained at least one obscene, yet hilariously funny story or joke. His brother Robert was now a magistrate and worked about 16 miles outside of Baltimore. Everyone called him "Judge" and Eugene was sure his brother walked around very dignified with his chest sticking out. Eugene would often try to get Norman involved in some venture or other and the latest one was the purchase of some petroleum and natural gas leases. Currently they were trying to raise $250,000 to begin the drilling of a well. The various schemes usually amounted to nothing but it was still something to keep the friends amused. Eugene was planning his 1930 trip to Banff as usual and looking forward to seeing the old gang which included Norman, Lorne Orr, and Bill Potts. This year Eugene hoped to drag his brother Frank along. Besides hunting and going riding in the mountains with Norman, Eugene loved his drink. This year would be a little drier though as Norman had decided to give up drinking entirely. Still Norman would supply his friend with a welcome drink when he arrived by train later that month.

One day in May a long letter arrived from Norman's friend, Peter Whyte. Peter was from Banff but had decided to make a journey around the world. Peter had known Norman for years but had only heard the rare mention of the little canoe trip Norman had taken with Voss. As Peter's trip continued it soon became apparent that the little "canoe" was more famous around the world than he had ever imagined. Every country he visited seemed to know of the famous *Tilikum* and it came as a shock to Peter that his friend Norman and Voss were huge celebrities around the world. While in Honolulu, Peter had met a Mr. Steinwasher who was a shipmate of Voss. Seems this man and Voss had worked on a sealing vessel in the Bearing Sea. Voss had given Steinwasher a copy of his book and now Peter had read it. As Peter continued on his trip he was even more astonished when upon reaching London, England, he picked up the local paper to find a picture of the *Tilikum* on the front page. That very day the *Tilikum* was being loaded onto a ship bound for Victoria. Peter quickly made his way to the spot on the Thames where the *Tilikum* was to sail from but found he had just missed the boat. Some weeks later, Peter made his way to China and once again, on the front page of the local paper, another picture of the *Tilikum*. Peter felt sure that not even Norman realized the important place the *Tilikum* and its journey had in nautical history. Peter wrote to Norman begging him to start writing the story from his recollections. What Peter didn't know was that Norman had written his story over the winter of 1927-1928 for his newspaper serial. Somehow Peter had missed those issues of the *Crag and Canyon*. Norman had the story typed and bound and gave it to his wife for her personal interest. Other than the serial, Norman had no further plans to publish the story in any form. The bound copy was dedicated to his friend, Captain Winchester, who he'd met at Penhryn Island those many years ago.

There was always something to do and the curio shop hadn't been promoted for awhile so Norman took an ad out in the *Calgary Albertan* newspaper. Then there were the Indian Days coming up plus Eleanor would soon be home again. She had just received her Bachelor or Arts degree from the University of Alberta. The Calgary Stampede was also approaching but the Banff Band had pulled out of the competition. Norman got a letter from E.L. "Ernie" Richardson, general manager of the Calgary Stampede, urging Norman to get the band to reconsider. They had pulled out as they were unhappy about the previous year's judging but Norman was reminded that their participation was good advertising for Banff. Besides, they would be given $75 just for showing up and that should be incentive enough.

George had written that Ed and Ollie had come for a visit and he sent the photos off to Norman. Ed looked to be in great shape but Ollie didn't look well at all. Ed and Ollie's boys, Bill and Louis, looked in excellent shape. They were both over 6 feet tall and it was obvious the height must have come from Ed's side of the family. All the Luxton boys were quite a short lot. Norman was only 5 feet, 7 inches. Norman always enjoyed hearing about his niece Pat, and George mentioned that she had recently taken up stamp collecting. It had been an interest that George and his sister-in-law Georgie shared and he had given Georgie his entire collection. Very diplomatically he asked Norman that if Georgie was not collecting anymore, and if the collection did not have deep sentimental value, that she might be persuaded to let Pat have it. George was happy to announce that his heart spells had improved. Even so, Ada had decided it might be in her best interest to take up a trade so she enrolled in a local business college to study stenography. George knew he likely wouldn't outlive Ada but was adamant that as long as he was alive she wouldn't have to work.

The Calgary Stampede parade was held on July 7, 1930, and Norman rode in the Indian section, right after the parade marshall and Stampede officials. It was quite a parade with many local celebrities including Colonel James Walker, Harold Riley, and Guy Weadick.

Eugene had visited Banff back in May and the latest photos arrived in his most recent letter. He didn't know if Norman wanted them but in his usual zany style he said,

"If you don't want the photos you can give them to the blind asylum."

That was Eugene, crazy as ever. Frank, Eugene's brother, had come to Banff with him and enjoyed his visit so much he was already talking about going back again in '31.

The depression seemed to have little effect on Banff in the summer of 1930 and business was steady. The Banff Indians Days were scaled down to just one day that year but still went ahead. The United States was starting to suffer and poor George was out of work at the movie theatre. The theatre owners were on strike again. Norman sent off some money, unsolicited, which George gratefully accepted. George wrote to thank Norman and in the same letter mentioned that, some years earlier, a memorial tree had been planted in Minneapolis in memory of Malloch. This news came as quite a surprise to Norman who had never heard any word of it.

In Minneapolis, back in 1921, it had been decided that a tree would be planted for every soldier that died in World War One. The trees would line Memorial Drive and would stretch for approximately 3 miles. Some 6000 trees had been planted and each one held a plaque with the name of a soldier from Minneapolis that had died in the war. George felt that although his brother Malloch had only lived in Minneapolis a short time that he should be remembered and so George had arranged to get a tree for him. The bronze plaque in the shape of a cross was affixed, along with the soldier's name, country, and army. Malloch's name would appear on the large war monument as well. George's intent was to visit the tree every Memorial Day with flowers and a Canadian flag. George felt it was the least he could do for the poor kid and knew it would have pleased their mother. (Malloch's tree still stands today, over 80 years after it was planted.)

In August of 1930, the *Tilikum* arrived back in Victoria and was placed in the Crystal Garden just across from the Empress Hotel. An old acquaintance of Norman's by the name of Mr. Fox was the contractor and ensured the *Tilikum* was placed in the best spot. The publicity made mention of the canoe's journey and her captain, John Voss, but nothing was said of Norman. Now Mrs. Kent, whose daughter Marjorie had been engaged years before to Norman, suddenly appeared on the scene. She had come back to Victoria and she remembered clearly Norman's involvement and was quick to point out the oversight to the local papers. Ollie had kept quiet, as he didn't really know the exact details regarding the financial end of things. He couldn't quite say for sure if Norman owned half of the *Tilikum* or not. He did know that Norman certainly was the first mate and that he had himself sailed on the *Tilikum* with Norman on a little trip from Oak Bay to Victoria. He begged Norman to write him of the exact financial details in case he should be in the position to defend Norman in the future. Ollie's other fond memory was of the photo taken onboard the *Tilikum* on May 20, 1901, when he posed with George Luxton, Captain Voss, and the Voss family. The *Tilikum* had sailed the following morning.

Apart from the *Tilikum*, Norman was very well known in Canada and the United States for his taxidermy and fur business. Norman had received a letter from the Detroit Zoological Park Commission requesting him to find them skulls and horns of bighorn mountain sheep. Norman was also known as someone who might invest in just about anything that would attract a tourist. He had been approached about his possible interest in the purchase of a miniature golf course. These golf courses were designed for installation in hotel basements and were easy to assemble. You could buy an 18-hole course or a 9-hole course and they came with 72 putters, balls, and 1000 scorecards. They were very portable and could be had for as little as $2500. Norman didn't really have anywhere to put the contraption but he kept the information and tucked it away.

Eugene was usually busy off on some holiday but that summer he attended the wedding of one of the Dupont girls. His son Bill was best man and even Eugene had not experienced this kind of wealth. It was certainly the social event of the season and Eugene said the wine flowed like water.

Norman did enjoy driving about town in his car, but his short temper and lack of patience often caused a stir in town. Rumour was that when stop signs were introduced in Banff that Norman ignored them. He had had a little accident back in 1929, but hadn't heard anything further until a letter arrived in November of 1930. It was from Calgary lawyer, A. L. Barron. The letter indicated that a certain Katherine Ethel Gallop had been injured by a car that Norman was driving. She was now looking for compensation and said that she had been confined to her home for 3 months and required the services of a nurse. Although there didn't seem to be any serious physical injury she claimed she now had a bad case of nerves and was high-strung and somehow that was Norman's fault. Norman, to his credit, didn't fight the charge and settled out of court. The woman agreed to accept $100 cash upfront, $200 more in one month and another $200 in two months.

George wrote again trying to get Norman to reconsider writing the story of the *Tilikum* for the general public. Just recently in Minneapolis, a vessel known as the *Roald Amundson* had docked in the city where it would remain until the following spring. The ship had travelled the world and would soon be on its way home to Norway. George had gone out to talk to the crew and found that they too were very familiar with the *Tilikum*. The Swedish crew considered the *Tilikum*'s journey to be the best and most dangerous voyage made in the history of the world. George gave them a photograph of the *Tilikum* and a copy of the *Crag and Canyon* that Norman's story had appeared in.

Although Norman had not suffered from the current Depression the Stoney Indians were having a tough time of it. The Indians had approached Norman as they wanted to replace the current Indian agent immediately. They asked Norman to write to Ottawa on their behalf so they invited him to Morley to discuss their issues. Rev. E.J. Staley from the Indian Residential School of the United Church of Canada also wrote to Norman. The Indians in Morley were destitute and he didn't know how they would even survive the winter. He knew how helpful Norman had been in the past and asked him if there wasn't something the two of them could do to help. The government officials continued to insist everything was fine.

The Depression was affecting Vancouver Island and Ollie wrote that all the lumber mills and lumber camps were now closed down. Still they had not yet had to resort to bread lines so perhaps they shouldn't complain.

One day, a representative showed up in Banff with instructions to slaughter all the buffalo in the Banff Paddock. The story that was given was that the meat was to be sent to the Northwest Territories for "Eskimo relief." It didn't seem to worry the government that the Eskimo diet did not include buffalo meat and it would likely make them sick. The other problem was that these were the buffalo used for Banff Indian Days. Every year, six buffalo were given to the Stoneys to slaughter and consume during the festivities. The government offered cold storage buffalo meat in place of the live buffalo but Norman pointed out that the stored meat made the Indians very sick. He suggested that perhaps a few buffalo could be sent down from Wainwright to feed the Indians during Indian Days. Norman's pleas fell on deaf ears. Norman wrote to Ottawa insisting that cold storage buffalo meat was not an option. Does the government just not get it? Banff Indian Days are important to Banff and result in a large number of tourists bringing income to the town. Typically, between 350 and 450 Indians would come and set up over 100 teepees. Their attendance meant increased business for the hotels and restaurants. It also gave the Indians an opportunity to sell their wares, providing them with some desperately needed money.

Along with the buffalo issue was the continuing problem with the current Indian agent. Norman wrote to the Minister of the Interior pleading for some financial aid. The current Indian agent continued telling the government that everything was fine. It wasn't! Norman wrote that he had lived among the Stoneys for over 35 years and his wife's family lived among them for 65 years. That is the reason that the Indians had come to him for help. What they needed at Morley was someone who knew the problems and lived in the area. Norman suggested that perhaps Howard Sibbald would be better able to appraise the situation and he could submit a report. Howard had served previously as an Indian agent for both Morley and Gleichen and was currently serving as superintendent of Kootenay Park at Radium Hot Springs. The government could trust Howard to give a true and accurate report that would show no favouritism to either side. Along with the letter, Norman included the petition that the Indians had drawn up to get rid of their current agent and sent off the package.

Christmas came with the usual flurry of activity and with it came greetings from family and friends. Norman's sister Nellie had written that her husband Fred was very sick but was hanging on. Guy Weadick, who Norman had met while working with the Calgary Stampede, also kept up regular correspondence with Norman. Guy had written that he was down in San Diego with his wife Florence and they were busy promoting the Calgary Stampede, Banff, and Lake Louise. Guy was trying to round up some new entertainment for the 1931 Stampede. He was hoping to get "Pawnee Bill" along with Will Rogers and his wife. If he was lucky maybe he could convince Two-Gun W.S. "Bill" Hart and Hoot Gibson to come. Guy mentioned that he had driven some 7000 miles and was thankful for the pair of driving gloves that Norman had given him. Eugene sent a wonderful letter saying that on both Christmas Day and New Year's Day, in New York City, he had gone outside with his compass and a drink and aligned himself northwest. Raising his glass, he had toasted Norman and all his friends in Banff.

Eugene and Norman had recently found another interest they had in common. Airplanes were becoming more and more popular and both Norman and Eugene did their best to go up flying whenever they could. The airplane of choice was a Gypsy Moth, the rage at the time.

Among other Christmas greetings was a letter from the Minister of the Interior regarding the buffalo problem. He would hear Norman out but needed more information. Just 2 days later another letter came from Indian Affairs acknowledging Norman's letter about the poor conditions at Morley promising that they would look into it. A few weeks passed when another letter arrived, it said the government would no longer allow buffalo to be slaughtered as they felt this was not in the best interest of the park. For tourists to see this spectacle would not be very pleasant and might result in bad publicity if a newspaperman decided to criticize the practice. They again confirmed that they would supply only cold storage carcasses for the occasion.

Norman was furious. The whole point of setting up the Banff buffalo paddock initially had been intended to supply the Indians on Indian Days with fresh buffalo meat. He sent off an angry letter saying that he couldn't believe the government would think so little of them that it believed they would slaughter the animals in front of the tourists. Each year the six buffalo needed were cut out from the herd, a mile or so from spectators, where they were shot by a warden. They were then butchered on the spot and rationed at the Indian Village after the sports were over. He said that if the government's only objection was the utterly disgusting assumption they slaughtered the buffalo for the entertainment of the tourists that in fact the opposite was true. The buffalo were for the Indians only. This letter would prove to be Norman's undoing. Norman continued his campaign and wrote the Honorable R. B. Bennett about the buffalo problem. Unfortunately for Norman, the Minister of the Interior had kept every letter Norman had ever written over the years. It seemed that Norman had written them back in 1926 boasting about how the Indians continued the tradition of preparing the buffalo from slaughter through to the skinning and consumption. The tourists would gather to watch how the Indians used every part of the buffalo, something Norman felt was important to show the tourists for historical reasons. In his earlier letter he had said how this tradition was watched by a large number of visitors and proved to be quite an attraction. The letter from the Indian Department asked how in 1926 Norman said the buffalo slaughter was an attraction and now he claimed the opposite. Norman knew he'd met his match and that July the Indians ate cold buffalo meat.

Ever since the turn of the century, Norman had always kept at least one hunting dog. His dog of choice was a red setter. He always named them either Larry or Barney. Being good Irish Setters he even gave them the good Irish surname of O' Toole. Over in Vernon, B.C. there was a man named Alex Green and he had heard about Norman's wonderful hunting dogs. At the time, Norman had just one dog by the name of Larry. Now these red setters made excellent hunting dogs and Alex had the perfect "girlfriend" for Larry. He was hoping that Norman would let Larry come to Vernon so that the two could breed. The puppies could then be trained to hunt. Several hunters in the Vernon area had already expressed interest. Alex knew that there was no dog finer than Larry. Would Norman consider putting Larry in a boxcar and sending him off C.O.D. to Vernon? Norman agreed and soon Larry had packed his bag and boarded the train to B.C. to meet his "lady." Larry was a huge hit in Vernon although the first day he didn't eat well. The likely cause was due to being locked up in a boxcar. The next day Larry bounced back and did his duty. Alex loved Larry and thought about "forgetting" to send him back but Larry was eventually sent home along with a snapshot of his new girlfriend.

Eugene had been flying again and wrote Norman all about his latest excursion. He'd flown over Pennsylvania in the sister ship to Lindberg's *Spirit of St. Louis*. The plane was called *The Sister of the Spirit of St. Louis* and Eugene was thrilled to have been able to fly in her.

The telegram arrived on March 13, 1931. Fred Foster, Nellie's husband had died. He had been feeling great that Friday, better than he had in awhile, but at 8 pm he had a heart attack. He fell unconscious and was dead by midnight. The funeral service would be held in Winnipeg and then the body would be taken to Montreal. The plan was for Nellie and a nurse to accompany the body. George and Ollie would go up to Winnipeg to help their sister in whatever way they could. Fred had always felt that he wouldn't live long and his business affairs were all in order. The funeral service was held at the Holy Trinity Church and it was decided that Ollie would accompany her sister to Montreal. Nellie was holding up well, but although many people came to the house to pay their respects, the family only let Nellie see those people that were her closest friends. Nellie had no plans for the future so after Montreal she came back to Minneapolis with Ollie. The closest friend to the family was Fred Pace and he made the travel plans for the two women. The house was locked up and Nellie and Ollie left for Montreal. They would travel back through Chicago and then on to St. Paul. The family told Norman to stay in Banff; there really wasn't anything he could do anyway. Just a few weeks later, Norman was laid up with a severe case of the flu.

The flying bug had caught Norman's interest and he made some inquiries as to purchasing an airplane. Second-hand Gypsy Moths could be had for around $2,400 with most of the engines having anywhere between 250 and 400 hours on them. It was only a dream for the time being.

It was always a surprise when the mail arrived, Norman never knew quite what it might bring. April brought a strange request all the way from Hertfordshire, England. The local school there known as Caldicott School, in the town of Hitchen, wanted a teepee. They had written to Ottawa and were immediately given Norman's name as a possible source. Norman was happy to help and after determining the costs involved he sent them the details. Other mail came from *Harbour & Shipping*, a monthly marine journal out of Vancouver. They had heard about Normans' voyage on the *Tilikum* and were currently writing a book on the maritime history of B.C. They were hoping Norman could help. Letters from family came as well and George was still working hard to try and make ends meet. He would take any kind of work he could get and along with being a projectionist at the local cinema he had also just been hired as staff photographer with the *Minneapolis Star*. He had been a newspaper photographer 18 years earlier for the *St. Paul Journal*. Now that he was older the work seemed harder, but he loved it. The letter also included some flower seeds for Georgie to try in her garden.

Good news arrived from Vernon with the announcement that Larry's girlfriend had given birth to 11 puppies. There were 8 males and 3 females and they were all beauties. Alex picked out one for Norman and would be sending him to Banff shortly. The little puppy was already picking up handkerchiefs and bringing them back to Alex and he was only 6 weeks old.

In early June, the latest addition to the Luxton family arrived from Vernon and they named him Barney. He was adorable and everyone fell in love with him. There would be time to train the new puppy in the fall but tourist season was upon them. Norman had arranged for the teepee to be made and it was ready to be shipped to England much to the excitement of Caldicott School. Banff Indian Days went ahead as scheduled despite the fact that an outbreak of chicken pox in Morley had threatened to delay the event.

His name was Earl Massecar and he was a handsome boy with dark hair and clear skin. He was in his mid-teens and had recently had a run-in with the law. His mother lived in Banff but there was no father and the lad had gotten into trouble. When most people would have been happy to simply let him go to jail, Norman decided that the boy was worth saving. At his own expense he took the troubled youth and sent him off to a Jesuit Boys' school in Regina, Saskatchewan. In the fall of 1931 the boy was sent off to the school. At first, it was difficult for Earl as some time had past since he had been a student. Still the boy was extremely grateful for the second chance at life that Norman had given him. He wrote Norman regularly and soon had quickly settled down to school life. Earl was hoping to make the rugby team that he had just tried out for. The drama class was very interesting and took its place alongside his regular studies in Latin, French, History, Geometry, Composition, Literature, Algebra, Science, Physiology, and Grammar. His letters to Norman always inquired after Barney and Larry. He sometimes missed his friends from Pincher Creek where he had lived, for many years, at the Pincher Creek convent.

More letters arrived from Earl but although he was homesick for Banff he was thrilled to have made the junior rugby team. He had come second in the weekly composition test and was doing his best to make Norman proud of him. Norman often sent $5 for the boy to spend as he pleased but even Earl thought it too much and did not wish to take advantage. Along with the spending money Norman had paid the boy's full tuition along with room and board. This did not come cheaply. The tuition alone had cost $120 for just a half year and books were over $12. Then came the room and board during the holiday season which brought the grand total to $235—all this at a time when the great depression was causing unemployment throughout the country.

George loved his job as photographer but the hours were tough. Evenings and weekends often found him called out to photograph a fire, murder, or some automobile smash up. Still he loved the rush of it all; being right in the middle of the most unfortunate events gave him quite a thrill. Sometimes when he did finally get back home to bed, he was too nervous to sleep. George had become closer to Norman after the death of their mother and he had told Norman that he had always been his hero. It was Norman who had succeeded well beyond anyone else in the family, Norman that helped out financially, and Norman that had all the brains in the family. George had often thought himself to be quite dumb but did his best to cover up that fact. It was important to him that his wife Ada and little daughter Pat thought him smart so that they could always count on him. He liked his place on the pedestal they had put him on and he never wanted to let them down. He knew that Norman worried about young Eleanor as she seemed more intent on studies than on settling into any sort of domestic life. George tried to assure his brother that it was good for a woman to be educated and would surely bring more to any future marriage. Norman wasn't so sure.

THIRTEEN

Friends

While working with the Calgary Stampede over the years, Norman and Guy Weadick had become fast friends. Both men had a passion to keep history alive for future generations and they both loved to show the tourists a little of their hometown heritage. Norman brought the tourists to Banff and Guy brought the tourists to Calgary. Norman had his Indian history and Guy had his cowboy history. The two men understood each other.

Guy was busy throughout the fall and winter promoting Calgary, the Calgary Stampede, and doing his best to rustle up entertainment for the following year's show. When he was home at his ranch in Longview, Alberta, he often invited Norman down for a visit. This winter Guy was down at Pawnee Bill's ranch in Oklahoma. He was still hoping to convince Pawnee Bill to come up for the next Stampede. Pawnee had been the partner of the late Col. W.F. Cody, better know as Buffalo Bill. The next Stampede would be its 20th anniversary and Guy wanted someone special to feature at the grandstand show. He hoped Norman could have the Stoneys send Pawnee Bill a special invitation to also attend Banff Indian Days. Norman was happy to oblige.

Christmas of 1931 was approaching, and came along with the usual pile of letters and cards. Earl was staying in Regina over the holidays and had done extremely well in school that year. He was always grateful for the money and chocolates Norman sent. Earl was happy to share the candy amongst his friends at school. He assured Norman that the chocolates were the best he had ever eaten. His grades steadily improved and things were looking up for the young man. He had also received a new pair of ice skates from Norman and he loved to go skating in his spare time. With the money Norman sent every month, he was able to afford a night out at the local cinema every 2 weeks to see the latest films. Norman had also sent some money to George who happily used it to pay off a few outstanding bills and buy himself a new suit.

Eleanor was still studying at the University of Alberta but would soon be home for Christmas and wrote her Dad to let him know she would be arriving shortly. Mrs. Alex Green in Vernon was astonished at the beautiful gift Norman had sent her for Christmas. She was the envy of all her friends including her husband. Norman had sent her a beautiful necklace.

January was quiet except for the bout of fleas that Barney and Larry managed to pick up. Norman used the time to write letters to old friends knowing it would be far too busy in the summer. Guy Weadick was down in San Diego staying with his friend Bill Hart. Bill was better known as "Two Gun" in the motion picture industry. He was a native Indian who had been raised among the Sioux in the Dakotas. In fact, Guy had only just learned that the Stoneys were actually an offshoot of the Sioux.

Earl continued to write regularly from Campion College. The college had been founded in 1917 by the Jesuit Fathers and was known as the Catholic College of Regina. The college served as a university preparatory school for students in grade 10 and beyond. It also offered a B.A. program in conjunction with the University of Saskatchewan and the University of Manitoba. Earl was now in grade 10 and doing very well. He referred to Banff as "Florida" when he compared the climate of Banff to his new home in Regina. He found the cold prairie winters very difficult and it always seemed to be snowing. Earl wondered how Larry and Barney were doing and was sad to hear that Barney had come down with a severe case of distemper although it sounded like he was improving. Norman had thought about sending Barney off to a training school in Strathmore but they offered no guarantees, as they had never had an Irish setter in all their years in business. Earl was starting to toy with the idea of becoming a priest but his Latin was poor so that decision would have to wait.

Norman's interest in flying meant he was a good contact for any plans to bring aircraft into the Banff region. The Chinook Flying Service approached Norman in April with tentative plans to fly floatplanes into the area. Their thoughts were that since there were so many lakes in the area that perhaps one might be suitable for landing planes on. They hoped Norman's knowledge of the area might help them decide on which lake would be most suitable.

The Depression continued and poor Eugene in Baltimore was at last suffering. He had recently made a trip to Bermuda and had taken his wife and his son. For the first time he actually worried about money and realized that he could no longer afford to take people on trips every year. Eugene had lost a great deal of money from depreciation and the fact was that now none of his investments were paying dividends. He kidded

Norman that maybe he'd just leave it all behind, move to Banff, and start a newspaper to compete with the *Crag and Canyon*. Better yet, he could start a movie theatre to compete with the Lux Theatre.

A few weeks passed when Eugene wrote again. He missed Banff desperately but that year he simply could not afford to come unless he came on his own. His wife was against the idea of him travelling alone so the trip was called off. For the first time in years there would be no hunting or trail riding trips with Norman. He hoped that perhaps Norman could come East for a change.

Norman would miss the annual visit from Eugene but summer was fast approaching and the tourists would soon be in town again. Money was tight in Banff although Norman still managed to surprise Georgie with a new electric washing machine. The Depression even affected Banff Indian Days, which were postponed for a month. For the first time ever, the Indian Days would run from August 19 to 21.

Georgie had been asked to join her mother Annie on a trip to California. They would be driving with Annie's grandson, David Ross, and a couple of Annie's friends including Mrs. Arthur Hall and Jean Graham. The 1932 Summer Olympics were being held in Los Angeles that year. Everyone thought that because of the Depression, it would be a huge failure but the weather was perfect and the opening ceremony set a record with over 10,000 people attending. Though only half of the usual number of athletes attended, there were many previous records broken. In the past, the Summer Olympics had never lasted less than 79 days, but this time only 16 days were scheduled. This would become the normal length of the Summer Olympics forever after, varying only by a day or two.

The little group had enjoyed the games and got a chance to visit Annie's sister, nephews, and nieces. They also enjoyed a trip to the old monastery at Santa Barbara where Georgie had attended school for one year. They planned their return to Alberta via the desert and the Grand Canyon. David Ross was driving that day as they drove a length of road that edged along beside the spectacular canyon. As they all enjoyed the magnificent view, a bee unexpectedly flew into the car and David panicked and lost control of the car. It was only for a few seconds but that's all it took for the car to veer off the road and plunge headfirst into the canyon. The car fell hundreds of feet until it came to a very precarious stop on an outcrop of rock. Everyone had survived the initial plunge but the car was hanging from a rock with the front of the car dangling over the edge. The only possibility to survive was if Annie, now

82, and her friend Jean could somehow crawl out the car window and manage to climb back up the canyon to the road. The others had to remain in the vehicle to keep it balanced. Annie and Jean made their way up the steep canyon walls and upon reaching the highway, managed to flag down a passing car. While Annie and Jean headed to the nearest town for help David, Georgie, and Mrs. Hall, waited for what seemed like an eternity for the others to return. A salvage truck was summoned to the scene and was able to hoist the vehicle out of the canyon. Much relieved, the car's occupants were taken to the hospital and although everyone suffered cuts, bruises, and broken bones they were lucky to be alive. As for the car, what was left of it was sold for scrap. The travellers were forced to continue their journey home by rail.

Norman was very relieved when his wife and mother-in-law returned home. Had Georgie died it would have been unimaginable to carry on life without her. At that same time just a few miles away in Longview, Alberta, there was another sad story unfolding.

Norman had just opened the mail and inside was a letter from his good friend Guy Weadick. Guy had been the manager and producer of the Calgary Stampede for 10 years. Back in 1922, the Calgary Exhibition Company had joined forces with Guy Weadick's Stampede to become the Calgary Exhibition and Stampede. Without any notice, Guy received a letter in August that said that due to cost-cutting measures they would be discontinuing the position of Stampede manager effective immediately. In a word, Guy Weadick had been fired. There were stockholders now and Guy knew that his opinion differed with a few of them. Still most of the directors and particularly Pat Burns were not happy about the decision. A.E. Cross had passed away from pneumonia March 10th of that year while in Montreal having surgery. It seemed the original founders had no control over the operation of the Stampede and the directors didn't want to make waves. Rumours began to fly that Guy had objected loudly to cuts to his promotion budget and to the prize money. Other more malicious rumours surfaced that perhaps Guy drank too much. The rumours were not true and the firing came as a complete shock to Guy. He was completely devastated. The Calgary Stampede had been his idea, his dream, and he had found the financing and built the world-famous event into what it was. He had travelled the world promoting it and his name was synonymous with the event. He had arranged the first Calgary Stampede Parade back in 1912. Before Guy, Calgary only had what was then known as the Alberta Provincial Exhibition. Guy was originally from New York but he loved the Wild

West and he alone convinced A.E. Cross, George Lane, Pat Burns, and A.J. McLean to put up money to start a rodeo. That first parade of 1912 saw a turnout of over 80,000 people, 25,000 of whom went to see Guy's new rodeo. The Stampede was Guy's life and he knew in his heart that the Stampede was his and his alone. In those early days, everyone said it couldn't be done. They said it would be a huge failure but Guy had proved them all wrong. Guy was certain of one thing— he would take all his goodwill and connections with him. If a few shareholders were going to turn on him in such a way he would ensure they had no further assistance from his many prominent friends including publishers, newspapermen, authors, and many others. If Calgarians didn't appreciate what he had done, he would take his dream elsewhere. Guy was hurt and angry and simply could not believe they had fired him without warning or good reason. They even had the audacity to tell Guy that since he was no longer employed with the company he would have to change the name of his ranch, the Stampede Ranch Ltd. He was stunned. This was his home, the Stampede his invention and they were telling him to change the name of his ranch!

As the months passed, Guy's shock did not go away. Every few weeks, another letter would arrive at Norman's home. Guy wrote how in 1923 the Stampede was in debt and they thought they could raise money buy running a winter carnival on the Stampede Grounds. Visions of iron ski jumps off the grandstand horrified Guy and he managed to talk them out of it. In his opinion, which was shared by many others, the Calgary Exhibition officials were a little clique who wanted to run the Stampede their way and not as it had been run in the past. Norman felt bad for his friend but he really didn't have the power to do anything. He had his own business to attend to. All he could do was offer his friendship and support.

Norman had acquired the reputation of being the one person in Canada that could secure an authentic Indian teepee and the National Museum of Canada in Ottawa wanted a teepee of their own. They got in touch with Norman and asked if he could order one and what the cost might be. Norman had a Stoney woman in mind for the tanning of the hides who could also decorate it with suitable paintings.

Work began on the teepee, which would stand about 18 feet high. Norman agreed on a price of $10 a hide to tan them, times 30 hides. Then there would be the sewing for between $50-$75 and finally the painting for another $25. The teepee was completed and sent off to the museum.

Winter was upon them again but that meant Norman could catch up on his reading. Acting on Eugene's recommendation he read Robinson's *10,000 Leagues* and thoroughly enjoyed it. Norman also had multiple magazine subscriptions so there was never a shortage of reading material.

Earl was still doing well at school and his mother Mary Massacre was now living at the King Edward Hotel. Mary and Norman had sent off a big box of cakes which Earl enjoyed sharing with his mates over the Christmas season.

A Christmas letter from George settled a misunderstanding that George and Norman had years before. George had always believed that Norman wanted him to leave Banff and go back to Minneapolis but Norman had meant only that he should go if he was happier there. He didn't want George to remain in Banff on his behalf. They both had not mentioned it before to spare the other's feelings. With that cleared up both were happier that the issue was now settled. Norman had sent George some of their mother's poems for Christmas, a gift he was well pleased to get.

January 1933 brought along the usual batch of mail from all of Norman's old friends. Among the usual letters came one from Freddie McCall. The government was now considering putting a flying field in Banff. They were thinking of perhaps using the animal-park area or at least part of it. Freddie was excited and saw huge possibilities for the little airstrip. There could be sightseeing trips, government work, and flights to Jasper and Calgary. Freddie thought maybe they could hook up with one of the transportation companies and make package deals. Certainly it would be difficult at first, time-consuming, and expensive, but if Norman and Freddie could obtain the concession for operating the field, the investment would certainly pay off. He hoped Norman thought this was a good idea.

As much as Norman loved flying he was getting older and his thoughts were how to slow down a little so the airfield idea would have to go on hold, maybe permanently. He still had the winter carnival to get through and that would keep him busy until the end of February.

Norman was starting to think more about his days on the *Tilikum* and decided to commission a model to be made. He found a man in St. John's, Newfoundland, by the name of Ernest Maunder and gave the model builder all the dimensions along with photos of the canoe. Ernest and Norman wrote back and forth and soon the model began to take shape. Ernest wanted to know if the *Tilikum's* sails should be hoisted.

Soon Norman received photos of the *Tilikum* model along with pictures of other models, including the *Bluenose* and the *Roald Amundson*.

Although Eugene could no longer afford to come to Banff, that didn't stop him from taking an annual winter holiday to somewhere warm. This winter he was off to Barbados, Trinidad, Curacao, Cuba, Venezuela, and Columbia. He also would be going through the Panama Canal. The word from Eugene was that the swimming in Barbados and Trinidad was the best in the world. Eugene was an excellent sport fisherman and loved catching barracuda, many weighing in at as much as 40 pounds. The one thing that amazed Eugene most of all was just how famous his little Banff friend actually was, sometimes even in very remote parts of the world. While on holiday Eugene had met a Captain Victor Campbell who was now retired from the Royal Navy. Campbell had been with Scott on the Antarctic Expedition and spent some time in Australia. Eugene mentioned that his friend Norman had actually sailed from Victoria to Sydney back in 1901. It was then Campbell questioned if, by chance, Eugene was referring to the *Tilikum*. Indeed it was and Campbell knew it well. He had been in Sydney at the time and met both Norman and Voss. It was Voss that stuck in his memory he admitted. He had last heard of Voss when he sailed around Cape Horn many years before. He had heard the *Tilikum* had made it to England and he thought the she was now in some museum in Essex. Campbell told Eugene he would love to hear from Norman and gave him his address in London, care of the Army and Navy Club at Pall Mall. Later on the same trip, while in Port of Spain, Eugene met another man who had met Norman when he arrived in Sydney and who also saw the *Tilikum* many times.

Norman was happy to send off a letter to Captain Campbell and let him know that the *Tilikum* had safely returned home to Canada and was now back in Victoria, B.C.

March of 1933, found the Stoney Indians extremely upset by the latest word from the Canadian government. All Indians were told that effective immediately they must have a permit in order to leave the reservation. This was never part of the treaty and now they had become prisoners in their own land. Understandably, they were upset. The government said the law was for their own good. It seems that many Indians, in particular the Blackfoot, would plant crops and then leave for some country fair or gathering and leave the crops to rot in the fields. Then there would be a shortage of food. Now even to attend the Calgary Stampede or Banff Indian Days they would require a permit. Norman wasn't worried for the Stoneys. The Indian agent at Morley had assured him that since the

Stoneys didn't farm due to the poor soil which made it next to impossible, that a permit would be no problem.

In April, the long awaited model of the *Tilikum* arrived by parcel post. Ernest had carefully packed it in a strong wood case but it still arrived broken. Ernest said not to worry about payment but instead would Norman send him the little brass totem pole he had earlier admired? The broken model was returned to Newfoundland for immediate repairs. Norman also sent along the totem pole in exchange and it arrived in St. John's in perfect condition. Ernest decided that the damage to the original model was too great and he would have to make a brand-new model. In the meantime he suggested to Norman that it was high time Eleanor Luxton got busy and went to work on the story of the *Tilikum*. She had always said she wanted to write the book for her father based on his diary.

Guy Weadick was busy down in the States trying to find a possible replacement city for the Stampede. Times were still tough financially and money for Guy was getting tight. He still had his ranch down in Longview and he'd try to find a way to keep it. He decided that worrying about his future wouldn't help matters any so why bother. He'd been through tough times before and always made out okay in the end. As he said, "The trail is pretty tough sometimes and there may be tougher ones ahead. If they should be tougher I'll try and make the grade anyway."

Norman had always been proud of his taxidermy work and had sent some of his game trophy heads to the New York Zoological Society. Some of his trophy heads were among the largest specimens known to exist and their measurements were published in the "Records of North America Big Game" files. Back in 1922, a special building had been erected in the New York Zoological Park to store some of the world's finest specimens and Norman's work was included among them. The Zoological Society had paid all shipping costs and the game heads were mounted behind glass along with Norman's name placed directly underneath.

Eugene had recently put Norman in touch with a woman by the name of Lulu Fairbanks who worked for the *Alaska Weekly*. This was Alaska's only territorial newspaper but was printed in Seattle. Lulu had heard of Norman and his journey in the *Tilikum* and she was anxious to publish the story. She thought the old timers in the Yukon and Alaska would love to hear of Norman's adventure in the canoe. While sitting in her office writing Norman a letter, a man walked into her office and asked her why she looked so serious. What was she working on? As she told him the story of the *Tilikum* a man in the outer office overheard the conversation. Since he was from Victoria he was anxious to join in the conversation and told Lulu that the *Tilikum* was now behind the Empress Hotel in Victoria and that in fact Captain Voss had died.

Norman had heard a rumour that Voss had died in California but he never believed it. He was certain that Voss died at sea.

Always a frugal man, Norman did his best to try to obtain things free, or at least for a discount. His theory was that if you asked you had some chance and there was nothing to lose by asking. Earl had been busy at school in Regina but Norman liked to bring him home for the summer.

Earl was a charity case, although Norman paid his tuition. Norman decided to approach the CPR and ask for a charity fare. Usually the CPR would consider a request for one fare, one direction only, but only one time. They looked through their files and found they had issued a charity fare the previous fall for the same boy but agreed to fund this second fare. Earl was ecstatic to learn he could come home for the summer. He just had his exams to finish and he'd be home at the end of June.

June also brought the return of the new *Tilikum* model and Norman was well pleased with it. He had a photo taken of himself, Barney his dog, and his new model. Another pleasant surprise came in the mail that June as well. Norman had received permission from the Indian agent at Morley for full hunting privileges on the reserve. This was to thank Norman for all the help and assistance he had given the Stoneys over the years. They had all agreed that Norman deserved those rights so now Norman could shoot ducks and prairie chickens on the reservation.

Norman's dog Larry had not been well for some time and he died in early October. Barney was still doing fine but Norman always preferred two dogs. He soon asked his friend Alex Green in Vernon to secure him another generation of his beloved red setter.

George had written from St. Paul about a little accident he'd recently had. George had been attending a baseball game when he was hit in the head by the baseball. He was knocked unconscious for a few minutes but was doing fine, although he had a lovely bump on his head. George had been to visit earlier that year and it was always a pleasure to see him.

Earl was back at Campion College and apologizing for his lack of letters. He had been very busy with his studies and was very involved in rugby. He was on the team and now had very little time for letter writing. He was very excited, though, as he had just learned that he had been accepted at a school in Toronto. Earl had finally decided to become a priest. He was very certain it was the right choice for his life. The school was also proud of the troubled boy who had turned his life around. They wrote Norman to thank him and let him know just how much Earl appreciated the chance Norman had given him. Earl was held in very high esteem, not just by the other boys but also by the entire faculty.

Christmas of 1933 was upon them and Ollie Ormond had received his usual Christmas gift of an assortment of prairie chickens from Norman's annual fall hunting trip. It was now the custom to have Norman's prairie chicken for Christmas dinner and this year Norman had included some cranberries in the package. Ollie had almost come out to Calgary that year for a biscuit manufacturer's meeting, but Mary's health had not allowed him to get away.

After Christmas Earl left Campion College and made his way to St. Stanislaus Noviate in Guelph, Ontario. He managed a quick stop in Toronto which he later described as a very big city. He loved Guelph and thought it a wonderful place with hills, orchards, and old-fashioned hedges. It was such a pleasure after the flat prairie land of Saskatchewan. The new school had a big barn full of cows, horses, pigs, chickens, and sheep. It also had a huge skating rink and a swimming pool for the summer. Earl knew he would be happy there and everyone seemed so nice. He had his friend Carey from Campion College with him but they were on 12-day probation and were not allowed to associate with the other novices during that time. They couldn't converse with the other students at all. The noviate had very strick rules about to whom the boys could write and when. The problem for Earl was that he considered Norman to be like a father, but technically he wasn't; therefore, the school would only allow him to write to his mother. There would be no exceptions.

Guy Weadick was trying out his hand at a new career. He'd taken up writing stories about the Old West. His stories began to be published in magazines like *Maclean's* and *Hollywood*. He wrote articles about famous cowboys he had known and Norman was behind his friend 100%. Guy was a little embarrassed by his writing and wondered if it was really good enough. He had only finished common school and he really appreciated that Norman gave him full support and encouragement. The winters in Longview were lonely, even with his wife Florence for company. He had been used to lots of visitors during his time with the Calgary Stampede but suddenly they all seemed too busy to visit or write. He realized they all had their own lives and troubles but only Norman ever bothered to write. In fact, only Norman had stood by him from the beginning. The fact was Guy was depressed and with the long cold winter stretching out ahead it was easy to fall into depression. Guy felt he was just too old to start up a new line of work and the one thing in his life he was most proud of was the Calgary Stampede. He hoped that he would be remembered for that if nothing else.

Ernest had stayed in contact with Norman after building the *Tilikum* model and had sent off a photograph of a giant squid that had recently been caught near St. John's. The only squids Ernest had ever seen were little ones that weighed maybe 6 or 7 ounces. This giant squid weighed in at 575 pounds. It looked identical to the tiny ones but as decay had set in it was turning into a gruesome mess. It made Norman even more sure that strange creatures did live in the deep and that his experience with the sea serpent was real.

With the passing of time Norman thought perhaps he could invest in businesses or buildings and then lease them out. With that in mind, he decided to erect a new building that would serve as a funeral home for Banff. He was no undertaker but would lease out the facilities to make a little money. Norman wasn't getting any younger and already was in need of a hearing aid. He purchased the latest model for $150 from the Sanotone Corporation of New York. All his friends were getting older now but Eugene always seemed to be in great health and off on some tropical holiday somewhere. This year Eugene was on a sailing and fishing holiday in Long Key, Florida. Eugene's letters were full of bawdy humour and good for a laugh and Eugene was making quite the name for himself in the fishing world. His photograph had recently appeared in the *Elks Magazine,* describing him as the "Fisherman Extraordinaire of Baltimore." Seems he'd caught himself a 60-pound "Amberjack" in the Gulf Stream near Matacumbe, Florida. Eugene looked a little like Ernest Hemmingway minus the beard. He was certainly cut from the same cloth. He was short in stature, often sporting a moustache, and always had a grin on his face. Eugene was an old man who knew how to have fun but Norman was starting to feel his age. He bought himself a book called, *Old Age Deferred.* It had advice from French doctors on how to delay the aging process and Norman figured it was worth a look.

With the coming of the spring of 1934 came news from Guy Weadick. Alone on his ranch, he had time to think and decided that he wanted his name cleared. He was going to sue the Calgary Exhibition and Stampede. He wanted his story told and he wanted to know who fired him and why. Mostly, though, he wanted his reputation and good name back. When they fired him, he hadn't even been asked to appear before the board of directors. He knew in his heart the Stampede was his show, his idea, and he had all the proof he needed. It wasn't about the money or getting his job back— he just wanted the truth to be told and to quash all the bad rumours, once and for all. He filed the suit and again thanked Norman for his ongoing support.

That summer of 1934, Norman decided to see if he could recapture his past glory by entering the Championship of Western Canada. He'd won first place 40 years before and he figured he was still as good a shot as he had been in his younger days. Norman was right and he easily beat out all the "youngsters" to win the title again. His brother-in-law, Ed Hoskings, was very impressed. It helped that he went on his annual hunting trip every year. He sure did miss Eugene's company and wished his old friend would come back to Banff again. Maybe right after *Indian Days* they could follow the Indians north to the Saskatchewan River, a trip that would take about 5 days. Then they could head over to Nordegg and take the train back to Calgary. They would get lots of fishing in and perhaps a little fresh meat as well. Norman's friend Sophy Smith would outfit the group. Norman was getting worried that Eugene might never come back to Banff. There had been an ongoing financial battle between Eugene and a well-known Banff resident and it made it uncomfortable for Eugene in case he should run into this person. Norman promised Eugene it need not be an expensive trip and he had asked Sophy Smith to be the outfitter as the problem that existed was between Eugene and another prominent outfitter.

Many friends had promised to come to see Norman that summer; even Guy hoped to make it up from Longview but it didn't happen. They always had the best intentions but something always came along. It was hard not to be disappointed but Norman never held it against them.

Financially people had not yet recovered from the Depression and local artist Charlie Biel was having a tough time of it. He had heard the government was building a new post office and administration building and thought they might need some ornamental modelling. He wondered if Norman could put in a good word for him. Maybe the buildings would need ornaments, a coat of arms, or even some human figures. He could work in any material including bronze.

Georgie was delighted when she received an unexpected but wonderful bouquet of flowers from the Stoneys. They had decided it was time to thank her for all she had done for them. When Guy Weadick heard about the flowers, it reminded him of an old toast.

"One little flower in the sick room is worth a million dollar's worth of flowers on the casket".

Along with the flowers, the Stoneys decided to honour Georgie by making her a blood sister. They gave her the name "Mac-a-Zeo-Mungahi-Wia." They dressed her in full Stoney costume and the picture of the ceremony appeared in newspapers as far away as the *Toronto Star Weekly*. It was truly a great honour.

Just before his annual hunting trip, the steering gear broke in Norman's car. It was a miracle that he did not have a serious accident. The Diamond Motor Company repaired the damage and told Norman that some people are just born lucky and that he should consider himself one of those people.

Eleanor often begged her father to write the full story of his voyage in the *Tilikum* and he finally agreed. His intent was never to publish it but it was to be a gift for his daughter to know more about her father's great adventure. Guy Weadick was desperate for a copy of his own and kept trying to talk Norman into publishing the story and selling it. Guy happily announced that a court date had been set for December 10, for his suit against the Calgary Exhibition Company. It was later postponed until the New Year but Guy was just happy it was on the docket. He was actually relieved that the court case was postponed as he had developed a huge boil on his neck and it was very painful. It was the first boil he ever had and he hoped it would be the last. He would have been in no shape to attend the court case had it been held earlier.

Another Christmas was upon them and Earl got his chance to write his annual letter to Norman. The school had been in need of money and Norman stepped up to the plate with a large donation as usual. Because of this donation, Norman was now a life member of the Jesuit Seminary Fund. Earl felt so terribly bad about never being allowed to write, he assured Norman that he prayed hard for him every night. At least the seminary had a hockey team and Earl soon learned how to handle a hockey stick. As a novice he hadn't been allowed to play hockey but now he was a juniorate that meant he could play.

Guy wrote again just after Christmas with more good news. He'd just had another article published in the *West* magazine. It was a story about Will Rogers. Not only that, but the magazine was giving him his own column starting in March. The *West* magazine decided to start a club among their subscribers called "Range Riders." These clubs would form in various towns and cities and unite people who were interested in the Old West. Guy was eager to see if Norman would start up a Banff chapter. To start a club you had to buy two subscriptions to the magazine. Each local group would be called a "Chuckwagon." Two memberships would only cost $3 and Guy was sure it would be a success.

Although Norman cared deeply for all his family he mostly kept in touch with George. His sisters very rarely wrote and Lou he saw every day as they worked together at the curio shop although they now just called it the "Trading Post." George liked to write but with his job as photojournalist, he was always busy. His only free time was every other Saturday after 3 pm. Even Sunday mornings were busy as there was always some auto accident from the previous night to cover. There always seemed to be a murder, train wreck, or fire to cover. The crime rate and accidents had shot up 75% since the taverns had reopened in the Twin Cities. Prohibition was officially over and that made for lots of news stories.

The spring of 1935 was a busy time and Norman had yet another idea up his sleeve. He had decided to design a buffalo that would be made of metal, about 2½ inches high, to be sold as an official Banff souvenir.

FOURTEEN

Titles, Trials, Treaties, and Trademarks

On March 15, 1935, it was official. Norman had his very own trademark for his little buffalo design. It had taken 6 months of work but the trademark for one "Industrial Design of a Statuary Buffalo", serial No. D-2460 was his. The tiny metal buffalo was now ready for manufacturing. The tricky part would be to find a good price and a light metal in which to cast the buffalo. A heavy metal would cause the shipping price to increase so Norman wanted a light metal to be used. He began to search the world for an inexpensive manufacturer. It wasn't long until the various companies got back to him. There was a slight design flaw. The buffalo head was so heavy that any light metal would not support the heavy head of the animal. The little 2-inch-high buffalo was not stable and would pitch forward, even when set on a base. Norman wasn't worried; he would find someone to make his little buffalo.

Guy Weadick was now sending letters weekly and a new trial date had been set. The case would be heard on Friday, March 22. Guy desperately wanted to clear his name and the horrible rumours that circulated about his departure from the Stampede. He was fairly certain that it was not the fault of the Stampede or its directors but he wanted to know the real reason for his dismissal. He had a good idea who was behind his being fired and was sure that it would all come out in court.

The day of the trial was a "who's who" of Stampede officials. None of the witnesses wanted to speak against the Calgary Exhibition Company. As each witness took the stand they spoke so softly that the judge often had to ask them to speak up. It didn't take long for the true story to come out. It seems that Earnest "Ernie" Richardson had hired Guy back in 1922. At the time Earnest was the general manager for the Exhibition Company. Ernie had approached Guy after he was told that he would lose his job unless he could turn the exhibition around as under his management the Exhibition Company had lost $24,000. Ernie knew that Guy had run a successful Stampede back in 1912. He also knew that Guy was well respected and a great promoter. Ernie decided to take a trip out to Longview to the Stampede Ranch to see if perhaps Guy would come and work for him. Ernie liked his job and knew if anyone could help save the exhibition that Guy could. He offered Guy the sum of $4,500, with an increase if the gate and grandstand exceeded their previous high record of $77,500. If Guy could achieve that goal, he would receive a bonus of $500. This was still less than the salary Ernie was being paid but Guy agreed.

The following July the show was the biggest ever and all previous records were exceeded. Ernie kept his job and he kept Guy Weadick on as well. Although Guy had brought his Stampede as part of the attraction, the Exhibition Company was its own incorporated company with 180 shareholders. The actual incorporated name was the Calgary Industrial Exhibition Company and legally Guy never gave the name "Stampede" to them. They could use it to promote and advertise but the Stampede name belonged to Guy.

For 10 years, all went well but after the Depression in 1929, the gate receipts began to fall once again. The company wanted to cut back and Ernie knew of a quick and easy way to save $4,500 plus expenses. After the 1932 Calgary Exhibition he would simply fire Guy Weadick. Since he had been the one to hire him and had all the authority, he simply told Guy to get out. The directors were not happy but no one really said anything although they all felt horrible. Soon rumours spread that Guy had been fired for being a drunk but they were completely unfounded. There had been a party at the Palliser Hotel on the final evening of the Stampede of 1932. The liquor flowed freely and everyone took advantage to the point that the Palliser Hotel refused to ever again host the closing night party. Guy was only one of many at the party that night but he was in no worse condition than most of the other party guests. He did want to catch the final grandstand show and had left the party with a couple of friends, one of whom was Pat Brewster. Guy had decided to go onstage at one point but the microphone was turned off to avoid any potential embarrassment.

As the trial continued, the judge learned that Ernie had stolen the name "Stampede" from Guy and had tried to coerce him into changing the name of his ranch. The judge was furious. Guy had allowed the Calgary Industrial Exhibition Company to use his "Stampede" name in order to benefit the people of Calgary. The city was famous for its Calgary Stampede and Guy would never have considered taking the name away from the wonderful people of the city. The judge offered to let Guy have the name back but Guy declined. To take back the "Stampede" name was never his intent.

Many witnesses sat in their seats waiting to be called to the stand on Guy's behalf. They included men like Nat Christie, Cappy Smart, and many others. The judge never did call them up on the stand; he didn't need to hear any more. Poor Guy had not only lost his livelihood and his passion, but also his reputation. All this just to benefit Ernie Richardson. Guy had also taken the fall for the drunken bash at the Palliser Hotel, which was reported to be one of the biggest drunken brawls in Calgary's history. The property damage came in at $1,800 and Guy wasn't even there when much of it occurred.

The judge ruled in Guy's favour and awarded him half a year's pay plus all trial costs. The grand total came in at $5,000. Guy was ecstatic and was at last vindicated. In the original suit, Guy had asked for the "Stampede" name back but he withdrew his demand. He wanted to be remembered for his contribution and the name would be a gift to the city. The Calgary Stampede was the one accomplishment in his entire life that gave him the most pride.

Guy wrote to Norman and said that throughout those difficult years after he was fired that many of his so-called "friends" dropped by the wayside, but Norman stuck with him through the bad times. Norman was one of his very few "real" friends. The other friends were with him when he was popular, when they could get something from him.

At this point Guy's life was up in the air. He thought he should sell the ranch because he couldn't really afford to keep it. Perhaps he could find work in the States but as long as he had his ranch, he hoped that Norman would come and visit. In the meantime, he was off to El Rene, Oklahoma, to stage the Stampede & Pioneers Reunion of the old 89's. These were the folks who had made the great run for land when the Cherokee, Cheyenne, and Arapahoe lands were opened for settlement. After the reunion Guy was asked to stage the 50th Jubilee Celebration of the Lethbridge Exhibition so he had a few things lined up to keep him busy.

Norman's little buffalo was still looking for a manufacturer and inquiries were sent off as far away as Bangkok and Siam but without much luck. There was a place called Silverware Products of Canada down in Toronto that offered to make 6 gross for $40 to which Norman finally agreed.

Eugene LaPorte had been on his usual holiday in Atlantic City, when much to his surprise, he stumbled upon a copy of Captain Voss's book, *Venturesome Voyages*. This was the third printing, published in London in

1930. He wasn't sure if Norman had read the book yet but he would happily pick him up a copy if he had not.

Both Norman and Eugene still had their interest in airplanes and had their eye on the Auto-Gyro planes that were all the rage. It was really nothing more than a dream, they both knew they were a bit too old now to become pilots. Eugene was hoping to get up to the Calgary Stampede and had invited his friend Lulu from Seattle to join him but she was unable to come as she had a convention scheduled for that week. Lulu was an interesting girl and was friends with Archbishop Vladimir Alexandroff who had been the private bishop to the Czar of Russia in the "good old" days. She had previously introduced Vladimir to Eugene who was most impressed.

Norman was often too busy to write in the summer but he always found time for Eugene and Guy. The Lethbridge 50th Jubilee Celebration was a smashing success. Lethbridge only had a population of 15,000, yet attendance for the 3-day celebration came in at 42,000. That just went to prove Guy's talent as a promoter. The grandstand sold out for every performance and the Lethbridge Jubilee was more successful than Guy had ever dared dream. The Indian displays were spectacular with hundreds of Blackfoot, Bloods, and Piegans attending. Even the Piegans from Montana came up. Along with the Indians came the "Oldtimers" who hadn't seen each other since the 1880's. The hotels were packed and the only person Guy wished could have been there was Norman. It just hadn't been possible, though, between the trapshoot held the first week of July, the Calgary Stampede activities, followed by Banff Indian Days. All that plus he still had to run the Trading Post and entertain visitors.

The highlight of that summer was that the Stoneys had decided to make Norman a honourary Stoney chief. Although many people are made blood brothers and sisters, the honour of chief is extremely rare. They had hinted for years that they wanted somehow to thank Norman for saving them during the flu epidemic of 1918. That, plus his continued support over the years. Every time they hinted, Norman would tell them not to spend the money. If they felt they must honour him, then wait until after he was dead so there would be no expense involved. They ignored his request and during Banff Indian Days, they surprised him. After a full day of visitors at the Indian grounds, the Stoneys put their plan into action. Norman was kidnapped, by force, and taken into the teepee to prepare for the ceremony. Norman, who had only gone back to the grounds to hand out the food rations for the day, was caught completely off guard. They hadn't wanted to embarrass him and so waited until the end of the day when the tourists had departed.

The moving ceremony was conducted and Norman's official status was raised from a blood brother to chieftainship. He was dressed in the most beautiful beaded and ermine buckskin suit with a headdress of eagles and ermine. The outfit was complete with belts, moccasins, gloves, shield, bows and arrows. Norman knew the outfit cost several hundred dollars and he knew they could not afford it. It was the first time the Stoneys had ignored Norman's pleas. They had all agreed this was something they wanted to do, regardless of cost. Norman was given the name "Waa-Chunga-Scon" meaning "White Shield."

Back in Baltimore, Eugene had also recently been honored. He was made "Aide-de-Camp" to Governor Laffoon and given the title of Honorary Colonel of Kentucky. The title was in recognition for his accomplishments in the Alaska Gold Rush of the 1890's. Eugene had gone to Alaska in 1893 and remained there until 1904. Now the letters that Eugene and Norman exchanged were between "Colonel" and "Chief."

George was very pleased with Norman's new honorary position as Stoney chief. Norman had always been his hero and he looked up to his older brother with great admiration. He knew that as Norman got older that he would be cutting back on his many activities. It didn't surprise him to learn that Norman had pretty much decided to lease out most of his business ventures, including the King Edward Hotel. He didn't doubt that running the Trading Post would be enough to keep Norman and Lou busy. Norman also had his hunting and numerous books and magazines to keep him occupied. Norman loved to read anything on the history of the Native people or general history of the Old West. George was still at the paper but hoped to travel more with his daughter Pat. She would be out of high school in just a year. She was not a stunning beauty but she had her Mother's eyes and beautiful skin. That and a strong dose of the Luxton temper. Now that Pat was all grown up George began to feel old. His hair had long ago turned gray but his biggest complaint was a very undeserved red nose.

Eleanor had now returned to Banff and was teaching at the local school. Norman and Georgie were glad to have her back in town. That fall Norman decided to take a trip out to the Stampede Ranch and pay Guy a visit. Guy was still trying to start up his Range Rider Clubs across Alberta but the idea just never seemed to catch on.

The New Year of '36 came with an invitation to the grand opening of the Stoney Indian Hospital and the new addition to the Morley Indian Residential School. The population of Indians in Morley had declined rapidly in the last few years and stood currently at just 688. The government, in their wisdom, decided that the reserve was far too big for such a small number of people and wanted to take back some of their land. Norman immediately started a campaign to stop the removal of Stoney land. He pointed out to Ottawa that unlike most of the other tribes, the Stoneys' land was nothing but gravel. There was virtually no suitable land for farming or raising stock. Other tribes had received land they could make a living from but what little useable land the Stoneys had could not be taken away. Chief David Bearspaw and Chief Jacob Two-Young-Men asked Norman to help them write to the Minister of the Interior to help them defend and keep their land. Norman also wrote of the deplorable conditions on the reserve. As usual, the government offered no help but the reserve remained intact for the time being. Norman asked his lawyer friend, Mr. Peacock, for his advice on the Indian problem. Peacock suggested that if they could get a representative to come out from Ottawa it might help but in his opinion it was really John McDougall's fault. John should never have convinced the Stoneys to settle on land that was nothing more than a gravel bed. Peacock also advised Norman that going to the press over the Stoneys' problems wouldn't help the issue either. The white population were still suffering from the effects of the Depression and he felt that there really wouldn't be much compassion at this point. Perhaps it would be better to just wait things out.

Norman had invested a little money in the new oil business and had shares in Hylo Oils Limited. They were drilling in Turner Valley and at first seemed to be doing quite well. In the beginning, they had pulled out 140 barrels a day but the well was not very deep and now they were down to only 30 barrels a day. The company submitted a plan to their shareholders that if they took half of the revenue they paid out in royalties and reinvested it they could drill another 200-300 feet deeper. Most of the other wells in the area were at the 600-foot level, drilled directly down through the limestone. If Hylo could deepen their well, that should increase production. Hylo Oils kept trying to convince their investors that the new plan was the only chance at success; otherwise the well would soon dry up. To Norman it wasn't much of an investment. He only got a cheque for about $7.00 a month.

That winter of 1936 found Norman taking up curling again. It always seemed that around Christmas, or just shortly after, that poor Norman would be laid up with some illness or other. He took comfort in the fact that his friends were also getting older and letters were often filled with the latest physical complaint. Guy always seemed upbeat and never complained about his aches and pains. Guy's latest word of advice was that many times people say things they don't mean and that we should all learn to take everything we hear much less seriously. Was it not better to take nothing seriously and treat most of what we hear as a joke? What was life anyway without a few jokes and it was high time that everyone just stopped complaining. Guy thought humans were a funny lot and would all be better off if they just realized that fact and appreciated how silly they all were.

Guy was right of course but that didn't make Norman feel better. He'd just had another car accident of which he was entirely at fault. He'd been driving on the wrong side of the road. As far as his insurance company was concerned, they didn't want anything further to do with him. They asked Norman to please cancel his policy immediately and find someone else to insure him. If he didn't comply, they would simply cancel his coverage anyway. Norman got the message and soon began his search for new coverage. It took some time before he could find a company that would agree to take him on.

Occasionally a letter would come from Ernest Mauder, the builder of the *Tilikum* model. This time Ernest was bubbling over with excitement. He was now in contact with Parker Christian, the great-grandson of Fletcher Christian. Parker had long been fascinated with the story of the *Bounty* and after 160 years, he had gone on a salvage mission to find his great grandfather's ship. Parker had recovered the rudder and Ernest hoped that perhaps a tiny portion of that original rudder could be obtained to build a tiny rudder for his *Bounty* model. Although Norman knew Ernest had seen the film about the *Bounty* starring Clark Gable, he decided to send him a copy of the book.

In June, a little parcel arrived from Eugene. Since Norman's Trading Post had originally been a curio store he thought perhaps Norman might enjoy a little something odd. He couldn't let customs know what was hiding in the parcel so the box packed inside had a false bottom. A letter was sent in advance of the parcel advising Norman to open the special box very carefully. When Norman got the box and opened the false bottom he found samples of the Cicada, better known as the 17-year locust. Once every 17 years these locusts appear in the millions and they last from 7 to 8 weeks. When the eggs hatch the locust looks like a worm. This worm then burrows 15 feet into the ground and once they arrive they turn around and burrow back up to the surface. This trip takes the little worm exactly 17 years. When they emerge from the ground, they have grown a shell on their back but no wings. Shortly after, this shell breaks open and two pairs of wings come out.

Norman had some little curios himself—his first shipment of little buffalos of his own design had arrived. He had ordered 15 cases from the Moritomo Trading Co. of Tokyo, Japan. They came in at a cost of $405. The Trading Post sold the little buffalos as did Birks & Sons in Calgary.

Eugene hadn't been very well of late but told Norman he should come out to Banff anyway as he had the perfect plan. The two old boys could rent out the top floor of the King Edward, put a good looking gal in each room, buy out all the liquor venders in Banff and then just go at it. He pretty much figured it would cure them or kill them. Eugene figured it would likely be the latter and told Norman just to ship his body back in a boxcar. Then Norman could live happily in the great Happy Hunting Grounds. Naturally, there would be an article in the *Crag and Canyon* describing the great time they had, while it lasted. Of course, all the girls would shed tears because they would miss Eugene and Norman so much. The letter gave Norman a good laugh; it really wasn't such a bad way to go.

Lou's daughter, Minota, came to her Uncle Norman for a letter of reference. She had helped in out at the Trading Post during the previous summer and Norman knew she was industrious, conscientious, and reliable. She had a good strong character and Norman didn't hesitate to give her a wonderful recommendation.

Another year had passed and by January of 1937, it was time to start curling again. Norman had his own "rink" and its members were all 60 years old or over. The New Year had started with a trip to Morley to deliver clothing to the Stoneys. Norman always had a collection going in Banff and all the old clothes would be gathered up and given to the Indians. Norman made a point that the clothes he took were in good condition and the Indians were always grateful. Eugene always sent a bunch of old Christmas cards so the Indian children could use the pictures for decoration. January always brought letters and cards from old friends who usually wrote once a year. Ollie was still in Victoria working hard at the Ormond Biscuit Factory. "Ollie's" wife Mary suffered from rhumatoid arthritis and had recently had another bad attack. She now found it difficult to move about and could just manage to shuffle along on canes inside the house. Ollie would get her up and ready for the day, then spend a full day at work, then come home to clear up supper. After dinner, he would take Mary for a drive just to get her out of the house. Ollie rarely had the time or the inclination to write anymore and his own hands were so stiff he found it difficult to hold a pen. He had missed another convention in Winnipeg because he could no longer leave Mary on her own. Still they had their cabin at the lake and hoped to be able to spend the summer there. They had thought Norman might have stopped by for a visit the previous summer to see the little cabin but it never happened. At the biscuit factory things seemed to change back and forth. Sometimes the company kept going just on candy sales and other times it ran only on biscuit sales. This year it seemed no one was buying any candy.

George usually wrote at least twice a year with all the family news. Norman's sisters, Nellie and Ollie, were fine. Ollie's daughter, Mary, had married Ed Graeber just 8 months earlier. Now that Pat was finished high school it would have been nice if she could have continued her education and gone on to college but the fact was George simply didn't have the money. Norman knew his brother was too proud to ask so he sent off a cheque for $250 specifically for the Pat Luxton Education Fund. She could start college in September. She had already missed the start of the January semester.

With spring came the purchase of a new car and Norman now had himself a 1935 Graham Sedan for $1,575. Maybe it wasn't a brand-new car, but it was new to him. Spring also brought the arrival of the latest Luxton. Norman's niece, Mary, had given birth to a baby girl who they named Susan Mary. The little family lived in Guttenburg, Wisconsin. Little Susan arrived exactly 8 months and 29 days after Mary's wedding. This was the first grandchild for Ollie and Ed Hoskings.

George made the news on national radio in April, 1937. He had been in Missoula, Montana, covering the story on the Gopher football team. George had been travelling with the team when they stopped in Missoula for a practice. The hotel where the team was staying caught fire and George had been the one responsible for getting the team members and guests out of the hotel. After everyone was safely out, he went back inside the burning building to get pictures of the fire. The team had been on their way to Seattle to play the University of Washington.

Although Norman was generous, he sometimes had difficulty accepting gifts from others. Eugene had got in the habit of sending books on a regular basis along with other little items that he thought

Norman could use. Norman asked him to stop because he felt guilty, but Eugene would have none of it. Eugene didn't care what Norman thought. If sending books to Norman to read and pass along to the other Banff residents made him happy then he would continue to do so. He didn't want anything in return from Norman, he just felt good about giving and so he ignored Norman's pleas to stop.

Summer would soon be upon them and Norman decided to do something special for Banff Indian Days. This year would mark the 60th anniversary of the signing of Treaty No. 7. Norman thought it might be nice to recreate the signing of the historic document. Norman got busy inviting the various chiefs of the Blackfoot, Blood, Sarcee, Peigan, and Stoney bands to come. Annie McDougall was still alive and was the only remaining witness alive who had signed the original treaty. It didn't hurt that she was Norman's mother-in-law and he figured he could convince her to come. Norman also sent invitations to the Duke of Windsor and the Duke of Connaught. To complete the picture Norman would ensure there were some RCMP officers present. The affair would be quite short and it would be a commemoration rather than a complete recreation.

Letters were sent and preparations were underway but Norman had waited too long to get the royal guests he had wanted. The Royal Palace refused to pass along anything to Edward and they told Norman to contact Edward through Indian Affairs. As for the Duke of Connaught, he had to decline the invitation. Then the various chiefs began to refuse only because they could not afford to travel to Banff. The Peigans agreed to attend if Norman could arrange to get them there. As for the Blackfoot, they would come by car if Norman would pay for the gas and the park permit. Norman agreed and it looked like things would go ahead as planned even without royal representation. Guy Weadick was sending a party of 29 people up to attend. The group had been visiting his ranch and he was busy arranging their transportation up to Banff. A Brewster bus was hired to go and collect them. Another guest at the Stampede Ranch was George Lyon, a writer for the *Buffalo Times* of Buffalo, New York.

Banff Indian Days were held July 23-25 and the event was a smashing success. The chiefs were all together for the first time since the signing of the original treaty. There was a lot of publicity and the Calgary papers were full of the story. Even the *New York Sunday Tribune* carried the story. The special guests were treated royally up at the Banff Springs Hotel by Mr. Deyell. He held a luncheon out on the lawn for the chiefs just above the swimming pool followed by a proper dinner held inside in the dining room. Norman was overwhelmed by the hospitality of Mr. Deyell and was also very grateful to the Blackfoot Agency. He wrote them a special letter of thanks and their Indian agent returned the compliment, praising Norman for the wonderful treatment given them. They had all thoroughly enjoyed the visit.

Later that summer a letter arrived in reference to the *Tilikum*. When the old war canoe had been built up the work was done by Harry Volmer. That August the son of Mr. Volmer, aged 7, had saved the life of a 5-year-old child. The little boys had been wading in the millstream when Neil Nicholson, the little one, had wandered out of his depth. The young Volmer wasn't strong enough to get him out but he was taller and was able to lift the little one over his head and hold him above the water until help arrived. Sonny Volmer had held on to young Neil and screamed until someone at last heard him. The local police were so impressed that they recommended that Sonny be awarded a medal for bravery, given out by the Canadian Humane Society.

The letter about Volmer wasn't the only interesting piece of news that summer. George had long suspected there were a few ghosts in the Luxton family closet. Their father had always been very secretive about his past and never spoke of his family or the relatives that remained in England. This sparked George's curiosity but, try as he might, he could never seem to get the story. He had decided to travel with Ada up to Ontario to visit their father's boyhood home of Palmyra, Ontario. George found no new information there but wasn't about to give up. He decided to hire a lawyer to find out, once and for all, the family secret the Luxtons had kept hidden for so long. It didn't take the lawyer long to find out. In England there had been a Luxton estate in Devonshire. It seems that William F.'s father was non-other than the impoverished Lord Luxton. He had lost all the family money and land so there was nothing left but the title. The lawyer believed that William F. may have had a younger brother who took over the title. The title of Lord Luxton dated back 500 years. In the famous Battle of Trafalgar it was Lord Luxton who had received Lord Nelson's hat after it fell from his head during battle. The hat was now on display at the British Museum. From what the lawyer could understand, William F. must have obtained the title at some point as he was invited both to the funeral of Queen Victoria and then to the coronation of Edward VII. William F. never spoke of these invitations or that the Luxtons had any title. He did not want his children to think themselves special or in any way superior to others. It didn't mean much anyway since there was no money or estate. George figured that since Norman was the oldest living Luxton, that was a direct descendant, technically he might now be Lord Luxton although he wasn't exactly sure how that all worked.

The arrival of fall meant it was time for the annual hunting trip. Norman usually went for several weeks and stocked up his supply of meat to send his friends at Christmas. This year the hunting trip was cut short when Norman got a severe case of dysentery. He'd heard that blackberry brandy was helpful but even after he had been home for 2 weeks he was still suffering. He wrote Eugene about his troubles and they exchanged stories on their ill health. Eugene had been told that he had high blood pressure and had to stop drinking. He agreed to do so only up until Christmas. What was Christmas without enjoying a few drinks with your friends? You had to live when you could; Eugene's brother Frank, had just had his fifth stroke and was in the hospital. Norman had also decided to give up the drink for a while, much to Guy Weadick's surprise. In Guy's opinion, drinking too much was bad for you to be sure but not drinking at all was bad as well. All things in moderation was the key.

Down at the King Edward Block the gentlemen's clothing store had been taken over by Gourlay's Drug Store. Lorne was still managing the hotel and there was a huge reunion coming up to commemorate the Klondike Gold Rush of 1898. The veterans would reunite at the hotel. These old-timers included the likes of Dan McGrew. Another one of the veterans was none other than Normans' good friend Eugene LaPorte. Eugene had been the first man to discover gold at Last Chance Creek.

Norman was still leasing many of his business interests, including the Lux Theatre. The theatre had been leased to Frank Christou but he didn't want to renew. Norman leased most of his businesses now but he still had to collect the payments and take care of the buildings.

Norman was coming up on another birthday; he'd be 61 this year. He would have preferred to skip the day altogether. He got a nice birthday letter from his friend Red Cathcart who was currently living in Vancouver. Red didn't know anyone out there and was feeling a little lonesome so had started writing some of his old friends in Banff. Actually old Red was a more than a little lonesome. He was downright depressed. Some of his Vancouver associates noticed but he just waved it off as a headache. Other friends sent birthday greetings to Norman including Guy Weadick who had missed Norman's annual visit. The roads were still clear so Norman was encouraged to come down for a visit. Guy was still bugging Norman for an interview about the journey on the *Tilikum*. Guy wanted to write up the story for one of his magazines. It would have been nice but Norman had some other work to do. A rather vicious form of measles was killing the Indian babies out at Morley. Norman got busy writing the House of Commons looking for help.

Christmas meant it was time for Norman to send off a cheque to cover Pat's college education. She had found college a lot tougher than high school but she promised not to let her Uncle Norman down. All the family was doing well. Norman's niece, Mary, loved being a mother to little Susan. Mary's husband, Ed, was a good father and had been made superintendent of the local school. George was busy travelling with the local football team covering their games. It seemed he was always up in Chicago covering some game or other.

Ollie Ormond was still in Victoria and had been following the world news of late. Things were not looking good overseas. Ollie thought the world had gone crazy and where it was all headed he didn't know. Perhaps it was best not to think about it and just drift along with the breeze. Whatever happened there was nothing he could do about it anyway. Ollie always enjoyed the birds and moose that Norman sent for Christmas and this year was no exception. Instead of eating Christmas dinner at home they had gone to his brother's place. His brother had been very ill and had begged Ollie to come until he finally agreed. Then on January 2, 1938, Ollie's sister-in-law died. Mary's sister, Flo, had died of a massive stroke. Mary was in such poor health that it worried Ollie, he wasn't sure she would survive the shock but she soldiered on.

Eugene wasn't in much better shape back in Baltimore. His liver was shot, his heart often skipped a few beats now and he was mostly "on the wagon." Not a place he enjoyed at all. In Vancouver, poor Red Cathcart had managed to break a rib and then caught a bad cold. He'd been laid up in bed and felt so awful that he'd dropped 40 pounds. It didn't help he was broke and he wondered if Norman could loan him $25. There was word of a new gold field on Vancouver Island and Red was planning to head there soon to strike it rich. Well, he lived in hope anyway. Norman soon sent off the money; Red was a good guy and he'd come out all right.

Norman was starting to feel old that winter. He had entered a shooting contest and came in second. That was quite a blow to one of the best shots in the country. He figured he was just getting too slow.

Down in Ottawa, R.B. Bennett was retiring. He had been one of Norman's most helpful contacts when it came to Indian issues. The two men had known each other since the 1890's when Norman met R.B.

while working for the *Herald*. Bennett had been running in the election in West Calgary in 1898.

The *Crag and Canyon* had been running along reasonably well for the last few years but suddenly in March, Norman found himself without an editor. Mr. Duncan, the paper's editor, had died. It didn't take long for the news to spread and various men began applying for the job. There was Victor Ball of Drumheller who had previously leased the paper from Norman, and Duncan's son Norman, who also showed interest. Norman would have to think about it.

Norman managed to get down to the Stampede Ranch that spring for a quick visit with Guy. He had taken Mary Massecar down with him who told wonderful stories about the Cree and Blood Indians.

That summer Eugene finally managed a short visit to Banff. He stayed a week and the two old boys had a great time. It was also a chance for Eugene to see other old Banff friends like Bill Potts and Lou Luxton. Eugene's friend Lulu had really wanted to come but she was up in Alaska at the time.

Eugene wrote as soon as he returned home to thank Norman for the wonderful visit. There were other things on his mind now. Stories of Hitler were all in the news and as far as Eugene was concerned, they should just blow Hitler and his high-up followers off the face of the earth. He didn't understand what all the fuss over the Jews was all about. The American, French and German Jews were all good people although he did understand there might be issue with the "Kike" Jews. These Jews had recently come into Germany from Poland. There were about 100,000 of them and they didn't belong there. If Hitler had a problem with them it might be understandable but what was wrong with the rest of them? Eugene had no time for communists and thought communism and socialism had no place whatsoever in North America.

FIFTEEN

The Return of War

The beginning of 1939 found Guy still writing for the magazines; his latest article appeared in *Hoofs & Hounds*. Still he bugged Norman for the *Tilikum* story and still Norman ignored him. Ollie was spending January in the garden; the flowers were still growing in Victoria. Ollie's brother wanted to build another biscuit factory and was thinking about expanding to Vancouver or Edmonton. Eugene had sent another parcel of books for the "L.L.L.," better known as the LaPorte Luxton Library.

Norman was busy with the winter carnival and the writing of an article for the RNWMP magazine, *Scarlet and Gold*. The *Crag and Canyon* was without an editor so Norman took over full operation in May. He was still hoping Norman Duncan would take over as business manager. Duncan's job would be to work alongside Norman and handle the staff and their work. Norman would take over as editor and try to clean up the mess.

With the approach of summer, young Pat was really hoping to visit her Uncle Norman in Banff. Some years earlier Pat had gotten surgery on her eyes to correct a severe double vision problem but it had returned. Glasses no longer helped and she had already lost 50% of her vision. It was possible another surgery would be necessary so, much to her dismay, Pat was forced to cancel her trip.

That summer those people who could afford it, were off to the World's Fair in New York. One of those visitors was Norman's mother-in-law, Annie McDougall. It had been a marathon trip as Annie first went to the San Francisco Exposition. From there she and her companions, George and Mary Ross, drove across the country to New York. The World's Fair was exceptional and soon the happy group was heading back to Banff by way of Montreal. Annie had wanted to go to Montreal to visit her grandson, David Ross. It was June 13, 1939, and it was George's birthday so they planned just a short drive that day. They would quit early and find a nice place to stop for a birthday dinner. It was 5:46 pm and as they drove along the highway near Cohoes, New York, a car approached from the opposite direction. What they didn't know was the driver of the other car should never have been on the road. At the wheel of the approaching vehicle was a student driver who should never have been practicing on the highway. His car collided with Annie's car on the Saratoga Springs Highway. George and Mary were rushed to the nearest hospital but Annie did not survive the crash. Annie's body was returned to her home in Calgary. Her funeral was packed with people, both whites and Indians.

The death of Annie had been a huge shock and papers across Canada and the United States carried her story. Annie had been the first white woman to set foot in Calgary and had signed Treaty No. 7. She was the last witness to the Treaty to die, thus taking a part of history with her. Georgie was completely devastated by her mother's tragic death and would not leave her house. Eleanor did her best to convince her mother to go out but Georgie refused. It would take someone very special to bring Georgie out of the little house on Beaver Street. That someone special would turn out to be Helen Keller.

Norman didn't have time to grieve the loss of Annie McDougall as there was a very important event coming up at the Banff Indian Days. Guy Weadick had asked Norman for a favour. Guy's wonderful friend, Helen Keller, was staying at the Stampede Ranch for 3 months and Guy wondered if the Stoney Indians might agree to make her a blood sister. Helen had a great love of the Indians and Guy knew it would mean a lot to her to be given such an honour. For all this woman's amazing accomplishments, he hoped that Norman could convince the Stoneys to do this. Guy stressed the fact that Helen would take it very seriously and that the ceremony must be done with the utmost solemnity. It could not be for commercial gain or publicity. Norman understood and arrangements were soon underway.

The Stoneys were happy to oblige with Norman's request and Georgie was called in to assist. Only Georgie knew the details of the ceremony, as she was the only other white woman to have been given this honour. Would Georgie, even in her despair, agree to help Helen? Even Georgie knew the importance of the event and she said okay. Plans were made and Helen agreed to give a lecture for two evenings during Banff Indian Days. Her talks would be held on July 20 and 21.

Helen arrived in Calgary at 6:30 am, Saturday, July 15, along with her companion Polly Thomson. Guy and Florence Weadick would be coming up for the lectures and would help out where they could. Norman arranged for his friend Spike to meet Helen and her friend at the station in Calgary, from there Norman would bring Helen and Polly up to Banff.

The local papers were full of the news of Helen's upcoming lectures and huge crowds came to hear the remarkable woman. Helen was in top form as thousands gathered to hear her speak. By the end of her speech, there was not a dry eye in the crowd.

On the Saturday evening the largest crowd gathered to see Helen's initiation into the Stoney Tribe. Georgie had taken Helen into the teepee to dress for the ceremony. Helen was dressed in a long-beaded buckskin gown with rows of pink beads sewn carefully on to the collar. As soon as she was ready, Helen was escorted from the tent by Chief Jacob Two-Young-Men and Chief David Bearspaw. Emotion welled up inside her as she took her place onstage; it was a very special moment in her life. Helen took her vows of Indian sisterhood very seriously and as the ceremony drew to a close the crowd cheered. Helen took the opportunity to express her heartfelt thanks as the applause began to diminish.

"You're welcome, so full of spontaneous warmth and trust makes me both embarrassed and grateful. It awes me to receive such a salute from the descendants of the oldest dwellers of the kingdoms of the setting sun. It is an honour for me to be adopted into a tribe, who have a noble heritage of quiet courage, generosity, and beauty.

Since my childhood I have read all I could find about the Indians and my cheeks have burned with the shame at the terrible wrongs the white man has done to them, his violence against peaceable disciples of the Great Spirit.

I have learned much through wearing feathers of darkness and the moccasins of silence. Like you, I have in my heart the voice of the free wind, and faith strong with the mountain's strength.

Standing among you I feel the Great Spirit near and I pray that your people may long carry their message of life giving wisdom garnered from the sun, the waters and the stars."

Of those people who were present on that momentous occasion, all agreed that seeing Helen being honoured, on that special summer's night in Banff, was the highlight of their life.

Helen was not the only honouree that year. Her good friend, Guy Weadick, was made an honorary chief. The Indians bestowed upon him the name "Chief Long Lance."

Helen spent the remainder of the summer with Guy and Florence and finally left their ranch on September 13. It was time to return home to the States as Canada was now at war. Great Britain and Canada had just declared war on Germany on September 4, 1939.

Norman was just sick in his heart with news of the war. He'd already been through one war and lost his little brother. Eugene in Baltimore wasn't so sick as he was angry. Not angry at the war but angry that the United States stood by and did nothing. What the hell was the matter with the Americans? Why didn't they step up to the plate? Still he told Norman to try and not get too upset. Eugene figured the Americans should just find out where Hitler was and drop a flock of bombs on the guy. That would end the whole thing real quick. Of course they'd have to take out Von Ribenstrof, Goering, Goebbals, Forster, Danzig and Hess while they were at it. Still no point in worrying, Norman had been through a war so what was the big deal? Guy was the only one who thought perhaps Banff would come out the better for it. With Europe at war, the Americans were sure to visit Canada instead of going overseas. Guy tired to cheer Norman up by telling him it would be good for business and for Banff. Eleanor also worried that her parents were far too upset over the whole affair.

Norman continued to lease out most of his business interests and felt the time had come to slow down a bit. He was the owner of the Banff Funeral Home and had agreed to lease it to Mrs. Vera Jacques of Jacques Funeral Home in Calgary. She would take over on November 30, for the price of $250 a year.

Norman was off on his annual hunting trip but word from home was that Eleanor was sick again. She'd started getting ill after her trip to the World's Fair in New York. The war had not yet had any impact and Christmas came and went with the usual festivities. The only business that was suffering was Ollie's biscuit company out in Victoria. The biscuit factory was having problems due to working conditions. The factory was just too overcrowded. The problems were not because business was slow but quite the opposite. It seemed everyone wanted chocolates and cookies that Christmas and, if anything, they needed to build a new factory and expand.

It wasn't until early January of 1940 that the local boys began to head off to war again. Norman's friend in Vernon sent news that his son, Gregory, had been accepted as a pilot in the RCAF and would be training in Calgary.

Norman was glad that Earl was still in school; in fact, the boy was now at the Jesuit Seminary. He'd been studying with the Jesuit Society now for 6 years but wrote often of his fond memories of his time in Banff in 1933. He would soon be given a teaching position and hoped for a posting at his old alma mater, Campion College. After a few years teaching he could then be fully ordained as a priest but that wouldn't happen until 1946. Earl considered Norman to be his best friend for giving him the opportunity to make something of his life. Earl's mother had the difficult task of asking Norman for money, clothing, and supplies for Earl. Norman was always happy to oblige.

Norman was always very generous to his friends. He'd just sent Guy had a wonderful birthday present. Guy turned 55 on February 23, and received a wonderful buffalo coat from his friend. As for birthdays, Guy always said the first 100 years were the worst.

Just as in the First World War there were a few boys that sent Norman letters so he could pass along their news in the *Crag and Canyon*. One of the young boys was William "Billy" Addison. He was in the 1st Division Armoured Company, Regimental No. 20785. Many of the Banff boys were in the same division. He was impressed with his training and had already driven trucks, motor bikes, and had completed his Lewis Gun training. He loved the machine gun because it was incredibly accurate. There was that little down side in that they tended to jam up at very inopportune times. Many lives had been lost in World War One due to that problem. Billy's mother had lived in Scotland and he was hoping to visit her once he was in England. He figured he could get leave and take a trip up to see her. Unfortunately, she died just 3 weeks before Billy was shipped off to Britain. Billy was happy to have Norman write to him but was hoping that some of the Banff girls would drop him a line. He figured Norman could charm the ladies (he had talent in that respect) and encourage them to write. Everybody knew that Norman was young at heart, and Billy figured if anyone could get the girls to write, Norman could.

Eugene was at it again. Why didn't those English and French find Hitler and blow him up? They had airplanes. Why not drop a few bombs on the guy? What was everybody waiting for?

One of Eugene's friends, Donnie Caster, had already gone missing in action. Eugene hoped that maybe he was a P.O.W. Norman knew Donnie as the boy had joined Norman and Bill Potts on a trip. Before Donnie was shipped out, he had spent many afternoons in Baltimore visiting Eugene. Eugene was angry that Roosevelt continued to do nothing about getting into the war. What kind of a man did nothing? If he didn't want to fight he could at least make a deal with Prime Minister Mackenzie King and give him a few thousand airplanes. Well with any luck he could discuss his concerns with Norman in person. He hoped to come up for a visit that summer. He was planning a couple of days up at

Radium Hot Springs to help ease his bad shoulder pain. Maybe Norman could come up and join him for a couple of days.

Eugene's plan fell through in June when his doctor said he wasn't in any condition to travel alone to Banff. He couldn't find anyone to go with him; they were all too busy. As for his wife, she never had any interest in visiting Banff. He resigned himself to the fact that he would have to spend another summer at his usual hotel in Atlantic City. Maybe if he lay out in the sun it would help his shoulder but he doubted it. Norman was upset as he missed Eugene and really wanted to see him again. He'd actually given Eugene a darn good "cussing out." Eugene said he deserved it and he was sorry. There was still no word on the missing Donnie Caster. Eugene didn't even want to listen to the war news any more. What was the point? Roosevelt was a loser—in fact, it was likely worse than that. What possible excuse could he have unless he was a communist? Eugene was embarrassed to be an American.

Good news arrived in July when Eugene got word that Donnie had been in a P.O.W. camp but was released. Donnie had worked as an ambulance driver but because he was American the Germans released him. He managed to get out of France and into Brussels. From Brussels he made his way to Lisbon, Portugal, where he was able to send word to Eugene's son Bill. Bill immediately wired money over so Donnie could pay for passage home. Eugene was thrilled with the good news but even angrier with Roosevelt.

Banff Indian Days was held in July as usual, but, what should have been an enjoyable celebration, in the midst of war, turned tragic. A young boy died during the bucking horse contest. He was a Kootenay Indian from St. Mary's in B.C. He was in no condition to have taken part in the event but the family thanked Norman for all his kindness during this difficult time.

In August, the Stoneys were busy giving the honour of blood brother to John Burns. John's company, Burns & Co. Limited Calgary, had always stored all the buffalo meat free of charge. Storage would have cost a great deal and this was their way of saying thanks. John was very happy to show off his new headdress at a garden party his wife was having. The party was being thrown for the actress Gracie Fields who was in town. Gracie borrowed the headdress and had her picture taken wearing it.

On October 5, Eugene was sitting at home listening to the football game on the radio when there was a knock at the door. He opened it and standing there was Donnie Caster. Eugene wanted to ask questions about the war but Donnie seemed a little "jittery" and he didn't want to make him uncomfortable. Eugene was just glad to have him back, safe and sound.

Norman had decided he could show his support for the local boys overseas by sending them cigarettes. Billy Addison was glad that Norman took the effort to write and he was very pleased whenever cigarettes arrived. Billy was in England and said that the bombs were dropping on them regularly.

Eleanor was now in Montreal, teaching at a private school. The girls all came from wealthy families and Eleanor didn't understand her students or the way she was treated by her employers. She found it very stressful. She didn't understand these people; they were nothing like the people she had known back in Banff. Out east, they were all so conservative and narrow-minded. Never had she met so many snobs in her life. She fought for what she believed was right and usually got her way but it was taking its toll on her health. She regretted not being able to be home for Norman's birthday. She couldn't remember the last time she wasn't in Banff to bake him his birthday cake.

Billy Addison was a great letter writer and whenever he bumped into another Banff boy he shared Norman's cigarettes. He had run into Bob Neish who had worked at the King Edward Hotel and his brother Bill who was in the artillery. Unlike Eugene, Billy was happy to hear that Roosevelt was re-elected. Billy was anxious to see some action; he wanted to actively fight against Hitler. He had joined up immediately after Hitler destroyed the World War One monument at Vimy Ridge.

Christmas was approaching when Norman received a very disturbing letter from his nephew David Ross. David was living in Montreal and saw Eleanor on a regular basis. David knew Eleanor never told her parents about her problems but he knew, and could no longer keep quiet. Eleanor was very ill. She had told David that he mustn't write to her parents but he didn't care, he knew it was the right thing to do. At first, it seemed as if she had the flu and she tried to continue at work. The only thing her doctor could find wrong was that she had very low blood pressure. Even so, that hardly explained her illness. Dr. Mohr said she was just "highly strung" and that the flu made her nervous condition worse. Even if it was stress and depression, she was still a very sick girl. David thought perhaps Eleanor should take a 6-month holiday and go back home to Banff. Maybe she just took her job too seriously but David figured her stress was more likely money related. She really couldn't manage on the salary they paid her.

Norman immediately sprung into action. If money was the problem, he would just send her a big Christmas cheque but early so she could cash it right away. Perhaps that would get her back on her feet. Eleanor was shocked at the amount but grateful. She missed her folks and the mountains but tried to reassure them it was just the flu and that she was in the infirmary for the moment. She did need Dr. Jennings in Banff to send her records but she was under a nurse's care and just needed to sleep.

Eleanor didn't remain in the infirmary for long as her conditioned worsened. She was transferred to the Civic Hospital in Ottawa. She still insisted she was feeling better and told her parents there was no need to worry. She felt sure she would be back to work by January. Norman and Georgie knew if their daughter was in the hospital it was more serious than she was letting on. Georgie decided to head off to Ottawa and Norman wrote his daughter to say that her Mom was on the way. Georgie would stay through Christmas and hoped to be back in Banff in early January.

At least there was some good news. Young Earl had indeed been given a teaching position at Campion College and he was thrilled to be heading back to Regina. He would be teaching there for the next 3 years. He had been ill that year with two boils on his arms so he was quite rundown. He attributed the boils to stress as the third-year exam had been extremely difficult. Part of the exam included writing a four-page essay in Greek. Earl reminded Norman that the Jesuits were the highest order of the Roman Catholic Church.

David Ross had found his Aunt Georgie a place to stay in Ottawa. It was a room in a private home with its own bathroom for just $1.25 a night. She could get her meals at either of the two little inns across the street. With luck she could eventually move into one of those inns as soon as a room became available. Georgie arrived in Ottawa on December 15, and David picked her up at the station and drove her directly to the hospital. Eleanor was thrilled to see her Mom but felt very guilty that she had come all that way. David was happy to see his Aunt again after 6 years. Georgie told her daughter all about the wonderful train trip out and the many friends she'd made on the journey. She also loved eating in the dining car.

Georgie hadn't said anything to her daughter but she was horrified at the state in which she found Eleanor. The staff at the school had promised Eleanor they wouldn't write her parents but they had been very worried. Eleanor assured her mother she was in the best hospital and hoped to be out by the weekend, but Georgie knew by looking at her daughter that there was no way that was going to happen. She spoke to the doctors who assured her Eleanor was much better but Georgie had never seen her daughter so ill. The doctor said she'd improved 100% since Georgie arrived.

The little room where Georgie stayed was two blocks from the hospital but even with it so near it proved a very difficult walk the next day. There was a terrible blizzard and Georgie had never felt so cold in her life; the ice blew directly in her face as she walked the short distance to the hospital. Once she arrived, she asked if Eleanor could possibly have a private room. In fact she thought it would be best if they found a room close to the hospital and Georgie would take care of Eleanor herself. The hospitals always had that annoying habit of waking people up all the time and away from the hospital Eleanor could sleep as much as she wanted. Besides, a repeat of that icy walk to the hospital was not something Georgie wanted to do again.

Norman had written Eugene a letter about how sick Eleanor was and, much to Eugene's surprise; the letter had been opened and censored. The post office was very strict now.

Eleanor was feeling well enough to write and sent her dad a letter. She thought her little family was quite queer. They were never in any way demonstrative with their feelings but they all knew how much they loved each other. She told Norman that she had just had her first solid food in a long time and had managed to sit up that day. Georgie was busy trying to find them a little apartment and Eleanor was desperate to get out of the hospital. She hoped her dad would be okay for Christmas and promised to phone him at noon on Christmas Day.

Norman was fine and already had an invitation from his friend May Ross to come down to Calgary for Christmas dinner. Would he be willing to play Santa at the school on Christmas Day? Norman assured them he would and agreed to spend Christmas with May and her husband.

George had not heard from Norman in a while and only got news that he picked up in the *Crag and Canyon*. It was in the paper he learned that Georgie had gone east to visit Eleanor. He wanted to know what the heck was going on. Why was Eleanor in Ottawa? His own family was fine, although Pat had to undergo more eye surgery. Her eyes had deteriorated to the point where she had trouble going up and down stairs and she had become very depressed. Their sister Ollie and her husband Ed had gone to Iowa for Christmas to be with their daughter Mary, and her two daughters. Nellie was coming to visit in a few days so the family was well.

Eleanor was finally released to her mother's care and they got a little apartment that belonged to a deaf/mute. That meant there was no radio or telephone so it was pretty quiet for a few days. Norman did send them a telegram saying he'd be in Calgary over Christmas. He also sent a cheque to help cover some of their expenses. Georgie was going to make Christmas nice for Eleanor, so had gone out and bought an 8-lb. turkey. She'd also picked up a little string of lights to decorate the apartment. David would be coming over to join them for dinner. On Christmas Day, David brought them each a gift and several of Eleanor's friends had sent her gifts so it might not be so bad after all. David also brought over flowers and holly to decorate and Norman had forwarded all the Christmas cards and gifts on to Ottawa. The little apartment was a very cheery little place indeed.

Norman heard from Ollie in Victoria who had wished Norman had come out to the Island for Christmas. Ollie said business was booming and that year surpassed anything they had done before. They couldn't even fill their orders so unfortunately there was no annual box of cookies for Norman. Ollie would send the package just as soon as he could.

Earl sent his annual Christmas letter and was now at Campion College teaching history to grades 11 and 12. He was also serving as the school's librarian. His mother, Mary, had come up to for Christmas and they went to Midnight Mass and shared Christmas dinner together.

As the war continued, Norman sent off copies of the *Crag and Canyon* to many of the Banff boys so they always had news of home. Billy Addison had managed to get up to Scotland on his leave and had just received the latest shipment of cigarettes. Jim Neish was now at Aldershot, serving as Corporal in the 23rd Battalion and he looked great. You couldn't beat the English spirit and the boys remained cheerful. Billy said there hadn't been an air raid for 10 days due to the miserable weather with its heavy fog and rain. It was a nice break. Still Billy was getting bored and anxious to get into the thick of it. At first doing nothing was a luxury, but now he was just plain bored.

Along with Billy another friend of Norman's had now signed up for action and was currently training in Nova Scotia. His name was Corporal J.G. "Red" Cathcart. He was with the Royal Canadian Army Service Corps, 3rd Division Supply Column. He hoped not only that Norman would write but that they would see each other again some day. His job once overseas, would be to supply the front line with supplies. It was an extremely dangerous position and he didn't hold out much hope for his own survival.

Another friend already in England was Lt. Corporal Howard Deegan. Howard had only received four letters since he left Canada and Norman's was one of them. Howard was happy to report that since Norman's last letter he had seen two German planes shot down in flames. It was more exciting than the fireworks at the Stampede. He knew it meant homes and perhaps people were destroyed but it was still an amazing thing to see. He figured the "Brits" were about the bravest people in the world. He'd received his package of cigarettes from Norman which were greatly appreciated. He'd already been offered 2 shillings a pack but his weren't for sale. He would only share them with other Banff boys that he ran into.

Guy had been right about the tourists and it seemed all the Americans were headed to Banff. George's daughter Pat was already planning her visit and her dad was coming up with her. Norman's house was too small so Pat would stay at the YWCA and George said he'd sleep anywhere, maybe even on the bench at the Trading Post if it was available. They all knew that life was uncertain with the war and George wanted to make sure he saw his brother again. George figured this war might well be the end of civilization or at least as they knew it. Maybe they'd all return to the Dark Ages. George was too old to join up and fight but the one thing he did know about was cameras. He'd been a news photographer most of his life and he had been working on an infrared "black out" camera. This would enable photographers to take pictures in the dark. They'd already tested the new process in New Jersey where they had a trial "black out." The test was a success and they wired the details to George. The newspaper photographs were perfectly clear, even though they had been taken when the city was in complete darkness.

George offered to lecture in Banff on the new camera process if Norman thought anyone might be interested in coming. It could be a benefit lecture, with proceeds all going to the Banff Red Cross. Already he'd lectured in Oklahoma to over 4,000 people including over 400 newspaper photographers and editors. He could bring the "black out" camera to Banff with him. His talk generally went for about an hour. Perhaps he could give a Sunday night lecture at the Lux Theatre? For the first time George was really proud of his "black out" camera; it was his way of helping the war effort. He was now working with the DuPont Company and General Electric to make it even more practical to use.

Norman's contribution to the war effort was that he was head of the Victory Loan Drive in Banff.

So George and Pat were coming but would miss out on Indian Days. They couldn't leave Minneapolis until July 19, but they were very excited. It was unfortunate because there was a lot of excitement at Indian Days that year.

England had been so grateful for all the support from Canada that they had decided to make a film as a sort of "thank you" card to Canada. The movie would star the greatest English actors of the day including Laurence Olivier and Lesley Howard. Raymond Massey also starred in the film. The original title was "The Invaders" and it was produced by the English division of Columbia Pictures. The story centered around a German submarine that was sunk. Some of the Nazis survived the attack and had to make their way across Canada from Halifax to Vancouver where they could hopefully escape to Japan. The Canadian scenery was spectacular but the film was a salute to all the people of Canada who made it the great nation that it is. The film included the Inuit, the Hutterites of Manitoba, and of course the Native Indians. Now what better place to find Indians in full native dress than in Banff during Banff Indian Days? The film crew arrived to shoot one of the scenes at the Banff Springs Hotel. Since Norman ran the Indian Days it was only fitting he should be given a small part.

In the Banff scene the escaping German Nazis had blended into the crowd of tourists up at the Banff Springs Hotel. Norman took his place at the microphone to thank everyone for coming. Suddenly a nearby Mountie interrupted and told Norman he needed the microphone. The Mountie then proceeded to tell the gathered crowd that hiding among them were the Nazi's from the sunken U-Boat. One of the Nazi's was spotted and captured by the Mounties, because of course, the Mounties....always get their man.

Pat was really having trouble adjusting to her eye problems and it had taken quite an emotional toll on her. While on her latest trip to Banff there had been a misunderstanding between her and her Uncle Norman on the last day of her visit. A train trip to see her cousin in Calgary had gone wrong. She had been mistaken on the time of departure and missed the train. Everything had been planned in Calgary and then she failed to show up. Norman had thought after all he had done for her that she was just an ungrateful and spoiled little girl. Pat was devastated because she loved her Uncle Norman more than anything in the world and could not stand to have him mad at her. The trip had been perfect and then everything was ruined on that last day. There had been an unpleasant scene at the station. When she got home she was so upset that George had to write asking Norman to please write his daughter a letter and say he wasn't mad anymore. It really had been an accident on Pat's part. George had enjoyed his trip immensely and really got to know Norman better than he ever had. They had both gone to Calgary to tour the new airfields and admire the city lights from up on the hill. They also visited the ice-fields and the two brothers enjoyed spending some time alone together.

Eleanor had recovered but was not comfortable with her employers or her students. She said there were no "real" folks out east. In her mind, the men of the day were all weak creatures compared to people like her father and those hardy men who had built Banff. The men in Banff were a tougher breed, yet they were full of kindness and a willingness to help out at any cost. She decided to quit her teaching job and because of the war, she was able to get on with the CPR. Eleanor worked in the drafting department, assisting in the design of the latest locomotives. She loved the work because she was no longer a mere teacher or secretary. She worked with men who were not petty like the women she had known.

With the war came the expansion of Lake Minnewanka as well as the dam. Norman's newest cabin would be sent to a watery grave some 60 feet under the new level of the lake.

Poor Howard Deegan wrote again from England. What was with the English and their sheep? All they ever got to eat was mutton. Mutton chops, mutton stew, roast mutton, raw mutton. If he never saw another sheep as long as he lived that would suit him just fine. Howard had met a nice lady at one of the dances who had lost her husband. She was from Portsmouth and was in the ladies' section of the Navy. He got an invitation to her mother's for dinner and he was looking forward to a proper English dinner. Hopefully it wouldn't involve mutton.

Another large Canadian unit had arrived and Howard could hear them all marching past the barracks. Billy Addison was happy to report that all the socks sent by the Soldier's Service Club of Banff had arrived.

In December, another 1,000 cigarettes had arrived safely in the hands of Howard Deegan. He got them regularly from Norman who he thought was far too generous. He promised to put a new roof on Norman's doghouse, as soon as he got back, to thank him. Billy also got his 1,000 cigarettes in December.

Eugene's son had signed up in the States now that the U.S. had finally entered the war. Bill was commissioned, as a Captain, and was nervously awaiting word on where and when to report for duty. Eugene was nervous too and soon fell off the wagon by way of some Christmas eggnog. Bill finally got word and was posted to Nassau in the Bahamas. His job was to inspect the fortresses in the Bahamas. Guy Weadick, who had been down in the States, was glad to see that the U.S. finally was taking some action. As soon as Japan attacked Pearl Harbor the Americans were immediately in the game. Now that Guy was back home he was having trouble getting help at the Stampede Ranch. All the good men were overseas.

News didn't come too often from Red Cathcart as he was really in the thick of things. Everyone else seemed to still be in England but Red was supplying the front lines. At the moment he was "somewhere in England" but that would quickly change.

The Christmas letters for Norman, had all arrived by the end of January, 1942. Ollie was still in the cookie business but all the workers in the factory were young and they didn't much know how to run the company. Ollie had hoped to retire one day soon but it didn't look promising. There had been labour troubles at the factory and production was slowed down to the point that many orders had to be cancelled. They had lost much of their help and hadn't had a chance to replace them.

It had been almost 8 months since the filming of the "Invaders". Since Norman had a small part he received an official invitation to the world première at the Capital Theatre in New York City. It was to be held on Thursday, March 5, 1942 at 8:30 pm. The theatre was located at 51st and Broadway. Norman didn't have any intention of going but tucked away the invitation. He hadn't even mentioned to any family or friends outside of Banff that the film even existed. It wouldn't be a secret for long.

What Norman didn't know was that his niece Dorothy was working as editor of a magazine called *Movie Story* out of New York. Before the world première she had been invited to the press screening in the projection room at the Columbia Pictures office at 729 Broadway, New York. She was sitting next to the editor of *Colliers* magazine and as the scene at the Banff Springs Hotel came on the screen she leapt out of her seat and shrieked,

"There's my Uncle Norm!"

When the film ended she proceeded to tell everyone all about her wonderful Uncle Norm. She loved the film and made sure she told everyone she met to go and see it.

The film was released and as friends across the country saw Norman up on the big screen the fan mail began pouring into Banff. All the Luxtons in Minneapolis went to see Norman the big movie star. Nellie, Ollie, Ed, and Pat were there. Pat was so thrilled she went twice. The film had been renamed in Canada as "The 49th Parallel" and played during 1942. It was an obvious gift of love from the English and was nominated for an Oscar in the categories of Best Picture and Best Original Story. The competition that year was fierce and Norman's film was up against "Mrs. Miniver", "Yankee Doodle Dandee", "The Magnificent Ambersons" and "The Pied Piper". On March 4, 1943, the Academy Awards were held at the Cocoanut Grove in the Ambassador Hotel in Los Angeles. Although "The Invaders" lost to "Mrs. Miniver," the film did receive the Award for Best Original Story.

The summer of '42 looked promising and the town wasn't really suffering. Norman kept busy sending cartons of cigarettes overseas. He had a few boys he sent to now including Billy Addison, Howard Deegan, Tony Leska, and Red Cathcart. They all thanked Norman for his generosity and all his letters. So many boys overseas received nothing so they very much appreciated Norman's efforts. Harold had been promoted to Corporal but was bored in England.

Norman was going to have a little help in the Trading Post as Pat was coming up from Minneapolis. Her Aunt Nellie agreed to pay her rail fare and George would pay for her room and board. Norman found her a room at Mrs. Charelton's house. Pat would be working along with her Uncle Lou and his daughter Minota.

Pat's summer working in the Trading Post was a huge success and when she returned to Minneapolis in the fall, her father hardly recognized the girl who stepped off the train. Her health had vastly improved and her poise and outlook on life had changed dramatically. He knew Norman was responsible for the change and couldn't thank him enough.

Red wrote from overseas and was "tickled pink" that the latest package of smokes arrived right on his birthday, November 3. Howard was getting all Norman's letters. There were now hundreds of bombers going over to Europe day and night. The skies were always full of planes now. Norman was about the only person to write to Howard. His wife had not written in over a year as she was a patient up in Ponoka. Howard still wrote to her regularly but heard nothing back. Half of all his pay went to her care and he heard nothing of his children. His dad wrote occasionally and was in touch with Howard's son who was in high school in Calgary. It was difficult being over in England and not even knowing where his children were. Sometimes months would go by when ships carrying letters went down in the Atlantic. Still Norman's always seemed to get through.

Eugene saw Bill while he was home on leave. Bill said that in the Bahamas they did see the occasional Nazi sub. Sometimes they blasted them to the surface but most just got sent to the bottom of the ocean, crew and all.

Ollie was still having problems at the biscuit factory. They had continued to lose staff during the year and many salesmen were now working in the factory instead of selling. They only managed to see their customers once a month now. With the young ones off to war the factory was full of older gentlemen who just didn't have the agility or spark of the young ones.

Norman's dog had died earlier that year due to the utter incompetence of a veterinarian in Calgary. It was a minor operation yet the dog died on the table. Norman was furious; this was Larry, one of his best hunting dogs! Not only were his dogs highly trained at great expense but they were also part of the family. Everyone agreed the vet should have lost his license but Norman lost his temper and punched the doctor. He regretted his actions immediately but word soon spread that he'd threatened the vet's life and punched him out. Friends who heard the whole story said they would have done worse than Norman did and that he ought to sue the vet for costs of training Larry. The problem was that Larry was the younger dog; Barney was too old to even hunt anymore. Norman let the matter drop, he felt bad enough for hitting the vet in the first place.

Earl was still at Campion College teaching but now had an additional course to give in aircraft recognition. He gave the course to the Air Force Cadet Corps at the College.

January of 1943 brought good news to Howard in England. His wife had finally written and he learned that his son had joined the cadets. His daughter was now teaching school in Millicent, Alberta. Harold had just received a nice pair of gloves from Norman along with more cigarettes.

In the spring, the Banff Springs Hotel announced that they would remain closed for the summer. Without the hotel's tourists and assistance it would be pointless to run Indian Days. For the first time in 40 years, there would be no Banff Indian Days. Norman would keep busy with the Calgary Stampede and the Trading Post. He arranged for Burns & Co. to sell the meat and the proceeds would be invested in Victory Bonds. Those bonds could be used to finance future Indian Days. The Stoneys wanted to again thank Burn's & Co and presented a chief's tent to John Burns.

All had gone quiet in Baltimore and there would never again be a letter, book or strange little parcel from "Pops." Eugene LaPorte died on April 21, 1943. Lulu had written Norman from Seattle. She was completely devastated. She had written Eugene almost weekly and Mrs. LaPorte had encouraged it. She said that Lulu's letters had brought real joy to Eugene's life. He always chuckled over the jokes. Lulu missed his letters more than she could have imagined. Mrs. LaPorte had lived the high life and her stylish clothes were often discarded after wearing them only a few times. Eugene would send them on to Lulu who appreciated the very lovely and expensive clothes.

Eugene had been a gentleman of the old school, never one to complain. He never put on airs or acted better than his fellow man. He was generous and kind to everyone, without exception. Lulu had confided in him and now he was gone. Only now did it occur to Lulu that she genuinely was in love with the man. Always he had written her and sent candy, often as much as 100 pounds at a time for her to share with others. Lulu was so lonely now without him. It was if the light in her life had been extinguished. She hoped that between her and Norman that they could continue Eugene's legacy of generosity and friendship.

That summer Earl moved to Montreal to continue his theology course. He had finished the teaching portion of his education and now it was back for more studying. He had now been with the Jesuits for over 9 years. He had managed to get to Calgary that summer to visit his Mom and her friends Mr. & Mrs. Garbutt. The Garbutts had taken them all to dinner at the Palliser Hotel. Mary had found it quite an ordeal, it was all so fancy, but she managed to struggle through it without any terrible faux pas.

Billy Addison wrote to say that he had at last left England and was now posted to Sicily. He found it incredibly hot there. The Sicilian people were very poor after the Italian and German troops had left. The people seemed friendly enough but you couldn't really trust them. Billy did enjoy exploring the island and loved the little towns and fruit groves. He also managed to get in some swimming in the Mediterranean. Perhaps some day he'd go back during peacetime.

Norman had always been an active member of the Calgary Gun Club but for the past 2 years it had been inactive. All the club's facilities had been offered to the Army and Air Force. This meant there was no income from memberships or activities but there was still rent, taxes, and insurance to pay and they were in trouble. They asked their members if they could still pay dues just to keep the place going.

The usual birthday greetings arrived that November including news of Pat's new job as a switchboard operator at a Minneapolis hospital. Even a birthday message came from Red who was in England temporarily.

Guy had been busy down at the ranch and was now writing a book about rodeos. It would be the history of rodeos in America and the writing of it took up most of his time. Norman also had a new little business venture. He was now running a livery booking office out in front of the Trading Post.

Norman had already decided that Banff Indian Days would definitely run in 1944. He'd already made up his "Things to Do" list.

SIXTEEN

Winding Down

The beginning of 1944 brought letters and cards from friends thanking Norman for his many gifts. Billy Addison, over in Sicily, had received his latest package of cigarettes; Howard Deegan got his chocolate; Earl Massecar had been sent his pocket money; and Red Cathcart was somewhere on the front lines but still alive and kicking. Red had been given the opportunity to return to Canada but chose to stay and "finish up." He wasn't leaving until the war was over. He'd come this far— he may as well stay until the end. Red was happy to hear his son had joined up with the Canadian Navy. Norman had already begun preparing for Indian Days. He always had to start early to get everything done by July. There were letters requesting donations, tickets and programs to be printed for the various transport companies, tickets for concerts, passes, and then the many phone calls to various businesses begging for donations. Next came organizing the volunteers, putting up posters, collecting props, arranging transportation for the Indians, and getting the groceries. There was a lot of work to be done.

Occasionally unusual letters arrived and the latest query was about the merman. The young lady had seen in it Norman's shop. Her friends assured her that it wasn't real, there was no such thing; it was just a myth. Was the merman real? She had seen it with her own eyes, after all. Norman always liked to keep the origins of his merman a mystery.

Eleanor was still in Montreal and was pleased with the new fur coat and the generous cheque her father had sent for Christmas. She had always wanted to eventually write books and her father's life would certainly make a great story. She knew Norman had kept many of his notes on various things, safely tucked away in the safe at the office. At least that's what she thought. She enjoyed her visits to his office at the Trading Post. There were so many pictures to look at. She wondered what would happen to the store once her Uncle Lou and her dad were gone. Maybe he ought to consider teaching Pat how to run the store. The one thing she was sure of was that it should remain in the family.

Eleanor was busy with her war work and the new locomotives she helped design were now being built. She was proud of her drawings and knew her father would be astounded at the number of parts required to build just one machine.

The war continued and more boys signed up. Ernest Mauder had written from Newfoundland to say that his son had signed up. The boy had joined the Air Force and the family had been proud to attend the presentation of their son's wings by the Governor General of Canada. Their son would now take commando training for a month before being shipped overseas. The Mauders' daughter had married a Canadian officer.

Norman continued sending cases of cigarettes and the boys overseas always seemed to get them okay. Howard, Tony, and Billy had all received the latest shipment. Tony hoped that when the war ended there might be a job for him at the *Crag and Canyon*.

Pat wrote from Minneapolis saying she had quit her hospital job at the maternity hospital. She didn't have any definite plans yet for future employment.

Summer of 1944 found Norman's friend Mary Massecar in quite a state. Her son, Earl, would be celebrating the biggest day of his life in exactly 2 years. That is when he would finally be ordained as a Jesuit Priest and take his final vows. The ceremony would take place in Toronto. Invitations would have to be sent to family and friends and the trip alone would cost Mary over $200. Then he would give his first High Mass in Calgary followed by a reception. Mary knew she would have to finance the reception and she didn't want to let Earl down. The problem was money. The job she currently had simply didn't pay enough to finance such a celebration. Perhaps Norman could help her find another job that paid better? As always, Norman came through and Mary was hired by Burns & Co. as a dictaphonist for $85 a month.

George and Pat came up to Banff over the summer and Norman gave Pat a job at the Trading Post. Pat loved selling the little trinkets in the store and was pleased to find it was as much fun as she hoped it would be. When she got back to Minneapolis in the fall her friends were glad to have her home but she really missed living in Banff. What she liked best about Banff was that her Uncle Norman always took her to the movies. Aunt Georgie was also a big movie fan. George enjoyed his visit and especially the trip he and Norman took to Lake Louise. He thanked Norman again for the big change in Pat. After working at the Trading Post the girl had more confidence and poise than ever. Norman must have given her awfully good advice to result in such a dramatic change in the girl. Pat was hoping to return the following summer.

By September Red Cathcart was "somewhere in France" until December when he was "somewhere in Holland." The man certainly got around. Tony Leska remained in England and wrote about the various kinds of bombs that flew overhead. There were Buzz bombs, V2's and Rocket Bombs. Howard Deegan was also still in England. He had learned that his daughter was now a teacher in Countess, Alberta. His son was still in the Navy but hoped to study forestry once the war was over.

Norman had not forgotten about his little buffalo souvenirs and decided to expand the line to include other animals native to the area. In the spring of 1945, he patented two more designs including that of a porcupine and a wolverine.

Ollie was having quite a tough time out in Victoria. His wife's rheumatism meant she could only just barely get around the house with the aid of two canes. They had hired a girl some years before, to help around the house. The problem was that she couldn't cook and had to be supervised every moment. If you told her exactly what to do she could follow orders but otherwise she would sit and do nothing.

Guy was still busy writing his book on the history of rodeos. As for the boys overseas, old Red was "somewhere in Germany" now. Actually he'd been in Germany for quite some time and said that there was never a dull moment. During their push to the Rhine they practically lived in water. He was in the 3rd Division and they had been nicknamed the "Water Rats." In Germany there was nothing but total destruction with towns literally wiped off the map. The country was nothing more than a giant rubble heap. Often under heavy shellfire Red would just get out his old kit bag, dig down and find the cigarettes Norman had sent. Norman really had no idea just how important his generous gifts were. He also wanted Norman to pass along his thanks to the folks at home who kept the wheels turning and the supply lines full. He thought Norman might like to know that while in Holland he had found a paddock full of buffalo which the Canadian boys had named "Wainwright Park."

Howard was in England and just received his latest package of smokes. Norman always sent them in packages of 1000. Howard could hardly wait for the day when he could walk into the Trading Post and thank Norman in person.

In March the Hudson's Bay was celebrating its 270th anniversary. The Calgary store's manager wanted to decorate the store windows with displays of the old pioneer days. He asked if Norman would consider helping him with the displays by providing him with beadwork, old guns, bows, arrows, and old Indian saddles.

More news came from Red in April; he was now back in Holland. He said how nice it was to be away from the death and destruction that was Germany. The northern part of the Netherlands was very beautiful. The trees here were green and had new leaves and there were wild flowers everywhere. Compared to Germany it was like a dream. Just hearing the sound of wind in the trees was to be treasured. Without the sound of constant shelling, you could hear the soft sound of the deep river as it moved along on its way to the sea. There were birds here, dozens of them, and their songs filled the air. In the marshlands were ducks and there were new and modern homes. New windmills took their place alongside the ancient ones and the older folks still dressed in the traditional costumes dating back hundreds of years.

Norman took part in the Stampede Parade and served in his usual capacity of Indian judge. He heard from Earl in August and was pleased to hear the boy was enjoying a holiday in Muskoka, Ontario. Earl said that there was less than a year now until he would be ordained and his mother was very excited. Mary had always dreamed that one day her son would be a priest. Mothers of priests were very highly respected and envied.

Billy Addison was home from the war and announced to Norman that he was getting married in a month. He said she was the sweetest girl he ever met and that they had decided to honeymoon in Banff so he would see Norman then. He would be there on September 22, and introduce his new bride. Billy had a new job in Calgary with McCosham's Storage down on 10th Avenue. He was glad to have been able to get work right away. Norman got busy and reserved a room for the young couple.

Norman had decided to take a little break and set out on a canoe trip from Banff all the way to Gleichen. He hadn't asked the Blackfoot Indians in advance if he could camp at the Blackfoot Crossing. They assured him that no permission was needed. Norman had done so much that they thought perhaps a marker should be placed on shore to read, "Norman camped here."

Guy was still working on his book and the project was much larger than he had anticipated. He was taking a break and heading off to Oklahoma with Florence to visit her dad. Charles Bensell was 91 years old and had been raised on a Sioux reservation in Minnesota from the age of 8 until he was 15. His father had been the Indian agent there. Florence (Grace Maud Bensell) was his only child.

The Weadicks received word that Guy's cousin had been shot down over Tokyo back on May 24. He had been flying in a Super Fortress and

186

was now reported as missing. In August, they heard that he had not been killed but was in a prison camp in Tokyo. He would be returned to the United States shortly. Another boy shot down over Tokyo was not so lucky. Eugene's brother, Robert, had a grandson who had been killed.

August brought other sad news for the Luxtons. Norman's sister Ollie had just lost her husband. Ed Hoskings had died. He had been suffering from angina pectoris and had been in the hospital in St. Paul. He had died on August 26, 1945. Ed had been a newspaperman since 1900 and worked at the *St. Paul Dispatch*. Although born in England he had moved to Japan at the age of 5 with his parents. His father was in railway construction and helped build the Japanese railroad. At the age of 15, Ed moved to Toronto and attended the University of Toronto. One of his classmates there had been Mackenzie King who later became Prime Minister of Canada. After Ed graduated, he worked at newspapers in Victoria and Winnipeg. Later he became city editor of the *St. Paul Globe* until he took the job at the *St. Paul Dispatch*. He had been proud of his family. His son Louis still lived in St. Paul, William F. lived in Chicago and Dorothy was still in New York.

The Morley church had fallen into disrepair. A committee meeting of the Junior Board of Trade planned to meet and discuss a plan to restore the church. They came to the conclusion that it would take a few thousand dollars to fix the place up. The plan was that on the last Sunday of November, 12 of the members would drive out and inspect the church. The building had been constructed by David and John McDougall, Andrew Sibbald, and several Indians. They asked if Norman would join them at the church and help out. They were also looking for donations for the project and Norman gave $50 to the project.

For years Norman had been known for the Stetson he wore. He'd had his for over 20 years and it was time to replace it. He wrote off to the Stetson Company in Philadelphia and ordered one medium weight hat for the summer and a heavy one for the cold weather. He preferred them in gray and made of beaver or felt. His hat was custom-made with a brim width of 3 inches in size 7.

On New Year's Eve there was a surprise call to George from Norman. Since Norman never phoned, poor George was in such shock he could hardly speak. The real surprise was that George had been at his neighbours and the call was forwarded there so it was completely unexpected. Pat also got on the line to wish her uncle a very happy 1946. The family were all there except Ollie who had gone to Iowa to see her daughter Mary.

After the death of Eugene his brother, Robert, had continued to write to Norman. He kept Norman updated on Eugene's son. Bill had survived the war and was now working in a bank.

Guy was still at the Stampede Ranch but thinking of selling the place. He'd been there 26 years and it was time to retire. He'd already had two offers and was seriously considering them.

George wrote in February to let Norman know that their sister Nellie had suffered a bad fall down the stairs. She had broken her nose and blackened both her eyes but was feeling okay now.

Ollie wrote from Victoria to thank Norman for the Christmas chickens. He couldn't believe that Norman was still out hunting, trudging across the snow trying to bag a few so Ollie would have a nice Christmas meal. He wouldn't blame Norman if he gave it all up and said, "Let that old coot in Victoria eat turkey." Ollie had given up smoking all but 4 pipes a day. He found that if he smoked after 5 pm he would get leg cramps.

Ollie had always wanted to retire to his little cabin by the lake but he'd recently been made an offer to sell it. They were willing to pay twice what Ollie paid for it. He'd had it 10 years but they seemed so happy that he let them have it. As for work, the Ormond Biscuit Company was looking like it might have to shut down. There was simply no shortening available. Just when they'd all but given up, a few barrels of shortening arrived so they were able to carry on.

The third week of March found Norman in the spotlight again. *Liberty* magazine had decided to run a feature story on him. The fan mail started to arrive again as people opened their latest issue of the popular magazine. It was the Canadian edition of *Liberty* so Norman got a hold of a few copies to send to his American friends and family. When Pat got her copy she immediately sent off to Toronto for extras. She sent one to her cousin Bill Hoskings in Chicago and his sister Dorothy in New York.

Pat was working for the Fire Brick & Insulation Co. where she took dictation from five different men. She wanted to come out to Banff again in the summer.

As more fan mail arrived Norman thought perhaps the magazine business might be interesting. Perhaps he could start a little mountain magazine. It was just an idea.

Dorothy wrote from New York and was very pleased to receive her own copy of *Liberty*. She left her copy out in the art department of *Movie Story* so her coworkers could read it. They all thought Norman was a fascinating guy and very handsome. She made sure everyone there knew she was Norman's niece. Dorothy had now been editor of *Movie Story* magazine for 8 years. She was happy that she and Norman were both in the publishing business. She would be happy to send him a few issues of her magazine. Dorothy had spent a month in Banff and had gotten to know her uncle quite well. She loved her Auntie Georgie as well. She wished they would come and visit New York sometime. Her summer in Banff was full of memories of going to the latest picture show at the Lux and then going to the drugstore afterwards for toasted cheese sandwiches. Norman had also taken her for a beautiful car trip through the Kicking Horse Trail. There had been horseback riding with Eleanor and dancing up at the Banff Springs Hotel. She hoped Norman would drop her a line one of these days.

Georgie was now serving as president of the Old Timers Association in Calgary and had been invited to a tea being put on by the Hudson's Bay Company. She was asked to come and receive guests. While in Calgary she also had tickets to attend the horse show along with Norman and her nephew David McDougall.

Dorothy wrote again in May to thank her uncle for his latest letter. Dorothy had sent away for another 10 copies of *Liberty*. She wanted to make sure her sister had a copy plus a few of her friends. She had also received a copy of Norman's diary from the *Tilikum* that her cousin Pat had sent to her. Once she started reading it she couldn't put it down. She thought it was simply fascinating. She still had the three pearls that Norman had given her mother, Ollie. Her Mom had broken her arm just before Easter and Dorothy wasn't sure if Norman knew yet. She had also been to see her cousins' Susan and Gail, Mary's little girls. They sure were cute.

Dorothy continued to think about her uncle and decided she wanted to visit Banff again. She called the CPR and booked herself a lower berth. She was going to leave from St. Paul on July 12 and would arrive in Banff on July 20. She was going to stay with the Charletons who came highly recommended by Pat. She also thought perhaps she would bring Mary's daughter Gail as she could still travel at no charge. Gail was only 6 years old but was extremely well behaved, got along with adults, and was very sweet. Gail pretty much loved everyone she met and loved stories about Indians. She wanted very much to see a real one. Perhaps Tommy Charleton could set up an extra cot in the room for the little girl. Dorothy had just spent the day on location at the Terry Tunes factory where they made the cartoon *Mighty Mouse*. The factory was full of artists and musicians. She had been to the Disney studio back in 1938 for a tour which was also good fun. She hoped to be able to tell Aunt Georgie all about the many movie stars she had met. After 8 years in the movie magazine, she had met almost all of Georgie's favourite film stars.

George planned to come to Banff in August and hoped to rent a room from Mrs. Charleton. Ada would not be joining him as she was off to Boston and New York for a visit.

Charles Bensell had been staying with his daughter at the Stampede Ranch since May 11, his 92nd birthday. He was planning to move in with Guy and Florence. First, though, he needed to return to Minnesota to clear up a few business matters. Guy and Florence would drive "Dad" back via Montana, North and South Dakota and they planned to leave in June. On May 25, they had all been sitting around listening to the news on CFCN Radio and Charles seemed to be in great shape. He lied down on the sofa when Florence went into the kitchen. He had just gotten up to walk to his bedroom to fetch a sweater when he gasped and sat back down on the sofa. A couple more gasps and he was dead. He'd only had a smoke from his pipe a few minutes before. The problem was that high winds had blown all the telephone lines down so Guy couldn't call anyone. He hitched a ride to Longview with his neighbours and called High River from there. Funeral arrangements were made and Charles was buried in High River.

Dorothy and little Gail were counting the days until they left for Banff. Gail had some new white sandals that she was sure would impress her Uncle Norman. She also had a new robe for the berth on the Pullman. Pat had sent the little girl some pictures of bears and Indians. Gail wanted to be made an Indian Princess. She had seen pictures of the film star Margaret O'Brien when she was dressed like an Indian Princess. Dorothy wondered if Norman had met Bing Crosby who had filmed *The Emperor Waltz* in Banff and Jasper. Dorothy had never met Bing but had met his costar Joan Fontaine.

Dorothy arrived in Banff on July 20 as scheduled with her little cousin in tow. The two of them had a wonderful holiday. Dorothy wound up staying at the King Edward Hotel and much to her surprise, Norman had paid the bill in full.

Pat had also spent time in Banff that summer but was off to Vancouver as she was hoping to find work there. As far as working and getting the papers needed for immigration, she asked Norman if he could help. With his letter of reference she was approved in 5 minutes and was able to start looking for a job. She had decided to continue on to Victoria and got a lovely room just one block from Beacon Hill Park. George was with her and they looked up Ollie and Mary Ormond and stopped by for a visit. George was happy to see his old friend again and Pat was very impressed with the lovely couple. George finally left Pat to carry on life in Victoria where she settled in very well. The *Tilikum* was only a ½-mile walk if she wanted to stop by and visit. The problem was that there didn't seem to be any work in the city and what was there didn't pay enough. By the middle of November, Pat decided it was time to move to Vancouver and try her luck there. She soon found work in a doctor's office as secretary and receptionist. She even wore a white uniform.

Ollie had written Norman after the visit from George and Pat. He admitted that had he bumped into George on the street he wouldn't have recognized him at all. It had been 45 years since he'd last seen his old employee. He hoped Pat was okay in Vancouver but she was welcome to pop by and visit any time.

Even by the spring of 1947, the food overseas continued to be rationed and there were still huge shortages. Norman decided to sponsor a family in England and began to send a huge parcel of food to supply them with products they could not get. A typical package consisted of pears, Oxo cubes, Lipton's Noodle Soup Mix, chocolate bars, meat paste, figs and lemon juice. Norman would continue to send these parcels for over 3 years to the Smythe family in Colgate, Sussex.

Robert LaPorte wrote to say that his other brother, Frank, had died. He'd been suffering from hardening arteries in the throat. This made it impossible for him to swallow solid food. Frank had become acquainted with Norman while on a trip to Banff with his brother Eugene years earlier.

Norman was thinking about reenacting Treaty No. 7 that summer and wrote up a script. He would try to set it up like the famous painting and got busy finding out just who everyone was in the picture. The man on sitting on the chair with the helmet was the Marquis of Lorne and in the other chair was the Hon. E. Dewdney (Lt. Governor of the Northwest Territories). Behind him the man writing was Col. DeWinton (military secretary) and the man standing behind him with the beard was Sergt. Bagley. Kneeling down in front was the NWMP orderly preparing medicine for sick Indians which was prescribed by the doctor sitting opposite the orderly. The man with the long hair, near the pole of the awning, was the interpreter, L. L'Hereux.

It was a start. As for financial help the Alberta Travel Bureau turned Norman down but he was still trying to get the National Film Board to cover the re-enactment. There would be the cost of costumes, actors, and the usual costs to bring Indians to the event. The show went ahead as scheduled and was a great success that year at Banff Indian Days.

In November the press relations officer of the CPR was going to be travelling to Banff with his young son who was crazy about Indians. He had asked Allen Bill (managing editor of the *Calgary Herald*), if something could be arranged. Allen contacted Norman and when little Johnny's train arrived in Banff he was met by Norman and Chief Enos Hunter and his brother. The little boy's eyes almost popped out of his head as he shook hands with Norman and the real Indian chief. Little Johnny and his father John Sturdy were travelling through to Vancouver so it was just a brief stop at the Banff station. The little boy talked of nothing else all the way out to the coast. John wanted to make sure Norman knew how much this little gesture had meant to his son.

Pat was still in Vancouver but managed to visit Victoria quite often. She liked nothing better than to go down to the waterfront and watch the boats go in and out. Whenever she did get out to Victoria the first stop was Thunderbird Park to say "hello" to the *Tilikum*. She had just spent Christmas out there and Tom Charleton from Banff was in town for a visit.

Eleanor was also out in Vancouver and was now suffering from fainting spells. Her cousin David Ross was also in Vancouver and kept an eye on her. He thought he would contact her doctors out there and see what they had to say. Eleanor had been so sick most of her life, yet every diagnosis was different, from every doctor. The latest guess was something they called "Egomania." It was said to be caused by personal problems giving her imaginary illnesses. They said sitting over a drafting table didn't help her. She needed to be around other people instead of alone thinking about her problems. Maybe she should learn her father's business and run the Trading Post. Eleanor considered the idea. If she did move back to Banff she wanted a separate apartment. She was too old to move back home.

At the end of December there was shocking news from Mary Massecar. Neither Mary nor Earl had written for some time and now the reason for the sudden silence was revealed. With less than a year to go until he was a priest, Earl had given it all up for a woman. He had his B.A. from the university and had left almost a year earlier but told no one. His mother had finally received a letter that said only that he was parting company with the society. Mary immediately phoned him in Montreal to see what she could do. Earl told her that while at a boarding house he met a French girl some years older than himself. He had fallen in love and married her. Mary was furious and a bitter fight ensued until Earl got hostile and finally hung up. The Jesuit Society was upset and Mary lost all her faith in prayer, religion, and almost in God.

Mary was scorned and ridiculed. Life was almost unbearable. She had taken the train to Montreal to see if she could talk any sense into the boy. Earl met her at the train station but the angry words were such that he left her where he had found her. Mary didn't really expect to ever hear from the boy again but Christmas brought an old photo and a note saying that Earl could take care of himself, his wife, and his family. He now had a son of his own. He also mentioned that he was now working at the Advertising Recording Company. Mary did not want to communicate with her son and wanted nothing from him. She took out an insurance policy to cover her burial expenses so that even in death she would ask for nothing from Earl. She would creep to the poorhouse on her hands and knees before she would ask Earl for anything.

January of 1948 found many of the Luxtons suffering from various ailments. Norman had the flu, Eleanor still was ill with her mystery illness, and George was in the hospital. At least the sisters were well and enjoying a holiday in La Jolla, California. George had gone in for some minor surgery and would be home soon. Pat was still in Vancouver and now working at a paint store.

In February, there was another letter from Mary. She had reached some sort of truce with Earl and he wrote to tell her that he had recently been made manager of his department. His wife was very thrifty and so financially they were doing well. Mary said her daughter-in-law always had money left over to put in the bank. The girl knitted her own socks and sewed all her own dresses. Perhaps Earl had done better for himself than his new wife had.

Pat wrote to say that she was leaving Vancouver and returning to St. Paul. She planned to stop in Banff to see Norman on the way. Norman met her at the station along with his brother Lou and his wife Elsie.

Eleanor had decided to go the Rochester Clinic in New York to see if they could help her. She arrived there in April and managed to fly up to St. Paul to visit George and the family for a weekend.

Ollie wrote in June, he was finding life quite difficult now. Mary had gone into the hospital the previous November and had stayed there for a month. It had just been for a cataract operation but the time in bed took its toll and she now had no use of her legs. Ollie knew that she could only barely walk and that a month in bed would destroy any chance of walking again. Now she could stand with crutches but would cry each time she stood on her feet. She could only manage to stand perhaps three or four times a day. Ollie was now a full-time nursemaid. Then just after Christmas he had caught the flu and was home for 6 weeks. Even though he was sick he had to bathe and dress Mary every morning and put her in her wheelchair. Then at night he had to reverse the operation. His strength, depleted from his illness, meant it was almost impossible to lift her. Every time he lifted Mary to her chair he was certain it would be the last time. He just didn't see how he could continue but he did continue because there was no choice. Every night he would go to bed at midnight only to be up again by 5:00 am. Then he would go to work from 9:30-5:30 and still have to do all the cooking and cleaning. He didn't know how much longer he could continue. The only good thing was that he had met a man by the name of David Ross and realized he was Norman's nephew. Ollie now suffered with rheumatism and wore a copper bracelet that was supposed to help. How he wished that he could just hop a train to Banff and visit Norman again!

On a rather happier note, there was also a letter from a man named Ray Maloney of Baltimore. He had been a good friend to Eugene, who for years, had read him every letter Norman ever sent. Ray had been a great friend to Eugene and they spent many days golfing, fishing, hunting and sometimes enjoyed a casual drink. The night before Eugene died he had called Ray and said he had three cases of whiskey to bring over. He promised to deliver them the next morning but they never arrived. Eugene died just after the call at 9:00 pm. Ray was glad his old friend had been in a great mood right up to 5 minutes before his death. Norman had been a hero to Eugene and through him Ray had heard all about Norman's adventures. He wished someday to meet Norman.

Norman didn't ever get to Baltimore but did decide to visit St. Paul and took a family trip with Georgie and Eleanor. Eleanor was still in New York and her parents were coming to take her home. On the way they stopped in to see George, Nellie, and Ollie. It had been years since the sisters had seen their brother but there was no mistaking that twinkle in his eye. He may have looked a lot older but he was no stranger. After leaving St. Paul the Luxtons made a stop in Winnipeg.

Eleanor was worse after spending time in the very hot and humid Rochester. She actually fared better in the mountains. David Ross wrote from Victoria not realizing just how ill Eleanor was again. The family in St. Paul had been very worried about her. Obviously, the doctors in Vancouver had been wrong in their diagnosis. Norman was starting to get desperate and was enrolling himself and Eleanor in something called

"Kabalarian Philosophy." It would cost $100 and they sent you monthly lessons. It was a philosophy of personal fulfillment based on a belief in the mathematical cycles. Practices included vegetarianism, physical exercise, and a belief in the mystical influence of numbers. It was a load of nonsense but at this point Norman would try anything to help his daughter.

In November there came a letter from Grant MacEwan. He was the Dean of the University of Manitoba and wanted to write a series of sketches on the lives of selected pioneers. He had met Norman while attending the Calgary Stampede the previous July. He was hoping Norman might have some diaries so he could do a story on him. He really wanted some anecdotes about Norman's voyage on the *Tilikum*.

In January of 1949, a friend of Norman's in New York sent him an article from the *New York Herald Tribune*. Ernest Kehr had known Norman for some time and the article caught his eye. It was a write-up on George and his career in the newspaper business. The article talked about how George had been a newspaper photographer for over 50 years. It mentioned how George helped develop the Howitzer camera that was now used for close-up sports shots. Perhaps the most interesting stories were of George when he worked on the campaign trains for every president since Grover Cleveland, except for Harding and Truman. There was a good story about the day that George was on the campaign train with Teddy Roosevelt. George always jumped off the train before it pulled into a station to get pictures of it arriving. He would do the reverse when it left and as the trains pulled away, he would chase after them. One day he was running as fast as he could but the train was getting away. Teddy Roosevelt watched as George desperately tried to catch the train and realized he needed help. Roosevelt reached up and pulled on the emergency cord to stop the train, ensuring that George got safely back onboard.

It had been years since Norman had heard from the Kent family in Victoria. His first love, Marjorie, was but a distant memory. One day a letter came from Herbert Kent and it spoke of the last time they had been together. Norman had come to their home in Victoria just after returning from Australia and they had enjoyed a wonderful visit together. Herbert was now 87 years old and living in Victoria. His son Aubrey was also living in the same city.

Norman had always had an interest in parapsychology after having a few ghostly encounters in his life. As a boy he and his brothers used to look out across the river from their house on Assiniboine Avenue. Where there should only have been prairie, there often appeared an image of a fully functional village. What was odd was that it appeared to be a very active Russian village. The homes were completely different than those in Canada and often the Luxton boys would wonder why this strange village would appear. They all saw it and it appeared on many occasions. Then there had been the visit from George Grieves on the *Tilikum*. The final story was to do with a goat hunt that Norman went on with Frank and Howard Sibbald, Tom Lusk, Jim Simpson, and Bill Brewster. Norman had been hunting in the high ridges to the west of Peyto Lake with an Indian by the name of Moses Bear. Norman was just crossing over to another ridge when a rockslide started. As the rocks swept him along, a stranger suddenly appeared and helped him. The stranger then walked back to camp with Norman. Just as Norman spotted the welcoming campfire he turned to the stranger and found him gone. There was no one there. Norman continued into camp only to find everyone in the middle of a wake. Moses had watched Norman be buried under the rock and had returned to camp to tell everyone that Norman had died. The strange man was never seen again. According to Norman, the house he had lived in back in Winnipeg was also haunted. Many believed Norman to be sensitive to these things which is why people and things would materialize in front of him.

George had finally given up the photography game and concentrated just on his gardening columns. He also answered all the gardening questions that readers sent in to the paper. The only excitement lately was that his car had caught on fire. He'd been visiting Ollie and Nellie in St. Paul and on the way home he saw flames coming from under the hood. Pat ran to a nearby house to call the fire department. The car was stopped in the middle of heavy traffic so Ada got out and directed traffic.

Guy had moved to High River after selling the ranch back in the spring of 1947. He was starting to get tired of the ice and snow. He was thinking now of moving south to somewhere like Arizona or California. First he had to attend the reunion of the Montana Cowboys Association down in Great Falls, Montana. That was in June; afterwards he'd see if his old Hollywood agent could find him some work. The agent said there might be work on radio or television down in California.

To his great surprise, Norman received a letter from an old friend by the name of Harry Wilson. Harry and Norman had known each other in Vancouver when one day Norman "popped" over to Victoria for a look-see. That was the last time Harry saw his friend. The next thing he knew he had a letter saying that Norman was going on a sea voyage with a

Captain Voss. He hadn't spoken to Norman since. Harry had moved to San Francisco later in 1901. He married, but in 1902 he suffered a severe stroke and never regained the use of his legs. He found work with Kelly, Douglas & Company where he went on to become the originator of the "Nabob" brand. Norman was glad to have heard from his friend and hoped they would keep in touch.

The CPR contacted Norman in August inquiring about Eleanor. She had been on a leave of absence since December of 1946 and they assumed she had decided not to return. They wanted to close her file and return her pension fund to her. They had forwarded her pension cheque of $298 but to their surprise she returned it in July. Clearly she didn't understand, they were not taking her back after such an extended leave. She expressed interest in returning but they wanted matters closed and would send the money back in care of Norman.

Norman still wrote to Eugene's friend Lulu and told her he planned to end his affiliation with Banff Indian Days on its 60th anniversary. He learned from Lulu that Eugene's wife had suffered a heart attack. Neither of them ever heard from her or Bill anymore.

In September, there was a surprise visit from Guy Weadick and it would have been great except for one small problem—Norman hadn't been home or at the Trading Post. Guy had gone to the house and knocked on the door but found no one at home. He then went to the store but found the place locked up tight. There was no one around, no sign was posted, and the customers waiting outside were wondering why the place was closed. Guy told them maybe Lou and Norman had gone to lunch and to try back later. What Guy didn't know was at that very moment Norman was knocking on a door in High River and finding no one at home. The two men had decided to surprise each other on the same day at the same time!

Norman went off on his annual hunting trip in October but had to cut it short. He'd been out with his friend Alex Green and managed to overdo it in the first 3 days. He was starting to think his hunting days were over. After returning home he continued to have pain, later diagnosed as a double hernia. It meant he had to start wearing a truss. Unfortunately, there wasn't much else to do for the problem.

After the war, Red Cathcart had moved to British Columbia. He was now living in Sayward and reminiscing about his days sitting in Norman's office at the Trading Post. He loved to just sit there and chat. Red suffered from nerve trouble from his years near the front lines but he was starting to recover. The doctors just told him to rest but Red wasn't the type to sit around and do nothing. He dismissed the doctors as a bunch of quacks. He'd also hurt his back overseas while one day lifting a 245-pound. air bottle when he slipped. Norman had always wished he could help his friend and Red now wondered if perhaps Norman could find an old shotgun. Red had a couple of rifles but no gun. He also agreed to let Norman send him a buckskin coat that had been on offer. Oh yeah, and perhaps a pair of moccasins. Red figured he'd better not add anything more to the list or Norman would load his .44 and run him out of the country. Once in a while Red found his way to Victoria and boasted about Norman and the *Tilikum* to anyone he met. He wanted to borrow Norman's book on the voyage as a few friends wanted to read it.

Norman was happy to oblige his good friend and the large parcel arrived in early December. Included in the parcel was an Indian headdress, which was now the talk of the community. Everyone wanted their picture taken wearing it. Red was running the Salmon River Lodge now and planned to put the headdress on display there.

Mary Massecar wrote to tell Norman that she had made amends with her son Earl. The boy had written his mother and begged her to come and visit him in Montreal. She had forgiven him for giving up the priesthood and was waiting to hear from him. Earl and his wife Mercedes had moved into a 4-room suite in a house belonging to Mercedes' cousin. They lived in the district of Ville La Salle, close to the city centre. Earl was now supervisor of operations and programs with his own staff. His ambition now was to write for radio and he had been actively submitting scripts although they'd all been turned down. Earl had two daughters now. Mary was 2½ and Helen was now 1 year old. Both girls were learning French and English. It was still difficult for the older Mary to recover from 12 years of dreams but the grandchildren were adorable and her daughter-in-law was a lovely woman.

Lin Spiller called Norman in early January of 1950. He was the current publisher of the *Crag and Canyon* and was looking to expand. There was high demand now for printing services and Lin was looking to farm some of it out to Calgary. The little paper's circulation was now at 900, up from just 475 in 1944. The problem was that the profits were declining. He was going to drop by the Trading Post and discuss it with Norman.

George wrote in February to say that Nellie had slipped on an icy sidewalk and fell down into an 8-foot ditch. She suffered a dislocated shoulder and it took 2 hours in the hospital to pop it back into place. She had torn ligaments as well but was slowly recovering.

The *Crag and Canyon* was in bad shape and Norman was hoping to find someone else to take it over. He contacted Sid Betts who was now working at the *Edmonton Journal*. Norman was also making plans for a new office for the paper.

In April, Guy Weadick had completed his book on rodeos but his publisher told him it was far too large to consider. Guy was now trying to cut it down but it was hard work. In the meantime he was busy as the Duke and Duchess of Windsor had arrived at their ranch on the 12th. Guy had a lovely visit with them at their house and asked them if they would come to High River to see the new memorial building. Edward and Wallace Simpson agreed and were in good spirits. They were thinking seriously about expanding their ranch activities and perhaps going into commercial beef production. Edward already had a couple of oil companies drilling on his property. They both hoped they could start to spend more time at the ranch. This time they could stay until the middle of May but they were due to sail from New York on May 24. They made their permanent home now in Paris. Edward mentioned to Guy that they had known each other for over 31 years and it was sad to see so many of the old cattlemen gone now. Wallace Simpson was happy to do Guy a favour and dropped into the High River Community Centre to meet some of the local women. The women were surprised and word quickly spread that the Duchess was visiting and a crowd began to gather outside. The couple told Guy they hoped to be back again in September. Guy joked with Norman later, kidding that the Duke and Duchess had not lived in vain as they had met 3 Luxtons in their life.

Norman had gone into the Holy Cross Hospital in Calgary for a hernia operation. He charmed his nurses and even sent his favourite nurse a gift. She was Roberta Kelly and she very much appreciated the gesture but said that Norman was such a lovely man he was a pleasure to have as a patient.

Guy Weadick decided it was time to move south so in June he sold his house in High River. He still wasn't sure what he planned to do but for now he was storing his furniture in Calgary. Florence's doctors had suggested she might do better in a warmer climate. Meanwhile, there had been a huge party in High River to say farewell to the Weadicks. There was a large turnout with folks from High River, Calgary, and the foothills range country. Everyone had donated towards the farewell gift which included a cheque for $10,000, a solid gold cigarette case worth $500, and a lovely wristwatch for Florence worth $100. The engraving on the watch read, "Florence Weadick - A real partner." The cigarette case read:

"His countless Canadian friends and admirers will never forget that Guy Weadick originated and gave to the Province of Alberta, the world-famous Calgary Stampede." Norman was unable to attend but had sent $50 towards the gift. Even after the official party the cheques continued to come in. An additional $2,010 was forwarded to Guy and Florence. There was a scroll made up with all the names of those that donated plus some hand-etched Western and Stampede scenes.

Red was still in B.C. but was hinting strongly that maybe he could help in Norman's store. He'd drop everything if Norman just gave him the word.

At the end of August a letter arrived from George. Nellie had a blood clot and was in critical condition but the clot was now reducing. Eleanor was now in Denver at the Spears Hospital. She was having treatments but in the heat of summer she found them very tiring. She was having difficulty walking again but could get around now without crutches. Eleanor was still in the hospital in October but was cheerful and making lots of friends. Nellie was also still in the hospital and had even been on tube feedings for awhile. She was doing well enough to request that a radio be placed next to her bed for her to listen to. Poor George thought she looked so bad he didn't really think she'd pull through. There was a bright side as Lou and Elsie had come to St. Paul for a visit. They talked about George's last trip to Banff. Norman and George had gone to High River and Fort Macleod for the 70th Anniversary of the RCMP.

Eleanor's doctor at the Spears Hospital sent a letter saying that although Eleanor was improving that he didn't see much change in her paralysis. The latest diagnosis was "arsenical paralysis." Doctor Spears thought it to be the result of Eleanor ingesting some sort of arsenical solution. There was now sensory and motor degeneration. Her American visitor's visa was about to expire but the good doctor would see about having it extended.

On November 10, Eleanor wrote to say she'd booked a flight home on the 30th. She would fly to Calgary and then make her way home. She had been thinking a lot during her stay in hospital. The original plan was to return to Montreal and continue in engineering but it seemed unlikely her health would allow that. It might be better to return to Banff and learn her father's business. She could move back in with them but she wanted them to realize she was an adult and was used to making her own decisions. There was little doubt she had a strong will and temper, these were traits she was well aware of. She was willing to work regular business hours at the Trading Post and salary expectations would need to be discussed. In the meantime she had to return to Montreal to get her things out of storage.

News from St. Paul was that Nellie was still in the hospital and required three nurses but was now able to walk up and down the halls. She was hoping to be home in time for Christmas.

Norman's old friend, Harry Wilson, had been true to his word and continued to write. He had invented a card game he called "On the Nose" about horse racing. He was trying to publish it. As for Norman, he had plans of his own for a far bigger venture.

SEVENTEEN

The Luxton Museum

The old Trading Post had been around now for over 46 years and had done its best to serve as a museum for all of Norman's treasures. The intensive collection of Indian artifacts constituted an important piece of history. Norman worried what would happen to his things after he passed away. He certainly wasn't getting any younger; at the age of 75 how much longer could he really expect to be around?

Early in January of 1951, Norman was sitting in his office at the Trading Post when in walked Eric Harvie. Eric took a seat across from Norman and quietly looked around the room. After some time he looked over at his friend and said, "Norman, what's ever going to happen to all this collection of yours?" Norman didn't answer at first and there was a few seconds silence while he pondered the questioned. At last he looked back at Eric and said," Eric ... I don't know." With that Eric jumped up and said, "Let's build a museum!"

Norman needed no further encouragement. A deal was struck, with Mr. Harvie agreeing to finance the entire project. Eric trusted his friend so the actual job of building and setting up the entire museum would be left to Norman.

Norman had never built on the property adjacent to the Trading Post even though for years he'd thought of building cabins or some sort of retirement home for the older Banff residents. The land had remained empty and so it was chosen as the logical spot.

Norman thought that his Indian treasures deserved no less than a fortress to protect them. The Mounties had their forts and so did the Hudson's Bay Company and now Norman would build his own. A museum built in the style of a fort would easily capture the attention of anyone in Banff looking south across the river. Norman owned a 2-acre parcel of land on which stood his Trading Post but it was decided that it was safer to subdivide the property. The section on which the museum would stand would be registered as a business lot under a new corporation that Norman would set up. The benefit was that the new foundation would now own all the buildings associated with the museum and collection. The new Luxton Foundation would also ensure that the buildings could not be used for anything else other than public benefit.

The building would include a basement where exhibits could be prepared, mounted, and stored. It would also provide living quarters for the taxidermist. The main floor would become the workshop and showroom. The cost was not to exceed $10,000.

In February, a letter from George spoke of a rather bizarre occurrence in Minneapolis. According to the letter, there had been what appeared to be flying saucers hovering over the city for the past 3 years. No one ever paid them any attention anymore and they didn't seem to cause any problem. The General Mills Company had recently agreed to put up the money to investigate. It would turn out later that General Mills had good reason to finance the operation. The mysterious "orbs" were part of "Project Skyhook." A small division of General Mills had been involved in the project since 1947. The project involved the flying of large plastic balloons under contract to the Navy and Air Force. The polyethylene bubbles were filled with hydrogen or helium and could reach altitudes of up to 80,000 feet. That was twice what any aircraft was capable of at the time. These Skyhooks were 100 feet in diameter and travelling at speeds up to 200 miles an hours, could be easily seen from the earth. The problem was that sometimes the Skyhooks went missing and General Mills could only track them by reported sightings of UFO's in the area. So much for George's chance of any alien encounter!

The only thing alien to Norman was how exactly to build a museum. In March, Norman wrote a long letter to the Museum of the American Indian in New York. They thought all his plans sounded fine except for their concerns about fire when building a wooden structure. They could also offer to exchange some of their artifacts with Norman if he was interested. They wondered what he had to offer for a Crow medicine bag and its contents.

Red had sent Norman a letter saying he was very sick with the flu. Since there wasn't a hospital within 52 miles he was doing his best to recover at home. As he read Norman's letters about the new museum he wished he could be there to help.

Guy Weadick arrived back in High River in April after a 14,000-mile trip crossing America from coast to coast. He had learned all about the Indian tribes in Arizona where there were 15 reservations. Just in that one state there were the Navajos, Apache, Hopi, Zuin, Papago, and several others. He was back in High River for the dedication of a park in memory of George Lane. Lane had donated the property. Guy would be staying at the Riverside Motel until May 8 and then would be off to visit the old Stampede Ranch and meet Allen Baker who was the new owner of the Bar U ranch. He was hoping Norman could make it to the park dedication. Guy was also hoping to convince Norman to take a few weeks in the winter and come down to Arizona with him.

The *Crag and Canyon* had been running quite smoothly under the watchful eye of a man named Lin Spiller. Unfortunately the conditions at the office were very poor and the place was in dire need of some renovation. Lin didn't want Norman spending a lot of money to fix up the place, as the rent he paid Norman would not cover any extra costs. The paper was really too big for just Lin and his wife Madge to run and Lin's health was suffering under the strain. Madge remembered when they had taken over the *Crag and Canyon* that everyone had said they wouldn't get along with Norman. Madge had never understood the warning as she very much enjoyed the friendship she had with Norman. She knew he would understand that she and Lin might have to leave the paper. For the time being they would carry on as best they could.

Harry Wilson wrote from Vancouver to say that the *Vancouver Sun* had just run a feature article entitled "Around the World in a Dugout." It was Norman's story but Harry took offence with the article that said Norman was inexperienced in a canoe. As far as Harry was concerned, there was no one with more canoe experience. He had sent the paper a rather nasty letter saying that perhaps before they published the article from Voss's book that they should have called Norman and verified the information. Harry was still trying to find a publisher for his card game but so far was having no luck.

The Spillers gave Norman their final lease cheque in June for the *Crag and Canyon*. They had no immediate plans but Lin's health had just made it too difficult to continue. Norman found a buyer for the paper and after many years of leasing the publication, it was time to let it go. He wrote an editorial to say goodbye and thank-you to all his subscribers. The story said that the current management was leaving as of July 1, 1951. Norman had sold the goodwill, equipment, and the newspaper but he would still be owner of the building and property. Although Norman had not actively worked on the paper for the past 25 years he had always been behind the scenes. Just to help the new owners with a smooth transition, Madge had agreed to stay on briefly as newswriter. The new owner would be Mr. William I. Clarke of Calgary. Bill had considerable experience and had been running a weekly newspaper up in Leduc.

The telegram from Guy Weadick arrived August 9, 1951. Florence Weadick had died just that morning. She had suffered a heart attack in July but was recovering and had been told she'd be out in 3-4 weeks. Her condition improved to the point that she told Guy to head south as he was working on plans to develop the old cattle train between Fort Benton in Montana and Fort Macleod. Just as he was packing to go he got the call that she had died. Florence was buried next to her father in the High River Cemetery. Guy was devastated but decided to return to Phoenix.

The bad news continued when just 7 days later a letter arrived from Pat. She had been visiting Victoria over the summer and had gone to see Ollie Ormond. It had been a long time since Ollie had written and Norman wondered what had happened to his friend. According to Pat, Ollie's wife Mary had passed away the previous January. Ollie seemed very lonely in his large house all by himself. Ollie told her his nieces and nephews took good care of him. He had tried to write Norman for a long time and had started many letters but never finished any of them. He just didn't know what to say. The last time Pat had visited she had noticed Ollie was limping but he assured her it was due to him having fallen out of a cherry tree that afternoon. To prove his point he gave Pat a bag of cherries to take with her. Pat tried to talk Ollie into coming with her to Banff but he said there wasn't enough time to get ready. The only other news Pat had was that her aunt Ollie had fallen over a fence and cut her leg quite badly.

Work at the new museum was now underway. Logs were hauled down from the Cascade Valley and construction had begun. There was some 1,400 square feet of floor space to start, with room for expansion. The architects Wallbridge & Imrie of Calgary were hired for the job. All the lumber was purchased from the Timber Building Company of Calgary. The architects submitted their plans and by September of 1951 things were progressing nicely. Eric Harvie had not been in touch with Norman since July but the money was always there whenever Norman needed it. By early October the weather took a turn for the worse and construction slowed while they fought with the rain and unseasonable snow. The fireproof vault was already in place where the collections were stored.

At the end of the month a letter came from Guy Weadick. He had received Norman's letter and was excited to hear all about the museum. Guy's furniture had finally been shipped down from Calgary and most of it fit in the new house. He was very lonely now with Florence gone but he was trying to concentrate on his writing. He was still trying to complete his history of rodeos and stampedes. Guy's main concern was that Norman took care of his health because nothing else really mattered. He said, "You can't take it with you and being the biggest man in the cemetery don't mean a thing." Guy still hoped that somehow Norman could come down for a visit. The days weren't too bad but being alone at night bothered Guy. He missed Florence so much and it seemed he missed her more each day. She had been a true partner. Had she lived until November 17, they would have celebrated their 45th wedding anniversary. In all those years, because they worked and lived together he said they had only been apart for a few hours. Their amazing partnership was broken so abruptly and came so unexpectedly that Guy feared the scar would never heal.

A suitable name for the new museum had been discussed, with Norman's suggestions repeatedly turned down by Eric Harvie. A temporary sign had been erected outside the museum while under construction which simply read, "Free Museum-Indian Relics." Norman didn't care if his name was on the museum at all but Eric insisted and the new building was officially named the Luxton Museum. It would take just over a year and a half to complete the initial phase of the museum; at least to the extent it was ready for the public. During that time Norman acquired artifacts, prepared displays, and did research. He set out to purchase any books that would assist him in ensuring accuracy on the various descriptions he wrote up on the displays. The books would later become part of the museum library.

Although Norman had a large collection of Indian artifacts, many more would be needed. Forms were drawn up that would allow him to transfer artifacts from other museums and private collections on loan or as permanent donations. With forms in hand, it was time to start putting together the collection. Norman pulled out his feather headdress that had been given to him by Jonas Rider of Morley when he was made honorary chief of the Stoneys. The headdress was as long as a man is tall and included hundreds of feathers. For many years, it had been hidden away in the Curio Shop's vault. Along with the headdress, Norman had a large collection of Indian clothes and additional clothing was acquired from Mrs. Mary Warren, the widow of Dr. Schaeffer of Philadelphia. The McDougalls donated David's Irish elk horns and skull. What made these horns so special is that they had a 10-foot spread. Native Eskimo art was also obtained from Phillip H. Godsell, a fellow of the Royal Geographical Society, a collection containing over 300 pieces of Eskimo works. A gallery of pictures of some of the most famous local Indians was also assembled. One included the portrait of Sarah Two-Young-Men who was famous for having successfully removed her husband's appendix which saved his life.

In January of 1952, Norman wrote Guy a letter. He had very much wanted to come to Phoenix but Georgie wasn't well. Guy wasn't feeling much better and said his heart wasn't what it should be. The death of Florence had taken its toll and Guy preferred to hide away rather than go out and mix with people. He never drove after dark now anyway and the nights were the toughest on him. He missed the West and all the old-timers back in Alberta. He had no objective to strive for and nothing interested him anymore. Guy wasn't religious and didn't really know what happens when you die. He wasn't afraid to go when the time came because he always tried to be a fair and honest man. He had never knowingly hurt anyone and never would. Guy was thinking it might be time to sell the place in Phoenix. There was one thing he knew for sure and that was he would come back to Alberta. When his time came, he would be buried next to his beloved Florence in High River. It had been her wish to be buried close to the hills they both loved.

A few Canadian friends had dropped in to pay a visit to Guy in April and found his spirits somewhat improved. Many friends had called him and he was planning to come up for the Calgary Stampede in June. John Burns and his wife had come down during the winter and invited him up. Guy also had his brother Tom in San Clemente, California, who promised to stop by on his way to Wyoming.

Eleanor had decided it was time to write a book on her family but instead of working on her father's biography she chose instead to write about her grandmother, Annie McDougall. It would be an enormous amount of work with the final manuscript coming in at somewhere near 500 pages.

With the collection of artifacts increasing it was necessary to have safe storage facilities until the museum was ready. Norman found a place in Calgary and his collection filled four large vaults. It was time to find some additional help and Norman wrote to Red Cathcart in August. Red wanted to help but he had his work at the lodge for the rest of the summer. He hoped he could leave for Banff in the fall, he was most eager to help.

Lin and Madge Spiller had settled in West Vancouver and Lin's health had already improved. He landed a job at the *Vancouver Province* on the night shift. He would be home at 5:30 am and then Madge and Lin would go for a nice walk on the beach, have a swim, and then a rest. Madge was retired from the newspaper business and now was at home and feeling very domesticated.

George had been up to Banff for his annual visit and was very much impressed with the museum. In October, the two sisters Nellie and Ollie had built themselves a cute little house in Iowa. They seemed to be doing very well. Pat had a new parakeet named "Timmie" who could say over 60 different things and kept them all amused.

In January of 1953, work continued at the museum and Norman had hired his friend Jack Mitchell for taxidermy work. Norman was busy sorting, classifying, and labelling all the various beadwork that would be on display. The hours were long and Norman's health was not so good. He went for an electrocardiogram at the Calgary Associated Clinic. His doctor, Dr. E.P. Scarlett, told him he looked fine and that his problems were likely due to nervous tension. The shortness of breath was just due to Norman's age and the general wear and tear on his body over the years. He was, after all, 77 years old.

Norman still had not heard from Ollie in Victoria but he received word from a rather unlikely source. Her name was Lillian Horton and she had been a young girl when Norman left Victoria. Lillian had known Ollie and Mary Ormond and was still in touch with Ollie. After Mary died, Ollie had remarried but the woman was only 55. Ollie would be 83 on his next birthday and Lillian couldn't imagine why Ollie had married the woman. They didn't even live together which she thought very odd and Ollie was certain his new wife was seeing other men. He seemed obsessed and Lillian and all his friends were worried about him. She knew Norman couldn't do anything for his old friend but she thought he would want to know.

Red was still in B.C. but now at the Timber Valley Ranch in West Bridge. He had received a nice book on the Calgary Stampede from Norman at Christmas. It was interesting to read about the people he'd met like Colonel James Walker. Red really wanted to come and help with the museum but he had been sick over the winter and was not well enough to come. He was looking to buy some new land in B.C. and found 185 acres with a river bordering one side, a log house, log barn, henhouse, and root cellar. They were asking $3,500 and would hold the deal until spring. He was still debating on whether to come to Banff and was glad to hear that Charlie Biel was doing some work for the museum. Red remembered the many hours he spent helping Charlie; he had even helped him pour his very first bronze. Charlie had always promised to make Red a bronze packhorse but had never got around to it. If nothing else, Red would make sure he came to the museum's grand opening and wanted to know the date. Red had his own little museum of things he'd collected over the years. There were guns, swords, woodcarvings, pewter, and war souvenirs. One of his most cherished was the framed page of Norman's *Liberty* magazine profile. He also had a picture of Norman and John Hunter that had been in an old calendar. He even had a 9-foot totem pole from the Nootka tribe.

Norman decided that he wanted a couple of very specific things for his museum, one of which was a birch bark canoe. The problem was that these canoes were very rare and almost impossible to find. The word went out but some time passed and the news was disappointing. Several people told him to give up the idea of the canoe but Norman refused. One day the mail brought a rather surprising letter from a man named James G. McCrea of Toronto. He had heard of the search for a birch bark canoe and just happened to have a friend that had one. He said that he hadn't seen it for years but he would see what he could do for Norman. The canoe was soon found in a boathouse in Barrie, Ontario and belonged to a Harold F. Crang. Upon hearing of Norman's plight, Harold decided to donate the canoe to the new Luxton museum. The authentic birch bark canoe, made by the Chippewa Indians of Central Canada, was then loaded on a CPR freight car and shipped off to Banff on June 19, 1953. Norman was astonished at the pristine condition of the canoe. Except for the fact a little resin was needed it was in perfect condition. Harold even sent along the recipe for a special resin to be used on birch bark canoes. It was a mixture of spruce gum, beeswax, and lard.

The other display that was a necessity as far as Norman was concerned was an authentic Indian teepee. David Crowchild of the Sarcees came to the rescue and donated a 19th-century vintage teepee.

Near the B.C. coast in the town of Hope there lived a retired school teacher by the name of Mrs. Isabel Maxwell who had been collecting Indian baskets her entire life. Many had been acquired when she taught English to the many outlying Indian tribes of British Columbia. It was thought that this collection of baskets would make a fine addition to the museum so she was approached to see if she might consider selling her collection. Along with her baskets, she had some excellent bead work from the Sioux Indians. Mrs. Maxwell's collection was purchased in its entirety at the cost of $700. The collection included over 200 baskets and was soon on its way to the Luxton Museum.

At last everything was ready. Red Cathcart had finally decided to come to Banff and had assisted Norman in labeling all the exhibits. Of those exhibits, Norman was most proud of his whooping crane specimen. The crane had been in his possession since his childhood. He and his friend

Ashley Hines had found it one day just north of Winnipeg. Now it was mounted and displayed in a glass case for everyone to enjoy. Another specimen, a pigeon, Norman had shot when he was a young boy in Winnipeg.

Perhaps the most impressive feature of the museum was the amazing diorama built by Charlie Biel. The 3-D display portrayed Indians driving the buffalo over a cliff. By looking at the piece you could imagine the cries of the Indians as they led the thundering buffalo over the cliff. Indians near the bottom of the cliff sat quietly with their bows and arrows poised to kill the buffalo that did not die from the fall. The final cost of the diorama was $3,500 but it had been hard work and it was magnificent. A recess was built on the north wall to hold the display.

Near the end of June, a surprise visitor arrived at the Trading Post. Tanned, healthy, and looking full of mischief, the visitor saw Norman out in front of the store and jumped in front of his him. Grabbing his old friend he then administered a big hug. It was Ollie Ormond and he'd come to see Norman. They had a nice visit and Ollie told Norman all about his life up to date. He didn't get a chance to see Georgie that day but sent her a bouquet of flowers to say hello. He and Norman had a wonderful day in Banff and Ollie promised to write. He also wanted Eleanor's address so he could drop her a line as well.

A letter from Lulu in July advised Norman that Mrs. LaPorte, Eugene's wife, had died and that her son Bill was now living in Florida.

There were many visitors in the museum now although it wasn't officially open yet. In August there was another surprise visitor that was perhaps not an old friend like Ollie but much more of a treat to the eyes. Her name was Marilyn Monroe. The film star was in Banff making her latest movie and she was interested in seeing Norman's museum. Naturally, Norman was more than happy to give the lovely lady a private tour. It was a Sunday afternoon and Norman's accountant, J.F. Abercrombie, had come up to the museum to discuss bookkeeping matters with Norman. As he walked into the Luxton museum he saw Norman showing Marilyn around and thought he would never be forgiven if he interrupted them. Quietly he turned around, left the building, and drove back to his office in Calgary. Norman didn't know Abercrombie had been there until he received a letter just over a week later.

That summer over 25,000 people visited the Luxton Museum. It was far from complete and the next display that Norman set to work on was of a dog toboggan scene. Norman was still searching for an authentic

Red River Cart. Eventually a cart was found at the Hudson's Bay Store in Calgary and they agreed to let Norman have it. The cart wasn't entirely accurate from a historical standpoint as the wheel appeared to have been made by a wheelwright rather than finished with an axe and knife. The axle pin was iron and there was also an iron tire held on by rawhide. The original carts had no iron and were made entirely of wood.

Eleanor had returned to Montreal and was offered a professorship at McGill University. Her health seemed to be good and she was enjoying life down east. Ollie and Mary were doing well in Iowa and, for a change, everyone seemed to be healthy and doing great. Guy Weadick had sold his place and moved to California and was in Los Angeles taping radio broadcasts on famous Western personalities. He had remarried an old friend named Dolly who was a great girl although she didn't understand Guy like Florence did. Guy officially owned nothing but his burial plot in High River but was happier and taking an interest in life again.

A letter from Guy dated November 13, 1953, had been so upbeat that Norman was not prepared for what happened next. On December 15, Guy Weadick died. His brother Tom notified friends and family but it was never too clear what it was that had caused the untimely death. It seemed that he had finally had something to look forward to. There were rumours that his marriage to Dolly had been difficult and that they separated in October but Guy's letters never indicated anything of the sort. His body was returned to High River as he had requested, and was buried with Florence. Over 500 people attended the funeral and, in the cowboy tradition, his boots were placed in backwards in the stirrups of his horse. The horse's bridle had been a gift from the Prince of Wales, and the saddle was a wedding gift from the Big Four of the original Calgary Stampede.

In February of 1954, the Luxton Museum had its first official list of directors and officers. The directors were Eric Harvie, Norman Luxton, Donald S. Harvie, John Gorman, and J.R. Fish. Eric Harvie served as chairman of the board, Norman as president and managing director, and John F. Abercrombie as secretary-treasurer.

Norman continued to work on his dogsled exhibit and the toboggan, harness, and dog saddles were nearly complete. The saddles arrived in April and came all the way from Fort Liard where a native had completed a set of six. Even though Norman's display had only four dogs the man thought that was silly and refused to send less than the proper amount for a dog team.

Over the years, Norman had acquired friends around the world and one of those was Ernie A. Kehr, editor of the *New York Herald Tribune*. He had offered to write up a piece on Norman's museum as a feature for the paper. Norman loved hearing from Ernie as he always had an interesting story to tell. This time Ernie told him that after 3 years of fighting the American Postal Service and the government, they had finally agreed—with over a million signatures on the petition, to put the words "In God We Trust" onto the American stamp. The first stamp would be an 8¢ stamp in red, white, and blue. Ernie was invited to the ceremony and was introduced to President Eisenhower, Richard Nixon, and John F. Dulles. The ceremony was broadcast nationwide on television and radio. Ernie had organized the "Stamps for the World" campaign during World War Two. Ernie also told Norman that it seemed Broadway must be doing some sort of salute to the Rockies at the moment as they were currently running the films *Saskatchewan*, *Rose Marie*, and *River of No Return*.

Eleanor was still at McGill University teaching English and Engineering. Pat was in St. Paul but looking forward to visiting her Uncle's museum. It wouldn't be this summer though, as Pat and her mother had planned a trip out to San Francisco. They would then make their way to Seattle and Victoria. Did Norman know that Aunt Ollie was now suffering from severe headaches and was off to the Mayo Clinic in Rochester? George would be leaving for Banff on August 5, and would hopefully bring back lots of news about the museum.

After a 20-year silence, Norman received another letter from Caldicott School in England. The teepee he had sent them over 20 years before was now worn out. Norman quickly arranged for a new one at their request. Although they could only afford a second-hand teepee, Norman had a brand-new one made and covered the difference in cost himself.

At the Luxton Museum, the parking issue was the next thing on the agenda. To make it as inexpensive as possible, there would be no cement dividers but there would be wheel bumpers to stop people from driving onto the grass. The plan was also to plant a few trees between the cars and the walls of the museum. Signs had to be purchased to read "Museum parking only." There would only be two dedicated parking stalls, one for Norman and one for Red Cathcart.

September brought a letter from George that was full of thanks for yet another wonderful holiday in Banff. When George returned he found that his sister Ollie had suffered a stroke and had been found unconscious in bed one morning. She was sent to the hospital but luckily there was no paralysis. Still it looked like the two sisters might have to sell their house. Pat had enjoyed her trip to Victoria and she saw the *Tilikum* as her taxi passed right by it when they arrived.

Eric Harvie kept in touch with Norman and in October got all the updates about the museum while having lunch with Charlie Biel. Charlie told him that he was hard at work on the diorama and hoped to have it finished by Christmas. George Brown was working on a nice case to hold the whooping crane and would donate the case as his gift to the museum.

Norman celebrated his 76th birthday in November and received several greeting cards. Pat told him more about her crazy parakeet "Timmie." The bird ate toast, drank coffee, and liked to look in the mirror and talk to himself. Just a few days earlier Timmie had looked at himself and said, "You're impossible!" Sometimes he looked at himself and said, "Are you a bird?" Pat didn't quite know where he picked these sayings up but he always kept her laughing.

Eleanor was trying to get a truss belt for her Dad as his double hernia still caused problems. She had also found a beautiful jade ring and since Georgie loved jade, Eleanor wondered if she should buy it as a gift from Norman and herself.

More birthday wishes came from Harry Wilson in Vancouver who still wrote regularly. He wondered why Norman never complained about his health and questioned if Norman ever got sick. As for Harry he said he hadn't been sick a day in his life since his stroke back in 1901. He attributed this to his diet. He lived on Chinese Oolong tea (no milk or sugar), fish, oysters, eggs, and peanut butter. He said that his doctor told him his blood pressure was that of a 25-year-old. Perhaps it was also because he never ate pork, black tea, or coffee. Either way he had never had so much as a cold in all those years. Harry had grown up in Winnipeg and remembered stories from their childhood. He remembered Harry Luxton the most. Norman's brother had been quite a fat little boy back in 1894, and used to frequent the little fruit store owned by Harry Wilson's uncle. Harry Luxton and his friend Conklin would come into the store and have contests on which one of them could eat the most bananas. Whoever quit first had to pay for all the bananas the two of them had eaten. Conklin always got stuck paying as he could never eat more than Harry. Harry used to eat an extra banana just to prove his ability. He was a happy-go-lucky kid and it was hard not to like him.

At the end of the month, Norman was appointed as president of the Old Timers Association. In December a decision had to be made regarding the old McDougall church at Morley. Plans were made to demolish all buildings from the Morleyville settlement area including the old church. Some of the local old-timers wanted to save the church and volunteered to paint it but it needed to be restored not just repainted. Mr. J.R. Fish asked Norman if the church was worth preserving. Norman could hardly give an unbiased answer. It was in this very church that he had married Georgie. Norman wanted the church saved. The mission was all that remained in Morley of the McDougall legacy. Norman soon got Eric Harvie on board and the mission was saved. An entrance to the site was designed and it was decided to have a bible quotation on the sign. They picked Proverbs, Chapter 22, Verse 28: "Remove not the ancient land mark which thy fathers have set."

January brought the usual pile of cards and letters. Pat had been trying to teach Timmie to say "Merry Christmas" and on Christmas Day the family tried their best to get the bird to say it. Timmie refused but he had a little trick up his wing. The following day as they gathered for breakfast he looked over at the family and said, "Nuts to you and Merry Christmas!" The family howled with laughter. They all agreed he was a rascal but what could you do?

Though it was Ollie who suffered the stroke it was Nellie who was getting worse. Nellie was in fair health and tried to walk around the house a little every day but was soon exhausted. Ollie was having bad headaches but her daughter Mary helped them both as much as she could. The sisters were now back in their little house in Iowa.

At last the toboggan for the dogsled was complete and shipped out in February of 1955. The museum building, with the latest addition, was complete and the official grand opening was held on May 21, 1955. The *Calgary Herald* sent a reporter to cover the event and he was most impressed. The reporter considered the new museum to be one of the finest Indian and natural history displays on the continent. This was only Phase I of the Luxton Museum but plans were already completed for Phase II and expansion was soon underway. By the end of June, 1955, the Luxton Museum had already received over 3,000 visitors. Norman's plans for the addition were sure to impress any visitor lucky enough to stumble onto the museum. The extension would be added on the east side of the current site. The plan was to recreate the daily events in the life of a Plains Indian.

The Calgary Stampede Board approached Norman that month because they wanted to award Charlie Biel with a special honour. Charlie had made the trophies for the Calgary Stampede for years and they had ordered him to make a bronze chuck wagon trophy. What Charlie didn't know is that the trophy he was working on was actually going to be awarded to himself. Since Norman had been an associate director of the Stampede for many years and was such a close friend of Charlie's he was asked to present the trophy at that year's Calgary Stampede. Norman usually was onstage at the grandstand show handing out the Indian trophies anyway so Charlie wouldn't suspect anything. That year Norman was also elected to be on the Calgary Stampede Entertainment Committee.

Norman had sent the newspapers regarding the museum's grand opening to friends and relatives. George wrote in June to say just how very proud he was of his brother and that it was a wonderful thing to leave a part of history behind for people to enjoy. Harry Wilson never quite figured out how Norman had the time to run a business, build and operate a museum, and still work with the Stampede. Pat was jealous that her mom and dad would be off to see Norman again in July but it didn't look like she could make it out that summer. Nellie had been moved to a nursing home near Pat's office so Pat was able to visit every Thursday.

In August, the City of Calgary was throwing a reception in honour of the old Alberta pioneers. The awards ceremony would be held at the Palliser Hotel on September 6. The Prime Minister would be there to make the presentation of two scrolls in honour of Alberta's Golden Jubilee. One scroll would be presented to a pioneer man and the other to a pioneer woman. Norman was chosen to represent the pioneer man of Alberta and would be accepting the scroll.

George and Ada returned home in September with wonderful stories of Banff. Ada loved her thrilling ride up the chairlift and Eleanor was home so they all had a wonderful visit. Pat had enjoyed her time in St. Paul and her aunt Ollie had stayed with her while the folks were away. In October the sisters had sold the house in Iowa as Nellie was now in a nursing home and Ollie was planning on getting an apartment in St. Paul.

Harry Wilson wrote birthday greetings to Norman in November and announced that he'd moved into the Hotel Dobson in Vancouver. There was a café right across the street, which was handy, but the hotel was a little on the cold side. They only turned the heat on for 1 hour in the morning and 1 hour at night. Still it was across from the best seafood restaurant in Vancouver so it would do okay. Harry had a little Chinese house-boy now to take care of him. He had been friends with the boy's father for 15 years. The boy's name was Gin and he was a good kid.

Red Cathcart had gone down east for the winter and was in Montreal in January of 1956. A letter came from his wife saying that Red was ill.

He was in the hospital having x-rays but so far they could find nothing wrong. Still Red was in good spirits and they hoped it wasn't anything serious.

Later that month Red wrote a letter to Norman. The doctors still didn't know what was wrong but Red was having really severe headaches. He'd never had a drink in his life so that certainly wasn't the cause. Even the sound of a TV in the same ward bothered him. The reason he'd gone to Montreal in the first place was on the advice of his Banff doctor. Eleanor was living in Montreal so had met Red and his wife at the train station, taken them to breakfast, and then on to the room she had reserved for them. Red had then checked into the hospital for tests. He was in so much pain that at times he could hardly see.

Ollie Ormond was writing letters again and still working at the biscuit factory. They were negotiating for a new plant in Edmonton that currently was known as "Sunland." Now that Ollie was free to travel he had gone down to California the previous year and spent two winters in Arizona and Mexico. He'd moved to 1391 William Street in Vancouver so Norman could write to him there.

Red wrote again at the end of January and was now convinced he was just the new hospital guinea pig. He'd had every test in the book and still they found nothing wrong. The headaches were still there. He was happy that Norman gave him updates on the museum. Weren't they both so lucky to have Eric Harvie as a friend? Red had two men he considered his greatest friends and they were Eric and Norman.

On January 30, another letter from Red said that he was now in a private ward which was quieter and very much nicer. Now the headaches would come and go so he had some relief. The doctors had ruled out cancer but the headaches were still bad enough to cause Red to pass out. Luckily, since he'd been admitted to the hospital, he'd only passed out once, perhaps because he had no heavy lifting to do and very little activity. His wife Eunice came up to visit twice a day.

Red checked out of the hospital on February 2, with nothing more than a slight headache. He was still light-headed but was well enough to enjoy a nice dinner out with Eleanor.

The Jacques were still leasing the funeral home from Norman and were looking to expand. The government had offered other properties but none were suitable to expand the funeral home. Though Norman had repeatedly turned down offers to purchase his land next to the current funeral home he knew that there was no other logical place. He offered to sell the land to the Jacques for $6,000 although he had turned down $10,000 from another developer. The town needed a proper funeral home and it was something he could do for the citizens of Banff.

Red left Montreal on February 12, and boarded the train for his trip back to Banff. The train had barely left the city when Red became very ill. He got off in Ottawa and sat in the station until he felt well enough to call a taxi. He had friends in Ottawa and they offered to let him stay for a while. The man he would stay with had been his old company commander and a close buddy during World War Two. They had landed in Normandy on D-Day together and remained together until after ceasefire. His friend was a major now and still in the army. When he got to their house they put him straight to bed where he remained until noon the following day. Luckily the lady of the house was a nurse so he was in good hands. Eleanor took the train from Montreal to check in on Red and make sure he was okay.

Red knew there was a lot of work to be done at the museum and he felt awful leaving Norman in such a bind. He didn't want Norman to disown him and promised to be home just as soon as he could.

That April there was word from George that he had been asked to write a gardening book. For years George had written the gardening column for the paper and was now at work on a book. He figured it would come in at around 300 pages. With luck, it would be published in December of 1956. The asking price would be around $4. Luckily, George had no cash invested in the venture so the publisher would take on all the risks, costs, and promotion. George would have to visit bookstores for a few hours a day to greet people and autograph their books. George felt a bit foolish just sitting there writing his autograph but this might be a way for him to leave something behind for Ada and Pat. He would get royalties from the book which would help the family if he were to pass away in the next couple of years. He hoped the book would sell a few copies and his royalties would be 10% on the first edition and 15% on the second. The publisher would be the University Press.

Less than 2 weeks later George's appendix ruptured and he was rushed to the hospital. They operated immediately. He had suffered pains that Tuesday morning but the doctor thought it was just tension. When the pain got worse the doctor was called back later that same afternoon. It was obvious George was ill and by 6:30 pm that evening, he'd already undergone surgery. The doctor found a big mess in the abdominal cavity, which had to be repaired. Pat didn't realize just how popular her father was until the get-well cards started to pour in. Within 3 days, George had received 387 get-well cards, not to mention all the bouquets of flowers. His daughter, Pat, also mentioned that Ollie got $14,000 for her house and now was renting a small apartment near Nellie in St. Paul.

On April 28, Norman received a call. His friend Harry Wilson had died that morning. There was no cause given and the man had been in great health. It came as quite a shock.

Ernie Kehr had written again with yet more tales of adventure. He had visited Pakistan the previous summer and met Prince Musad of Saudi Arabia. Ernie had been staying at the house of Pakistan's prime minister and the prince was the other guest. Prince Musad gave Ernie a personal invitation to visit him in Saudi Arabia. At the time it was very difficult for newsmen to enter Pakistan so Ernie took advantage of the invitation. He planned to spend the coming June there and visit Yemen, Aden, Ethiopia, Sudan, and Egypt.

Ernie wrote again on October 14, to say he was happy to hear that Norman's museum expansion was coming along well. Ernie had been with Franklin D. Roosevelt the day before and had indulged in a little debate with him. He'd been up in Providence for a luncheon with Roosevelt, Gov. Roberts, and Senator Kennedy. He said the Kennedy boy had almost got the Vice-Presidential nomination at the Chicago Convention. The lunch had been good fun.

George's book came out the end of October. He had called it *Flower Growing in the North - A Month by Month Guide*. He had dedicated it to his wife Ada. On the cover was a silhouette of his grandmother. She was the one who got him interested in gardening back on the farm when they were kids. Many of her gardening hints were in the book as they had been in his gardening column. He had written his column "Grandma Said" from 1905-1956. The book was now out in a department store in Minneapolis and St. Paul so he was already busy with book signings. He'd send Norman and Lou a copy just as soon as he could. The other exciting news was that the book was not only published in America but also Great Britain, India, and Pakistan. George was now retired but he continued as garden editor. He was glad to hear that Eleanor was working on a book and she was to send him a copy as soon as it was published. Her book was on the life of her grandmother, Annie McDougall.

Eleanor had chosen to write about her grandmother Annie because in her opinion Annie was perhaps one of the greatest women to have ever lived, certainly in the early Canadian West. She decided that Annie's story should be written and published. For years, she had listened to the wonderful stories that Annie told and decided it was time to write them down. Although she had only just started the book, she let her father read it as she went along. Norman was very impressed by what he read and felt the book would be a huge success. Norman also enjoyed the stories of David McDougall, his father-in-law. Norman loved the old man and enjoyed their many hunting trips together in the early days. David was a great hunter and had never missed a shot.

Lou was still going strong even with his various aches and pains. All the Luxton boys were getting on in years now. Norman still worked hard but no longer did any heavy lifting. Even snow shovelling just about killed him but he still did it. Norman still loved driving his car and found it quite relaxing.

With another year winding down Norman found himself reminiscing. One of his favourite memories of Banff was the rainy evenings he used to sit next to the log fire in the King Edward Hotel and talk to tourists from around the world. He remembered those early days at the Lux Theatre and the old player piano he'd bought after it opened. The piano hadn't been used for years and was now in the home of Pearl and Hal Lambert of Golden, B.C. for safekeeping. It had been badly abused over the years but they were going to try to restore it. He remembered how when Voss finally did reach England back in 1903 that Voss had sent him a letter asking if Norman could arrange for him to get back to Canada. Norman had spoken with a Sir William to arrange the passage. Voss crossed Canada by train but though the train went through Banff, Voss didn't even stop off to say hello. Norman never got a thank you and never heard from Voss again.

With the pending arrival of 1957, there was a lot of work still to be done at the museum. It was time to work on the mannequins representing the Indians of the plains. Now just how did one person go about building an exact replica of a Plains Indian? The standard store mannequin was hardly suitable. Norman thought it over until the answer became obvious. He would have to build each Indian figure from scratch with the actual faces based on some of his Stoney friends from Morley. After researching possible artists who might consider such a project he was given the name of Ron Spickett. Ron was a talented art student from Ontario but was currently living in Mexico on an art scholarship. Could Norman convince him to come to Banff and recreate the life of the Plains Indian? The letter-writing campaign began and soon Norman had Ron excited about the idea. Ron had many ideas of just how such a display could be accomplished.

To create a full-size Indian figure one would need to make it light weight yet durable. It would be an experiment at first but after the first few were done and the best method found, it should be quite easy. Ron's idea was to use a type of dental cement, which was very hard but gave a beautiful finish. Each figure would take an estimated 1-3 weeks to complete. Ron needed Norman to draw up colour sketches of exactly what he wanted. The drawings must include the Indian figures and how they were to be grouped in their settings. What made the figures even more difficult is that they didn't just have to simply stand but had to be in action poses—everything from seated figures cooking over a stove to hunters and dancers. Norman was adamant that every scene must be as realistic as possible. It was felt that this would make the museum an even more popular attraction. Ron agreed to come and they would work on one group or setting at a time. He was due to arrive in January of 1957. Of course he had a wife and family so he left it up to Norman to find them a suitable house to rent.

Ron arrived and serious work began. A combination of materials would be used including plaster and papier mâché. Ron also had hoped for a painted background but the look of the logs was kept instead of plastering and painted murals. Ron also wanted an assistant that could do the "legwork" such as rough painting and running errands. As they began their work, they still threw out ideas about possible settings. Norman had thought seriously about a setting showing the arrival of the white man. He listed the early missionaries that might be suitable to include such as Robert Terrill Rundle, Pierre Jean de Smet, and John McDougall. While work continued another collection was added to the original display area. This was a collection of owls that had belonged to Marcel Houle. The collection included a great grey owl ($35), barred owl ($35), screech owl ($33), Richardsons owl ($27), hawk owl ($10), snowy owl ($12), short-eared owl ($10) and a sawhet owl ($10). They were placed just inside the showroom on the north wall.

Ollie Ormond wrote in March to say that he was still living in Vancouver and had been laid up for 3 weeks with viral pneumonia. He was very much hoping to get out to Banff again that summer.

The old McDougall church was in the process of being restored. That year the restoration committee had cleaned all the pencil marks from the walls, cleaned the floors, and completed most of the renovations. The pews were donated from a church in Calgary. The executive restoration committee included L.L. Gaetz, George Thorson, and Archibald Johnstone. Twice a year they held a service at the church and the next one was going to be on Sunday, May 26. They hoped Norman could manage to come and check it out.

Norman was still Associate Director for the Calgary Stampede but he really wanted to get out of the judging. He was so busy with the museum now but after all his years with the Stampede they agreed to make Norman more of an Honorary Director. His name would appear but he didn't have to do anything if he wasn't up to it.

That June a letter arrived announcing the death of Robert LaPorte. He had died back on March 13, his wife said he'd been very ill for 2 years. He had never mentioned it to Norman. It seems Robert had been married to Mary Clark back in 1899 and had been in the automobile and tire business with his brother Eugene. He had been an avid traveller and had met Pope Leo XIII back in 1903. He later became a judge and had two children, Molly Lu and George Clark. His grandson, Robert, had died on the bombing mission over Tokyo in World War Two.

By early July of 1957, the young Mr. Spickett received a rather lucrative offer to as an art teacher at an art college in Regina. He had actually refused the appointment once and decided to work with Luxton instead. The problem was that once his work at the museum was done there would not be enough maintenance work to keep him employed full-time. He agreed to stay but Norman knew that he would be unhappy and, with reluctance, he agreed to let Spickett leave. He did so only on the condition that Spickett would do a complete report as to the method used to make the mannequins along with problems he had run into. Also that if he had the time he could assist them part-time. In his place, Norman hired Mr. Jack Fuller to work as sculptor and modeller at a salary of $400 a month. The contract was for two years commencing on September 1, 1957. He would take over the house Spickett was currently living in and could have the house for $50 a month. Jack accepted the offer and the museum work continued.

The new displays at the Luxton Museum were complete. The characters and settings were life size and depicted Indian life as it was in the mid- to late 1800's. One setting included a woman making pemmican and another making buckskin. The entire addition depicted life around the teepees. There was even an old-time sweathouse. The chicken dance was depicted with nine figures dancing while one kept time on the tom-tom. Another scene was of a dog train hooked to a toboggan. The dog train consisted of different-coloured husky dogs. Other scenes included the Indians meeting with the early police.

Ollie didn't make it to Banff that year and had been suffering from an ulcer. He was hoping to perhaps make a trip to England but he was scared to fly so was checking to see if he could go by ship. The Ormonds had bought the factory in Edmonton but were thinking of closing down the business in Victoria. The unions out there were pretty much forcing them out of business. Ollie really wanted to get out to Banff again and looked forward to the day he would see Norman again.

In November there came a nice card from the Luxton School in Winnipeg. The school had been named after Norman's father and they were celebrating the school's 50th anniversary. Eleanor had decided to go to the celebration at the school to represent the family.

EIGHTEEN

Final Goodbyes

By early February of 1958, Norman was hard at work on another display. This time he was working on the set of an Indian on horseback killing a buffalo with a bow and arrow. The problem was that in order to have a scene featuring an Indian on horseback it meant killing a horse. Killing an animal just for display purposes was not an option for Norman. The problem was solved by approaching a slaughterhouse that had horses ready for slaughter and buying one from them. Although technically it still meant a horse would die, the horse in question was set for slaughter anyway. The difference would be that instead of using it for meat it would become a part of the museum.

Another set in the works was to be a depiction of the Sun Dance. This would show an Indian brave, hooked by throngs to the Medicine Post while the other ends of the throngs held hooks that were put into the brave's chest. The original plan called for some 50 Indians to be sitting around the Medicine Lodge watching the brave. The Medicine Lodge would be a replica of a real medicine lodge but made of artificial logs and natural cured tree bows with the leaves on. Norman's only worry was whether or not he would live long enough to see it completed.

During the year, Norman found himself starting to slow down a lot. It was difficult to keep up with the work at his usual pace. Still the museum was now complete and work was underway for some illustrated colour folders to promote the museum.

Red had recovered and worked at the museum after his return from Ottawa. He was now in New York on holiday and would be staying there for a while.

Ollie Ormond had made a stop in Banff one day in February only to find the Trading Post closed. There was no sign of Lou or Norman anywhere about. He was disappointed in having missed his friend. Just four months later, on June 21, Ollie was in a terrible bus accident while on his way to Victoria. He had left Vancouver and taken the Black Ball Ferry over to Nanaimo. From there, he boarded a bus to take him to Victoria. They had just gone about 3 miles out of Nanaimo when the driver saw a car coming in the opposite direction on the wrong side of the highway. The bus pulled off the road and stopped but the car was out of control and weaving down the hill towards them. The driver of the car saw the bus but he was too drunk to do anything about it. The car raced towards the bus doing over 85 mph when it slammed into the bus, right where the driver was sitting. Ollie had been asleep when the car hit. His head had slammed into the steel shelf that held parcels and bags overhead. Then his head came down and slammed into the seat in front of him causing him to fall to the floor. As he hit the floor he thought, "This is the end."

Ollie didn't remember anything until he found himself being led through a gate outside by two ladies. They took him to a house where he was washed up. His clothes were covered in blood but he decided to return to the bus. He was in a daze and kept wandering off into the bush when finally two Mounties saw him, picked him up, and headed back to the bus. It was then he saw the car and its driver. Ollie knew immediately that the driver was "dead as a doornail." The front seat had pushed up right against the back seat and the driver was caught in between. It took two large trucks to pull the car free from the bus. Acetylene torches had to be used to cut the driver out. Ollie was taken to Nanaimo by ambulance and luckily the hospital had one bed left. The doctors didn't get to Ollie until 11 pm when they finally were able to sew up the large gash on his lower lip and the inside of his mouth. His partial upper plate was broken and had jammed in his mouth so it took a lot of work to get it out. The final injury was to his right hand, which required a bandage and a splint. He would have to wear that for the next 2 months. Ollie returned to Vancouver but decided he didn't belong there anymore and chose to return permanently to Victoria.

George wrote more frequently now and often talked about the family and his past. He didn't know if Norman knew that he'd met Ada while she was working as a cashier at the old *Minneapolis Journal*. He'd also continued to find out more information on their father's history but hadn't discovered anything new. George had just celebrated his birthday and Pat had taken him to the movies to see *South Pacific*.

Still going strong at the age of 83, Norman never stopped working. When he wasn't at the Trading Post or the museum, he could be found sending off letters to his old friends. There were fewer of them but Ollie was still going strong in Victoria after surviving the recent bus collision. Ollie had been a most generous and kind man his whole life and Norman always wondered how such a big heart could be held in that little 5'7" frame. He wrote Ollie about his museum work describing everything in detail. He also told Ollie about Eric Harvie, who had now contributed over $250,000. Norman really couldn't quite believe that one man could be so supportive and generous. The tourists had come and given their support with over 100,000 people visiting the Luxton Museum each summer since it had opened. It was still free to the public and on a rainy day it was the best place to be. Norman enjoyed watching the school children and their teachers come through. They were taught the history of the Indians while walking past the displays. Even the Banff School of Fine Arts made the museum their headquarters for many subjects.

Ernie Kehr had written again with some photos he'd taken on his last trip in 1957. On that holiday Ernie had met with Pope Pius XII.

Though Norman and Lou still worked in the Trading Post, they were now assisted by one clerk and two part-time helpers. Norman knew he wouldn't be around forever and decided it was time to train one of the young lads to take over. The plan was to eventually leave the store to the museum and that its profits would assist in the continued running of the Luxton Museum. Although Eric Harvie would continue to finance the museum, he wouldn't be around forever either. Norman knew the museum would need some other source of income.

Eric Harvie had made his fortune in oil, buying up land that no one else seemed to want. These investments left Eric one of the richest men in Canada. Norman didn't know if Eric was the wealthiest man in the country but he was certainly the most generous. It helped that Eric and Norman had known each other since the 1800's from their early days in Calgary.

As for Lou, he was also on his last legs. Over the years, he had been the greatest partner anyone could ever wish for. Norman thought his younger brother was the finest tourist salesman in the West. Lou had a wonderful character and never got angry or upset. Norman felt himself the opposite and was always mad about something so the two brothers made the perfect team.

Red was still enjoying his holiday in New York City and while there had lunch with Norman's friend Ernie Kehr. When Red and Ernie discovered that Eric Harvie was also in town they all met up for dinner that same day.

In April, another friend of Norman's passed away. John Laurie had been very active in fighting for Indian rights, a passion they both had shared. Norman was asked to be a honourary pallbearer and he attended the service at the Cathedral of the Redeemer in Calgary. John had taken over the judging of the Indian activities at the Calgary Stampede and his untimely death left the Stampede in a bit of a bind. Norman was asked to come out of retirement to assist and he agreed to fill in.

Upon Red Cathcart's return from New York he had decided to resign from his position at the Luxton Museum. He had decided to retire so Norman found a replacement by the name of Doug Light.

Georgie, now 86, still took care of Norman and the little home on Beaver Street. Even at that advanced age she still did all the housework and prepared the meals. Eleanor, although never married, was a wonderful woman. She had returned from Montreal and now worked for the Glenbow Foundation of Calgary. Her job was to write up the histories of all the old timers who had arrived in Alberta before 1890. Eleanor adored her work and was now living up in High River. She still managed to get up to Banff twice a month to see her parents. Eleanor's health problems still plagued her and she had suffered a bad fall and subsequently and was laid up in bed with a bad back. She had never been a strong girl but that had never stopped her from working hard and being a success. There was a time when she was younger that she had been unable to walk for 3 years. Back then she had gone to many of the leading hospitals in the States but doctors held out little hope for her and none could help. With the help of crutches and a cane she had forced herself back on her feet and taught herself to walk again. What Eleanor lacked in physical strength she more than made up for in intelligence.

Most of Norman's friends had passed on but Alex Green and his wife, back in Vernon, were still hanging on. Their son, Murray, lived in Red Deer and worked for the Industrial Acceptance Corporation. Another son, Emory, lived in B.C. and worked for the Chrysler Corporation. The third son, Gerald, still ran the old garage in Vernon at 3401 Barnard Avenue.

Throughout 1960, the Luxton Museum was run by Norman and Doug. Norman had started having some lower back problems with pain that radiated into his right leg and knee. It was diagnosed as rotoscoliosis of the lumbar area, with secondary arthritis changes and disc degeneration. The only help they could suggest was a new lumbar support belt and some muscle relaxants. There wasn't anything the doctors could do; all Norman's problems were age-related.

There was good news that summer in that George was still able to make it up to Banff for his annual summer holiday. Pat was coming up too and after Banff, the two of them planned to go to Winnipeg. At long last Pat was going to get to see Norman's museum.

Georgie was ill that July and for the first time Norman would not be attending the Calgary Stampede. He was invited to the opening of the Calgary Aquarium by John Cross on August 25 and planned to attend.

By 1961, the years were catching up to the Luxton boys. Norman had already made all his funeral arrangements and told Georgie and Eleanor all his wishes. Originally Norman planned to leave $10,000 to his brother Lou but decided to give it to him early so he could use it right away. It also meant Lou would not have to pay gift tax on it. As it turned out the idea was a good one.

Lou Luxton passed away while sitting on the chair, behind the counter, in the Trading Post window. He was 82 years old. George could hardly imagine the Trading Post without Norman and Lou together. It was even harder to imagine Banff with no Lou. The funeral was held at Jacques Funeral Home in Banff and was one of the largest held in town in recent memory. Many of the Stoney Indians attended. Norman took care of and paid for all the arrangements. The bill came to a total cost of $333.45. The obituary was printed in both the *Calgary Herald* and the *Calgary Albertan*.

Nellie and Ollie were still alive but Nellie's mind was now that of a 2-year-old. Ollie's daughter Dorothy had never married and still lived in New York. Dorothy never had children of her own but adopted a 6-year-old girl. George was still working 20 hours a week editing the gardening column. He was having difficulty walking now as it caused him quite a lot of pain. It was due to problems with his sciatic nerve. All his doctor could suggest were cortisone shots. It had been some time since George had visited his two sisters as he didn't want them to know he wasn't well. It didn't matter so much about Nellie as she no longer recognized him anyway.

By August of 1961, it was difficult for George to even get out of bed. It didn't help that the summer had been cold and damp. He didn't want to bellyache about all his troubles though, there wasn't anything to be done.

Eleanor was having problems again and had been in the Calgary General Hospital for quite some time. She heard her father wasn't well and hoped he would feel better soon. Norman's health continued to deteriorate and in October of 1962 he was admitted into the Holy Cross Hospital in Calgary.

Norman Luxton died on October 23, 1962, at the age of 86. He was laid to rest in the Banff cemetery next to his brother Lou. The pallbearers were George Dutchick, Frank Copithorne, William McKendrick, James

Fish, Frank Gourlay and Jim Boyce. Honourary pallbearers included George Gooderham, William Hargrave, Bill Brewster, Norman Mackie, and C.H. McKinnon. Many of the mourners were Stoney Indians and they gathered around the gravesite to say their last goodbyes. They came out in their full regalia, sang hymns, and staged a benediction service at the cemetery.

Ernie Kehr wrote a tribute to Norman in the *New York Herald Tribune:*

"The passing of Norman K. Luxton will be mourned by friends far beyond the community of Banff, of which he was so dedicated a pioneer.

His friends who were privileged to know Norm over the decades appreciated his rugged determination and outspoken suggestions as honest, sincere, and civic-minded. A man with a tireless selfless purpose to make Banff and its grandeur the most interesting tourist attraction in the world. Banff will never be able to repay Norm for what he contributed. To make a better community for the residents without regard for personal gain.

I have met people in Argentina, Australia and Afghanistan who recalled their visits to Banff to see the Indian Days.

Norman has left our personal lives, but those things he did in Banff shall certainly remain as an eternal memorial to him and the countryside he so loved and from which he refused to depart while life coursed through his dynamic frame."

The shock of losing Norman was too great for his last remaining brother. George Luxton died just 9 days after Norman, at the age of 81.

Georgie Luxton passed away March 29, 1965, at the age of 95. Eleanor moved back into the family home on Beaver Street for her remaining years. After almost a lifetime of misdiagnosis Eleanor's illness was finally determined to be multiple sclerosis. In 1971 she took her father's diary from his voyage on the *Tilikum* and turned it into a book. It was titled *"Luxton's Pacific Crossing."* Eleanor died in the Luxton home on June 22, 1995.

Appendix I - Voss

Captain "Jack" Voss did continue his journey on the *Tilikum*. The story of his journey can be found in his book *"The Venturesome Voyages of Captain Voss"* which was published in 1913. The book has been republished several times with the latest printing in December of 2001. This latest version of the *Tilikum* voyage is entitled *40,000 Miles In a Canoe and Sea Queen*.

Voss did complete his voyage in the *Tilikum* and arrived in Margate, England on September 2, 1904 at 4:00 pm. Thousands of people had gathered to watch the *Tilikum* on its approach up the Thames. From the shore one person shouted, "Where are you from?" to which Voss replied, "Victoria, British Columbia." The crowed roared their approval. The journey was over. Voss was busy shaking hands once he had landed when he felt himself suddenly lifted above the crowd. Some men had picked him up and soon deposited him in a carriage. Voss was taken to a hotel where there was much celebration and the champagne flowed freely. The British Geographical Society hired him to lecture and he travelled around England giving talks on sailing. Voss was allowed to lecture because of one of the Society's members. Lieutenant Shackleton, had heard Voss lecture in New Zealand and was an ardent fan. Voss also had a letter of introduction from the British Consulate in Pernambuco. Although Voss often claimed he was elected a Fellow of the Royal Geographical Society in London, research indicates that he was not. Voss wanted very much to become a member of the Geographical Society but because of his checkered past in smuggling they never allowed him this privilege. There were those that honoured him and on January 4th, 1904, he was made honorary member of the Point Yacht Club in Addington, Durban, South Africa. Voss felt that he had more than proved himself and did not see the need to return to Canada. Although technically the voyage had not been a complete circumnavigation there was no doubt he had more than covered enough miles to satisfy the sailing community of the time. Voss's feat was compared with that of the famous Captain Bligh and he now had achieved the reputation of best small-craft sailor in the world. The *Tilikum* was shown successfully at the Navy and Marine Exhibition at London's Earl Court in 1905. Afterwards Voss decided to sell the *Tilikum*.

Having lectured his way around England, Voss decided the time had come to return to Victoria. He arrived back in the coastal city in 1905 only to find that his wife, Lillie, had left him. She had packed her bags and moved to Portland, Oregon, with their two boys. Caroline Voss had stayed behind anxiously awaiting the return of her father. She had been running his hotel interests while he had been away. Caroline was the most like her father and had greatly desired to join him on the *Tilikum* but her father considered it too dangerous. Caroline adored her father and understood his passion for the sea. Upon his return Voss got work as master of a lifeboat named the *Quadra* but soon had purchased a new hotel, the St. Francis, located at 550 Yates St. It had originally been called the "Oriental Hotel". It was a lovely building made entirely of brick and stood three stories high. On the top of the hotel was 25-foot high, wooden cupola. This "tower" was a local landmark and at night served as a beacon to ships in the harbour. A light was kept burning at its peak, as a guide for navigators. The St. Francis had 40 rooms and accommodation for 150 guests. On opening night, March 21, 1906, a band played outside while Caroline Voss served as hostess. It was during these two years that Voss also owned the *Jessie*, a small transport ship. On April 17, 1906, Voss married for a second time. The new Mrs. Voss was Mary Anna Croth of St. Louis but the honeymoon was barely over when she died on August 20, 1906. She was only 43 years of age. She was buried in the Ross Bay Cemetery, located on Fairfield Rd, in an unmarked grave (her plot can be found just to the left of a K. Tanimura). Voss remained at the St. Francis a few more months but he was not comfortable on dry land and sold the hotel in 1907. With a crew of eight men and two boats, Voss left on a coastal spring seal hunt. He journeyed up to the Bering Sea and returned with 262 sealskins. One of the sealing vessels, the *Ella G*, was registered to Voss. She had been built in Seattle in 1896 by John O. Whipple.

Voss was soon at sea again, sailing on the *Milton Stuart*. It left the Lizard in England and sailed to Santa Rosalia, Mexico, where it arrived in 1908. This voyage lasted 125 days. Then in 1909, Voss went to Japan to find work in the sealing industry. He was master of a sealing schooner in 1909, serving under the Japanese flag. In October of 1911, Voss was working on the sealing schooner, *Chichishima Maru*, which was anchored in Yokohama Harbour, after a recent trip to Siberia. Japan had just signed a treaty with the United States, Canada, and Russia that would prohibit sealing for the next 15 years. Some money was set aside to help the fishermen and Voss did qualify for some financial assistance since he had been sailing for Japan for the past three years. It was slow in coming but he was given some financial aid. Always looking for the next adventure, Voss set off on July 26, 1912, on a yawl called the *Sea Queen*. Voss returned to Japan in 1913 but with sealing now prohibited by law there was little to do. Voss decided that it was a good time to publish an account of some of his journeys. The book was published in Yokohama in 1913 and titled simply "*Venturesome Voyages*". Voss explains that to him the ocean was not a "barren desert" but a "source of life and wholesome joy".

With the coming of World War One, Voss again found himself at sea. He captained a schooner and travelled the North Pacific. By the end of the war, Voss was now a man of 60 and decided it was time to retire from the ocean waves. His cousin lived in a small city in California, just 60 miles east of San Francisco, and Voss decided that was as good a place to retire as any. Tracy (now a city of 65,000) had just been incorporated in 1910 but many found it hard to believe that Voss would settle into some quiet town in California. Tracy was anything but quiet though, and it certainly suited Voss's personality. The city was full of card rooms, slot machines, Chinese lotteries, and a brothel or two. It was here that Voss took the job as driver of a small Ford passenger car known as a jitney. It was a taxi service in a sort of mini bus. Voss was a character and made quite an impression around town.

Voss lived with his cousin, William Johnsen. William had lived in Tracy for 39 years and had helped promote and develop the area. William had been born in Holstein, Germany, on October 6, 1853. He was the son of William A Johnsen and Catherine Voss. The Voss family was quite famous in Germany for their Hamburg Shipbuilding Company, Bloom & Voss.

By early 1922, Voss's health began to fail. He often spoke of his adventures to new friends and told stories about his first sea voyage at the age of 30 in the American vessel, *Top Gallant*. He was proud that in all his time at sea he did not lose even one vessel although he was saddened to admit he did lose one sailing companion. That shipmate was Louis Begent from the *Tilikum*. He maintained until the day he died that Louis had indeed been washed overboard.

Voss's children had all remained in Portland and Caroline eventually married Frederick Hahn. On Monday morning, February 27, 1922, Captain John "Jack" Voss was found dead in his bedroom. The cause of death was pneumonia and a dilated heart. An autopsy had been performed by Dr. Powers of Stockton. The funeral was held at the Lutheran Church on the Thursday afternoon with Rev. A.H Wessling preaching the sermon.

Voss's son Harry gave his father's birth date as March 6, 1851, but further research in Germany gives his birth date as August 6, 1858. This would indicate that the gravestone is indeed correct and that Harry was mistaken. Voss was buried in the Tracy Public Cemetery. There lies a very simple gravestone that reads "John C. Voss 1858-1922" and on top of the stone it simply reads "Father."

A book entitled "The Life of J.C. Voss - Told by Himself" was written by a Werner Gilde in 1984. It is believed that most of its contents are fictitious. The book was printed in German and may still be available.

Appendix II - The Tilikum

Perhaps no single tree had quite the life of one particular Cedar from British Columbia. It was dug out and made into a war canoe that transported Canada's coastal Indians between the Islands off the coast of Vancouver. The war canoe was later abandoned on a beach after carrying 3 Indians, suffering from smallpox, to their final destination. Discovered by Voss and Luxton it was fixed up, built up, and then set sail on one of the greatest voyages of all time. By the time it reached London, England, it was the most famous canoe of it's time, perhaps the most famous canoe ever. You would think it would be content to retire peacefully, spending its days as a simple canal boat in England. But the little canoe known first as the *Pelican*, then the *Tilikum*, then later as the *Benlaric*, and finally the *Tilikum*, wasn't content.

After the Navy and Marine Exhibition at Earls Court she was sold and towed up the Seine to Paris on her final exhibition. She was then sold to Harold Ingersoll, fitted with a motor, and taken to the Orwell River, near Pin Mill in England. The plan was to use her as a canal boat but she didn't prove to be very useful for that purpose. She lost her figurehead during that time but it certainly wasn't for the first time. In 1911, the *Tilikum* was abandoned and left to rot in the Thames near Canvey Island in Essex. It was here she lay half-submerged in mud and water for five years, until two men found her.

Archie Campbell and Leslie Bentley noticed the wreck and decided to see if they could fix her up. The motor was long gone, there was no rudder but her three masts were still in place. Archie and Leslie managed to find the owner, a Mr. Price-Powell, and he told them they could keep the boat. Before removing the *Tilikum* from the river, they needed a permit. A letter was soon dispatched to the Commander-In-Chief's Office, The Nore, Chatham. The response and permit were received in September of 1916, stating that Mr. Leslie Bentley was now authorized to remove an "Open boat 37 ft. long from Oyster Creek, Canvey Island to the small creek under Railway Bridge at Benfleet." Leslie and Archie had to first remove several tons of mud so she could be righted and then moved. The *Tilikum* was restored, hatch covers replaced, and a coat of paint was applied. Archie decided to name her after a ship he had served on so he affixed a nameplate and called her *Benlaric*. The *Tilikum* remained with Mr. Bentley until 1920 when he sold her to the Byford brothers. Meanwhile there were those around the world that began to wonder about what had happened to the famous little canoe. Somewhere along the line, Harold T. Barnes of Victoria wrote to the British Columbia Agent General in London asking him to investigate the whereabouts of the *Tilikum*. Mr. W.A. McAdam didn't know but placed an ad in the *Yachting Times* requesting information about the famous vessel.

The Byford brothers immediately offered the *Tilikum* to Victoria as a gift, but only on the condition she never be used for financial gain. In addition, the city of Victoria must incur all the expenses of returning her to Canada.

In June 1930, the *Tilikum*, having survived Indian wars, a journey around the world, and the effects of time as it lay rotting in the Thames, was now bound for Canada. A freighter called the *Pacific Reliance*, part of the Furness-Withy Line agreed to put her on deck at no cost and bring her home. After crossing Canada by rail, the *Tilikum* made her first home at the Crystal Gardens in Victoria. She was later moved to Totem Park and then made her final resting-place at the Maritime Museum of B.C. in Victoria. In May of 2001, they celebrated the 100th anniversary of her great voyage with a special exhibition. The *Tilikum* was then repainted in her original colours and fitted with new rigging.

Bibliography

Bentley, David - Surrey, England.

Begent, Simon - Somerset, England.

Brewster, Pat

Bridge, Bonnie (researcher), Winnipeg, Manitoba.

Bumsted, J.M., *Dictionary of Manitoba Biography*, Manitoba, University of Manitoba Press, 1999.

Calgary Herald, 1901, 1953.

Calgary Public Library.

Canadian Gentlemen, July, 1955.

City of Victoria Archives

Crag & Canyon Newspaper, Anniversary edition, 2001.

Crag & Canyon Newspaper, 1901-1945

Daily Colonist (The), Victoria, B.C., December 12, 1940.

Freeborn, Susan - Calgary

Glenbow Museum Archives, Calgary.

Harris, Elsie - Banff.

Hart, E.J., *The Brewster Story*, Banff, EJH Literary Enterprises, Ltd., 1981.

Healy, W.J., *Winnipeg's Early Days*, Winnipeg, Stovel Company Limited, 1927.

Holm, Donald, *The Circumnavigators*, Place, Publisher, Date.

Jupp, Ursula, *Home Port: Victoria*, Victoria, Ursula Jupp, 1967.

Kent, Marjorie (personal letters).

Livingstone, Donna, *Cowboy Spirit - Guy Weadick and the Calgary Stampede*, Vancouver, Greystone Books, 1996.

Luxton, Eleanor, *Banff Canada's First National Park*, Banff, Summerthought Ltd., 1975.

Luxton, Eleanor, *Luxton's Pacific Crossing*, Sidney, B.C., Gray's Publishing Ltd., 1971.

Luxton, George E., *Flower Growing in the North*, Minneapolis, University of Minnesota Press, 1956.

Luxton, Norman, *50 Switzerlands in one-Banff the Beautiful*, Banff, Norman Luxton, 1913.

Maritime Museum of B.C. Archives, Victoria, B.C.

Mathias, Guy - Victoria, B.C.

MacEwan, Grant, *Fifty Mighty Men*, place, publisher, date.

New York Herald, 1904.

Observer (The), Adelaide, Australia, January 30, 1904.

Opie, Ellen, TAGS Cemetery Project, Tracy, California.

Ormond, Bill & Judi - Victoria, B.C.

Ormond, Oliver B. - (personal letters)

Parker, Patricia, *The Feather and the Drum*, Calgary, Consolidated Communications, 1990.

Paterson, Edith, *Tales of Early Manitoba*, The Winnipeg Free Press, 1970.

Pulscher, MaryLynn, Minneapolis Park & Recreation Board, Minneapolis, Minnesota.

Parker, David, (researcher), Victoria, B.C.

Resolution, The Journal of the Maritime Museum of British Columbia, Tilikum edition, May, 2001

Standard (The), St. Catherine's, November 30, 1974.

Star Weekly, May 17, 1958.

Tracy Press, Tracy, California, March 4, 1922.

Whyte Museum of the Canadian Rockies- Archives, Banff, Alberta.

Voss, John, *The Venturesome Voyages of Captain Voss*, London, Rupert Hart-Davis, 1950.

(First edition printed Tokohama, Japan - 1913).

Index

Greenway, Premier, 62
Grieves, George, 20, 34, 123, 196

H
Hall, Mrs. Arthur, 139, 140
Hamilton Ladies College, Montreal, 53
Harbour & Shipping magazine, 134
Harmon, Bryon and Mrs, 66, 109
Harris, Reg, 108, 109
Hart, W S Bill (Two-Gun) 132, 138
Harvie, Donald S, 211
Harvie, Eric, 202, 205, 211, 213, 214, 216, 225
Hayden, Charles, 122
Hind, Ella Cora, 16
Hines, Ashley, 20, 210
Hine, C F, 44, 61
Hollywood magazine, 146
Hoofs & Hounds magazine, 165
Horton, Lillian, 208
Hoskings, William F "Bill", 29
Hoskings, Ed, 38, 74, 88, 115, 116, 148, 159, 173, 179, 187
Howard, Lesley, 176
Howell, Chief Justice, 63
Hub Cigar Store, 96
Hunter, Enos, 92, 113, 121
Hylo Oils Limited, 156

I
Intruders, the, 178

J
Jacobs Creek, Morley, 50
Jacques, Vera, 168, 216

Jennings, Dr, 172

K
Kehr, Ernie A, 195, 212, 218, 225, 228
Keller, Hellen, 166, 167
Kelly, Roberta, 199
Kennedy, John F, 218
Kenny, John A, 15, 18, 62, 70
Kenora, Ontario, 21
Kent, Aubrey, 196
Kent, Herbert, 196
Kent, Marjorie, 28, 35, 38-40, 46, 129
Kerns, Johnny, 113
King Edward VII, 161
King George, 75
King Edward Hotel, 55-66, 68, 71, 75, 81, 84, 85, 87, 89, 191, 219
King, William Lyon Mackenzie, 169
Kipling, Rudyard, 20
Knight, Harry, 108
Kutenai (Kootenay) Indians, 58, 103, 118, 119, 131, 170
Kwong Lee Restaurant, Banff 59

L
Lafferty, Dr James, 54
Laggan, Alberta, 42, 74
Lake Louise, Alberta, 42, 73, 74, 85, 104, 132, 184
Lambert, Pearl and Hal, 219
Lane, George, 141, 203
LaPorte, Eugene and family (Bill, Mary, Frank and Robert), 111-113, 117, 119, 122-124, 126, 128, 130, 132, 133, 138, 139, 142-144, 147, 148, 153-155, 158-

Vancouver, BC, 24, 25, 32, 39-41, 97, 122, 134, 162, 163, 165, 176, 191-193, 195, 197, 204, 207, 213, 215, 216, 220, 223

Vancouver News Advisor, 25, 27, 39

Vancouver Province, 25, 204

Vancouver Sun, 25, 204

Venturesome Voyages of Captain Voss, 9, 32, 118, 153, 229

Victoria Daily Times, 30

Victoria Hotel, Victoria BC, 25

Volmers, Harry, Mrs. And Sonny, 28, 29, 161

Voss, Abel, 25

Voss, Anna, 25

Voss, Caroline, 26, 30, 232, 233

Voss, Harry, 26, 30

Voss, Heinrich, 25

Voss, Herman, 25

Voss, John, 25

Voss, Lillie, 30

Voss, Captain John Claus, 9-13, 25-34, 36-39, 57, 58, 106, 118, 123, 124, 126, 127, 129, 143, 145, 153, 197, 204, 219, 231-235

Voss, Peter, 25

W

Walker, John, 46

Walker, Colonel James, 53, 128, 208

Wainwright, Alberta, 70, 131, 185

Warren, Mrs. Mary, 206

Weadick, Florence (Flo), 132, 146, 167, 186, 187, 190, 200, 204-207, 211

Weadick, Guy, 128, 132, 137, 138, 140, 141, 144, 146-155, 157,

160, 162-169, 178, 182, 185-188, 190, 196, 197, 199, 200, 203-207, 211

Weadick, Tom, 207, 211

Western Canada Cement and Coal Company, 61

White, Dave, 93, 108

Whyte, Peter, 126, 127

Wilson, Eddie, 64

Wilson, Harry, 197, 201, 204, 213, 215, 218

Wilson, Tom, 45, 46, 104, 109

Winchester, Captain and Mrs, 33, 34, 127

Windsor, Duke & Duchess (Edward & Wallace Simpson), 160, 199

Winnipeg, Manitoba, 13, 15-18, 20, 25, 31, 34, 38, 41,42, 44, 46, 54, 56, 61, 62, 68, 84, 90, 93, 116, 117, 134, 159, 187, 195, 196, 210, 213, 222, 226

Winnipeg Free Press, 16, 18, 23, 74

Winnipeg Sun, 23

Woodworth, Fred, 94

Wright, Archibald, 15

Y

Young, J J, 22, 38

About the Author

Susan Warrender is a second generation, native Calgarian. She is the author of "Alberta Titans" a part of the "Amazing Stories" series (Altitude Publishing - 2003). Susan was published in the magazine *Resolution* in their special *Tilikum* issue, (spring 2001). Susan began writing for children's theatre with three of her plays performed at Calgary's Jubilee Auditorium, Medicine Hat College, and Yates Memorial Centre in Lethbridge. Susan's primary passion is travel so she can get, "Up close and personal with history." From the battlefields of Gettysburg to the Beaches of Normandy, Susan has been there, done that, and bought the souvenir mug (she has over 300 in her collection).